# Fighting Ships

# Fighting

Michael Joseph

# Ships

## Richard Hough

This book was designed and produced by

George Rainbird Ltd,
Marble Arch House,
44 Edgware Road,
London, w.2

for

Michael Joseph Ltd,
26 Bloomsbury Street,
London, w.c.1


Colour origination by Schwitter Ltd, Zurich, Switzerland
Text filmset by Oliver Burridge Filmsetting Ltd, Crawley, Sussex
Book printed and bound by Jarrold & Sons Ltd, Norwich


House editor: Caroline Lightburn
Designer: Judith Allan
Indexer: H. V. Molesworth Roberts



7181   4021   4
First published 1969
© Richard Hough 1969

# Contents

# Colour Plates

# PREFACE

Ever since the days of Phoenician sea power, the fighting ship has been the noblest and most splendid of all the weapons of war, inspiring reassurance and courage in those who sailed in them, and discouragement and fear in their enemies. Unlike the tank and the military aircraft, the fighting ship has always possessed in its design a measure of both the functional and the decorative. During some periods of extravagance, the decorator – the carver, the gilder, the painter – has in the past been allowed to exercise too great an influence, and bluff sea captains were known to chop off and with relish hurl into the sea heavy carvings, perhaps of saints, in order to improve their vessel's sailing qualities. On the other hand, to go into battle behind carved figureheads of fierce beasts has enflamed the fighting spirit of seamen over thousands of years of naval warfare. Right up to the last generation of battleship, the skill of the naval architect has had to consider how best the rig and silhouette of his ship may most effectively intimidate the foe. (The French quite recently made their guns look longer and more fearful by siting them in inconveniently small turrets.)

When the loving skill of the artist has been equally matched by the practical wisdom of the shipwright, the fighting ship has been an object of peerless beauty. When a Humphreys-designed frigate sails in all its elegance from the mouth of the Delaware, when a great Dreadnought of this century fires a full broadside at 30 knots, the proof is complete that the fighting ship is one of history's most beautiful and fearful creations.

It seems, then, that the visual quality of men-of-war is something to be cherished, and that a fully illustrated history of the fighting ship through the ages is a worthwhile object. But the number and range of illustrations in this book has demanded an economy of text which has represented something of a challenge. The subject of naval architecture and development is so vast that this cannot attempt to be much more than a summary of the most important trends and developments, with reference to the fighting ship's construction and embellishment, her weapons and how they were used, and her activities in war. Some omissions, especially among the smaller classes of ships, will be noted, and the medieval period is considered very briefly because the fighting ship was then really only a converted merchantman, and little is known about it anyway.

There are two obvious ways of extending knowledge beyond what is provided here. First, the world is full of maritime museums and preserved fighting ships, like the *Constitution* at Boston, the *Victory* at Portsmouth, and the wonderful *Wasa* at Stockholm. Second, the literature of the fighting ship and its battles in all languages is vast and fascinating – from Hakluyt to Jane. A few of the books to which I have most often referred are to be found on pages 293-4.

Richard Hough

# 1. EGYPTIAN ORIGINS

The master of the sea
must inevitably be master
of the Empire
        Cicero, *Ad Atticus*

The fighting ship propelled mainly by man's muscles had a life span of some 4,500 years, longer by far than that of the sailing fighting ship. It also developed through more forms than the sailing warship, or than the steam-powered warship, which has lasted for little more than a century. The oar-driven fighting ship was used by Xerxes in the Hellespont, by the Viking earls of Orkney in their raids against Ireland and England, by Louis XIV's captains in the Mediterranean. It thrived for centuries in a highly sophisticated form in the Baltic and took part in the American War of Independence. Its origins are to be found in the primitive Nile river craft of 3000 BC, its final flowering in magnificently decorated Mediterranean galleasses mounting 36-pounder guns and powered by some 500 slaves, all living in indescribable misery and squalor.

The Mediterranean, 'the cradle of oversea traffic and of the art of naval combats', as Conrad has described it, has seen more sea fighting than any other ocean in the world. There is evidence of a great sea battle between the Egyptians and the 'peoples of the north' around the time of the Trojan wars. In the Mediterranean Antony deserted his fleet at Actium, Nelson lost an eye and gained one of his greatest victories, and torpedo-bombers of the British navy signalled the end of the heavy gunned fighting ship 140 years later at Taranto. Although claims have been made for Crete and the Minoans, the cradle of the fighting ship was almost certainly the estuary of the Nile; and sea warfare began when bold armed mariners in strengthened river craft ventured forth into open waters for the first time – to explore, to

pillage, perhaps to trade, and certainly to confront new enemies.

The nature of the earliest sea fighting, and the form and characteristics of the vessels, are likely to remain obscure for ever. One of the few valuable sources of knowledge of the early Egyptian fighting ship is the relief carvings on one of the Abu Sir pyramids, which have been dated at about 2600 BC, and fragments of detailed reliefs dating from Pharoah Sahure (2700 BC). These show a basically Nile river type of vessel with bipod mast, upright stem and stern posts, and thick ropes, or 'hogging truss', stretched taut longitudinally by a 'Spanish windlass' over queen posts to ease the strain off bow and stern in heavy seas. The fourteen oarsmen are shown standing for greater purchase, and the mast is lowered onto a crutch as evidence that the wind is unfavourable for sailing. With a good wind from astern, the mast would be raised with the halyards leading aft to form an additional backstay. The square sail was loose-footed, although later it was laced to a lower yard.

The Egyptians were always handicapped by a lack of natural sources of supply of suitable shipbuilding timber. The native sycamore and acacia provided only short lengths, and until the later introduction of imported timber, the ribless hull was built up from thick wooden blocks, pegged and joined by flat sections of thinner timber slipped into the blocks. Support athwartships was provided by ropes lashed round the upper hull planking drawn taut by a linking woven rope.

There is little evidence of any radical improvement or elaboration on this primitive strengthened river vessel for the next 1000 years or so. By 1500 BC the oar remained the principal means of power. The power of the wind was still a doubtful factor in a sea noted for its long periods

Bas relief of an Egyptian rowing boat from the tomb of Ti near Saqqara *c.* 2650 BC. It is constructed of reeds bound together at the ends; the men working the paddles are under an awning; the steering oars are handled by the two men standing in the stern

Bas relief of an Egyptian ship of fifth dynasty from the pyramid tomb of Pharaoh Sahure at Abusir. The heavy cable running the length of the ship over the yokes prevented the ends of the ship hogging, that is, drooping. The mast is lowered onto a tabernacle

Bas relief of an Egyptian sailing boat from the tomb of Ti near Saqqara *c.* 2650 BC. The oars are drawn inboard whilst the tall masts and sail drive the ship upstream over the current of the River Nile; a man on the light upper deck handles the sail by means of two braces from the yardarms; in the top right corner two men carry a coil of rope over an oar

of calm. Oarsmen were cheap, their muscle-power was available at all times, giving the fighting ship a flexibility and reliability which the sail was never able to offer, even when the art of sailing had achieved its highest state of development more than 3,000 years later. A single simple square sail was, however, still sometimes raised when the wind was favourable. There were two steering oars in the bows with tillers near the upper end to ease the task of the helmsman. There is no pictorial evidence of ribbing, although the deck beams project through the hull planking to suggest that they are now offering greater structural strength than before.

Some 300 years later there took place the first naval battle of which there is pictorial evidence, in the tomb of Rameses III at Medinet Habu near Thebes. Tribes from the south coasts of Asia Minor and the southern Aegean islands engaged in sporadic but well organized raids against the Phoenician and Egyptian coasts, and made a major landing in Egypt. The fact that both friend and foe are depicted fighting from basically similar vessels suggests that warship design in

11

the eastern Mediterranean had become standardized, and that the Aegean shipbuilders had long before learnt from the Egyptians. A new shape is now becoming evident. The oarsmen – around twenty-four to a vessel – are seated on benches and protected from the elements and from enemy arrows and missiles by high washboards out of consideration for the main motive power and no doubt in the interests of efficiency rather than from delicate feelings for the oarsmen's comfort and safety. For the same reason naval architects 3,000 years later shielded the engines of great ironclads with armour plate a foot thick. The rigging, too, suggests a deeper appreciation of the benefits wind power could offer and the fact that it did not have to be blowing from directly astern to add pace to the warship. The rigging is more elaborate, the sail is furled by brails, thus avoiding the need for lowering the yard. A better understanding of hull design – although ribbing is still not evident – has obviated the need for the clumsy lengths of rope stretched longitudinally between and above oarsmen. The crow's nest makes its first appearance, for the advantage of being first to sight the enemy had now been properly understood. So also is the incalculable benefit to be derived from frightening the enemy by presenting an intimidating demeanour, a consideration in naval architecture that was to endure until the present century. The ram has not yet arrived, but the vessels depicted at Medinet Habu have 'fierce-face' carvings of heads of angry beasts secured to their elaborate prows.

   This great unidentified sea battle, between the Egyptians and the marauding 'Northmen of the Mediterranean', was fought fiercely at close range mainly with bows-and-arrows, slings and spears. It marks the decline of the Egyptian warship.

Egyptian rowing boat from a papyrus. Models of this type of boat have been found in the tombs. The two steering oars are clearly shown

# 2. THE GALLEY

By the beginning of the decline of Egyptian maritime power in the eastern Mediterranean, the Minoans of Crete (before their overthrow by the Mycenaeans), the Phoenicians, the Greeks themselves and the numerous scattered tribes of the Aegean, had all attained a similar standard of warship construction. An exception must be made for the Lindians whose appreciation of the finer aspects of naval architecture even at this early time has been made increasingly evident by excavations conducted during this century on Lindos. From 1100 to 800 BC, the chief initiative and enterprise in maritime power passed to the Phoenicians, and they were most influential in the development of the oar-driven warship. Some authorities, R. C. Anderson among them, insist that the definition of a galley must include the ram bow, the most formidable ship-destroyer before the refinement of the cannon, and one that was included in the armoury of the fighting ship until the present century. The advent of Phoenician sea power around 1100 BC marks the serious beginnings of the warship as a distinct species, rather than as a trading vessel modified slightly and equipped to carry troops. During this period the fighting ship acquired greatly increased speed, manoeuvrability and power to damage the enemy. Up to about 700 BC the oar-driven Mediterranean fighting ship was powered by a single bank of oars on each beam, each oar operated by a single oarsman, standing or sitting. Homer's larger ships, although he writes of them as trading ships or – for war purposes – as troopships for the transport of soldiers, were fifty-oared *pentekonters* – one man to one oar. The first evidence of the galley with oars in two banks and at two

levels – the *bireme* – has been found on Assyrian reliefs evidently depicting Phoenician fighting ships of around 700 BC. These suggest a long, thin hull dug out from a single tree trunk with oarsmen sitting in pairs along the centre line and each operating a single oar. But from each side of this lean, dugout-canoe-like hull there now project planked outriggers. On the thwarts supporting these there sits, on each beam, another oarsman at a higher level than his inboard companions and with his oar in a rough parallel line with the oar below him. In this way twice the power is developed for the same overall length, the additional weight being offset by the marvellous stability in heavy weather offered by the outriggers. The fighting men occupy a 'storming bridge', a narrow deck like a gallery, extending the full length of the vessel above the inboard oarsmen. A wicked-looking ram, projecting some eight to twelve feet forward from the bows like the horn of a charging rhinoceros is the vessel's main 'armament', the real killing weapon which may, at some 7 knots, slice clean through an enemy ship. A single square sail is still only an auxiliary means of propulsion. The overall length is about 80 feet, the beam no more than 10 feet.

On the evidence of Thucydides's account of Corinthian shipbuilding methods recorded in his history of the Peloponnesian war, it is now generally accepted that the Corinthians were probably the first

Bas relief showing an Assyrian galley of the time of Assur bani Pal, with its underwater ram, two banks of oars and protective shields. This important evidence is difficult to interpret. The Assyrians maintained their thalassocracy with these floating fortresses, but at face value their stability is open to doubt

shipbuilders to revolutionize the art of design by introducing the rib to ship construction. Up until 500 BC a ship's hull was either dug out from a single trunk or made up from lengths of timber secured together with deck beams providing athwartships support. Like most advances in marine architecture the impulse was provided by the needs of warfare. Greater fighting power, greater speed, and greater impetus to drive home the ram could be provided only by an increase in size. This could be achieved without a proportionate increase in weight only by a completely new basis of construction. Nature's rib-cage, which surely must have provided the inspiration, was the answer. It was light, offered enormously increased structural strength to meet the sudden strains imposed by tempest and the impact of the ram, and posed no constructional problems. Björn Landström shows the Greek bireme of this period with a full-length keel and storming bridge adding further support to the ribbed hull. The fifty oarsmen, twenty-five on each side, are disposed in staggered form, one bank of oars working through oar-ports, the upper bank secured between double railings. The ram is shaped to depict the head of a fierce fabulous beast, and Landström speculates that this may be detachable now that it does not form an integral part of the earlier dug-out, and would therefore tear loose without damage to the hull. The ram was almost impotent against the contemporary merchantman with its heavy-built, resistant hull, and the galley had to come alongside and board – if the wind was light. But unless the weather was calm, boarding was a difficult business and the merchantman, with its superior sailing

Fragment of a relief in the Acropolis museum showing a Greek trireme. This famous carving has so far defied interpretation. It is possible that the viewer is seeing the trireme from above, with the oars resting on racks outside the ship

qualities, might well escape. The fighting galley, then, was best equipped for combat with its own kind in short, sharp actions conducted in sheltered waters, usually in the spring or summer. A fleet which did not have the opportunity to leave their sails and masts ashore were at a severe disadvantage. These narrow, uncomfortable vessels were not intended for remaining at sea for long periods, and whenever possible they were drawn up on land at night. The art of blockade, which was later to become such a decisive aspect of maritime power, was rarely resorted to and scarcely ever effective. Nicias, commander-in-chief of the Athenian forces blockading Syracuse, sent home this bleak report:

> Our fleet was originally in first-rate condition: the ships were sound and the crews in good order, but now, as the enemy are well aware, the timbers of the ships, having been so long exposed to the sea, are soaked, and the efficiency of the crews is destroyed. We have no means of drawing up our vessels and airing them, because the enemy's fleet is equal or even superior in numbers to our own, and we are always expecting an attack from them. They are always trying their strength; they can attack us when they please, and they have far greater facilities for drying their ships, since they are not, like us, engaged in a blockade. (Thucydides, VII, 12.)

It is a curious paradox in the history of the fighting ship that the most famous vessel of ancient times, the Greek *trireme*, has always been the subject of most conjecture. This is because there is almost no

A Greek kylix showing war galleys. This graceful painting shows the rams, the lookout in the bow castle, the double steering oars and steersmen aft, and the ladders for landing every night. The galleys fought under oars, but cruised under sail

16

contemporary visual record of these speedy, slender, graceful fighting ships which dominated the Battle of Salamis in 480 BC: a fragment of a relief in the Acropolis, another from Lindos, a Greek vase or two, a sculpture in the Louvre, inadequately provide our only evidence of the shape and specification of this great fighting ship. R. C. Anderson lays some emphasis on the value of the Acropolis relief, and sees the ram as the *raison d'être* of the trireme at the height of its fame at the time of Salamis. 'Its presence,' he writes, 'entailed the complete differentiation of bow and stern . . . the keel runs up in a gentle curve to the water-line to meet the converging lower wales in a point finished off, at least in later examples, by a more or less faithful representation of an animal's snout. . . .'[1]

There is no fundamental conflict of opinion on the hull formation and general shape of the classical Greek trireme. Nor is it disputed that the facilities for substituting wind for manual power were still primitive, and that the sail was used only in a fair wind and never in combat. Anderson even asserts that mast and sail were left ashore before an expected action, although a smaller mast and sail could be hoisted at the stem for emergency use. The real conflict of opinion arises over the arrangement of the three oars and oarsmen. Landström makes the case that the double line thwarts were set obliquely, forwards and outwards from the centre line, two oarsmen on the upper bank sitting slightly apart, the inner oarsman's oar being the longer. These oarsmen used the outrigger as the fulcrum, while the single oarsman on the lower thwart and placed between the upper oarsmen made use of a port for his oar. Other authorities, from A. B. Cook and Wigan Richardson (*Triremes* in 'The Mid-Tyne Link', 1906) to Tarn (*The Greek Warship* in 'Journal of Hellenic Studies', 1905) to Anderson – the most scholarly and least dogmatic – put forward a wide variety of three-oar permutations, all speculatively based on fragments of sculpture or painting or graffiti and occasional quotations from con-temporary writers. Lionel Casson is confident that there were three rows of thwarts, the oarsmen being staggered with the upper oarsman forward of his fellow below. John Charnock, in his formidable three-volume work of 1800–2, demolishes the theories of the galley authority, Meibomius, who claimed that: 'In the Trireme, two rows, the upper and lowermost, were seated on the steps, or projecting boards, affixed to the sides, and the intermediate rank on the crossbenches,' the boards 'being fixed for that purpose on brackets fastened to the lining'. Vice Admiral William L. Rodgers, the American student, confidently propounds yet another theory: 'All the evidence from ancient writers,' he claims, 'from coins, sculptures, paintings and

inscriptions is that . . . oars were in three rows, one above the other.
. . . Taking any group of three rowers on different levels, the upper
man (*thranite*) sat well inboard pulling a long oar. The man in the
middle rank (*zygite*) sat 14 inches lower, 18 inches outboard, and
9 inches forward. Thus his head was between two oars worked by the
men above him. Similarly the man in the lowest rank (*thalamite*)
pulled the shortest oar and was 14 inches lower, 18 inches outboard,
and 9 inches forward of his zygite neighbour, so that his head was
under the oar of the thranite of the next group forward. . . . We
cannot doubt that this manner of rowing was used,' asserts the admiral,
'the evidence is too strong to reject.'[2]

The most valid conclusion that can be drawn from this long
controversy is that there was no standard seating and rowing arrangement for the Greek trireme, and that this – like the formation of the
hull design, the construction of the prow and many other features –
varied widely over the years and at any given time. History is never a
very tidy business, and there is no more reason for an Athenian trireme
fighting off the Arginusae islands in 406 BC to be identical to one of
Ptolemy's a hundred years later than that identical features should
mark, say, the design of French and American frigates in AD 1812.
It is very likely, too, that even the commonly accepted number of
oarsmen at 170 – thirty-one each side on the upper bank and twenty-
seven a side on each of the two lower banks – was not rigidly adhered to.

For many years a similar controversy raged around the correct
interpretation of the terms *quadrireme* and *quinquereme*, galleys with
supposedly four or five banks of oars. The writings of Pliny, Diodoros
and others have been cited as proof that five-banked fighting ships
were not uncommon, and that the number of banks rose to as many as
sixteen. Cecil Torr, who was for many years after the publication of his
*Ancient Ships* in 1894 accepted as an authority on the Mediterranean
galley, wrote: 'There were ships of six and seven banks in the fleet of
Demetrios Pliorcetes at the battle off Cyprus in 306 BC . . . while
there had been a few ships of nine and ten banks in a fleet formed in
314 BC by Antigonos. . . . Pliny states that ships of twelve and fifteen
banks were built by Ptolemy and Demetrios respectively: and a
fifteen-banked ship is ascribed to Ptolemy by Pollux.'[3] Until recently
few people bothered to question the practicality of, say, a fifteen-
banked galley. The uppermost oars of these mythical vessels, fostered
by misinterpretation and the fancies of romantic poets, would have
been about a hundred feet long, and the super-oarsmen would have
had to engage in a constantly reversing sprint race to keep up with the
lowest oarsman. Anderson is prepared to accept the possibility of a

Fragment of a Greek vase showing
a warship similar to those on page
16 but in the Geometric style

quinquereme; Landström stops short at the trireme. It is now likely
that these numeral definitions of the ancient writers refer to the number
of oarsmen in a group or one unit of three on each beam in a trireme.
Given sufficient beam, the seating accommodation on the thwarts
could be arranged to accommodate 3:3:2 (the smaller number for the
shorter oar). This would make the 'sixteen-to-a-bank' vessel of the
Macedonians referred to in the Treaty with the Romans in 197 BC. An
odd number, say fifteen, could be obtained by alternating the groups
of three along either beam 3:3:2 3:2:2 on the port side and 3:2:2
3:3:2 to starboard.

Everyone is entitled to his own definition of a quinquereme, but
there is no doubt that naval fighting in the Mediterranean in the 400
years before the birth of Christ was mainly conducted by biremes and
triremes. During this period, Carthaginians and Greeks, Phoenicians,
Macedonians and Romans all brought sea fighting to a higher degree
of refinement than was to be seen until many centuries later. The
vessels that fought – whether biremes, triremes or perhaps quinque-
remes – might be between 60 and 120 feet long with a beam of 10 to 20
feet. The ram, whether of hard, sheathed wood and detachable under
violent impact, or integral with the galley's hull, remained the primary
weapon of destruction, although the Romans tended to despise
tactical finesse and relied more on their larger complement of soldiers
and the bludgeoning weight of the boarding party.

'They did not understand,' wrote Shuckburgh, 'how to manoeuvre
a vessel so as to bring her beak crashing into an enemy broadside; how
to dash through the enemy's line, and turning rapidly to charge stern or
side; how to sweep away his oars by a swift rush past, or practise other
feats which required great command over the vessel and long laborious
training. They therefore determined on another method of fighting,
which, however rough and unscientific, would make the victory
depend on the fighting men on deck of whose superiority to the enemy
they felt confident. The object of the contrivance was to enable these
men to board an enemy's vessel and fight as though on land. To effect
this they constructed a wooden gangway or boarding bridge on each

vessel, swinging round a pole fixed in the prow.'

Above the ram rose the stem, concave in profile and passing gradually to the vertical. This was elaborate and highly decorated as 'a proof, and by no means an inconsiderable one, of the superior consequence attached in the minds of the ancients, to the formation of that part of the vessel, by which they considered themselves principally enabled to annoy their enemies, or return their attack . . . for show, splendour, and magnificence it attracted no inconsiderable share of notice.'[4] But although the prow itself, elaborate and gilded, was a fearful gesture of intimidation and challenge, the eyes set in the hollow of the concave represented the early mariners' vulnerability to superstition. The 'Horus symbol', the ignorant navigator's guide through storm and fog to his vessel's destination, seems to have had its origins in the ancient Egyptian fable of the killing and dismemberment of the ruler Osiris by his enemy, Set, and the search across the seas by his avenging son, Horus, for the scattered remains of his dead father.

Abaft the formal prow there was a forecastle ending – just before the oars – in two projecting timbers, which could have served the double purpose of catheads and protective buffers for the outriggers. A further projection, just forward of these buffers, was intended to prevent the vessel's ram from penetrating too deeply. Above and for the full length of the galley ran the storming bridge, its rails perhaps reinforced by shields; and there might be one or even two wooden castellated towers built up from it and painted to simulate stone, from which the archers gained a superior firing position. The stern was even more highly decorated than the prow. The head of a goose, other birds or beasts or fabulous animals elaborately carved, or gilded scrollwork, might be found rising up abaft the two great steering oars, while above would protrude a short pole carrying brightly coloured streamers. Another source of decoration was the 'hedolion', the seat of the steersman, which was often carved with such elaborate formality that it became a throne. The important status and comfort of the steersman was for many centuries recognized in this way, and Clowes reminds us that the steersman's throne can still be found today on the Irrawaddy rice boats. The Romans provided him with a richly woven awning. The fighting castle, too, was usually embellished with carving and was brightly painted, while the mask of the lion – the origin of the term 'cathead', from which the iron or bronze anchor ring was suspended – offered further opportunity for the carver.

The scouting biremes would, like the scouting cruisers of recent times, be camouflage-painted to blend with the sea and the sky. But the triremes, the 'capital ships' of their time, were proudly ostentatious as befitted their status.

'Even as early as the Trojan war, it was a custom, if the authority of Homer may be relied on, to paint various sections of the galley with the most gaudy colours, especially red, which is supposed to have been native cinnabar.' In some galleys the decoration, Charnock asserts, 'might easily vie with the most luxurious splendour of eastern magnificence. It was by no means uncommon to gild a considerable part of the vessel . . . the awning, and a great part of the inboard works were frequently inlaid with ivory; and, if we may credit the hyperbolic description of the ancients, have been sometimes studded with precious gems.'[4]

The sail, too, offered great scope for the lavish decorator from the time of the Trojan war, when an emperor's name might be embroidered on it in silver or gold. Violent striped contrasting colours were popular, purple being reserved for eminent commanders, whose rigging and even oars might be gilded. The ram, sheathed in iron or bronze, remained the most devastating ship-destroyer; but the real outcome rested with the courage and skill in close combat of the soldiers, so splendidly evoked by Aeschylus – himself a combatant at Salamis – in his *Persae*:

> . . . Not in flight
> The Hellenes then their solemn paean sang;
> But with brave spirit hastening on to battle,
> With martial sound the trumpet fired those ranks:
> And straight with sweep of oars that flew through foam,
> They smote the loud waves at the boatswain's call;
> And swiftly all were manifest to sight.
> Then first their right wing moved in order meet;
> Next the whole line its forward course began.
> And all at once we heard a mighty shout –
> *'O sons of Hellenes, forward, free your country;*
> *Free too your wives, your children, and the shrines*
> *Built to your fathers' Gods, and holy tombs*
> *Your ancestors now rest in. Now the fight*
> *Is for our all.'* And on our side indeed
> Arose in answer din of Persian speech,
> And time to wait was over: ship on ship
> Dashed its bronze-pointed beak, and first a barque
> Of Hellas did the encounter fierce begin.
> And from Phoenician vessel crashes off
> Her carved prow. And each against his neighbour
> Steers his own ship: and first the mighty flood
> Of Persian host held out. But when the ships

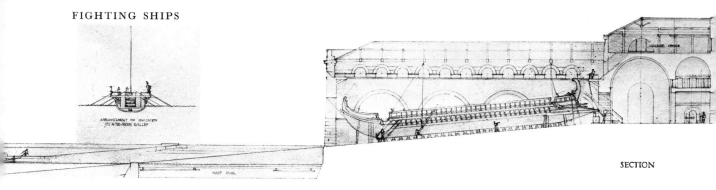

SECTION

Were crowded in the straits, nor could they give
Help to each other, they with mutual shocks,
With beaks of bronze went crushing each the other,
Shivering their rowers' benches. And the ships
Of Hellas, with manoeuvring not unskilful,
Charged circling round them. And the hulls of ships
Floated capsized, nor could the sea be seen,
Filled, as it was, with wrecks and carcasses;
And all the shores and rocks were full of corpses,
And every ship was wildly rowed in flight,
All that composed the Persian armament.
And they, as men spear tunnies, or a haul
Of other fishes, with the shafts of oars,
Or spars of wrecks went smiting, cleaving down. . . .

A drawing of the naval slipways a
Vitruvium and Roman galleys, b·
Ensir

Here we see in action the crippling, demoralizing effect of the ram,
followed by the hand-to-hand assault of the soldier; just as, in modern
times, the torpedo shattered the hull below water and laid the enemy
open to destruction by gunfire. A galley pierced below the waterline
for several yards, its oarsmen on one quarter wounded or in a state of
confusion, was either left sinking or crippled for later attention, or
at once boarded and taken by the sword. To assist in boarding, the
Romans equipped their galleys with an ingenious combined grappling
iron and gangway some twelve yards long, the *artemon*, hinged at the
base and lowered by a pulley from the masthead. The preliminaries
to combat might be accompanied by a haphazard, probably in-
effectual but morale-destroying bombardment of catapulted darts or
stone or lead shots from ballistae; and certainly by arrows or spears.

Fire was another effective killer at a range, but this was a clumsy
weapon which endangered the user almost as seriously as his enemy.
The sailors of Rhodes in the third century BC made effective use of
containers of fire projecting from the bows on long poles like the spar
torpedoes used by the Americans in the Civil War. When conditions
were favourable, blazing rafts were sometimes floated towards a
trapped enemy. The most effective recorded instance of the use of fire

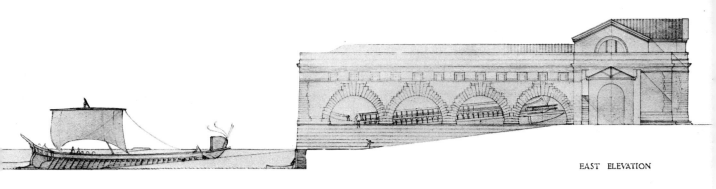

as a weapon is at Actium, in the last frightful stages of the holocaust, when Agrippa had already torn apart by ram the remnants of Antony's fleet.

'The assailants coming from many sides,' records Dio Cassius, 'shot blazing missiles and with engines threw pots of flaming charcoal and pitch. The defendants tried to ward off these fiery projectiles and when one lodged it was quenched with drinking water. When that was gone, they dipped up sea water, but as their buckets were small and few and half-filled they were not always successful. They smothered the fires with their mantles and even with corpses. They hacked off burning parts of the ships and tried to grapple hostile ships to escape into them. Many were burned alive or jumped overboard or killed each other to avoid the flames.'

Fire, the ultimate terror at sea, was decisive at Actium and it was an important weapon of Howard at Calais 1,600 years later during the Armada engagement. But it remained a hit-or-miss business in ancient times, used only occasionally, until the Byzantine Romans perfected 'Greek fire' – a form of liquid bitumen which at short range was blown by giant bellows through copper tubes and was only further activated by water.

Agrippa's victory at Actium was brought about by many factors. Materially, the most important was the first use on a large scale by the Romans of a new fast and very handy bireme called a *liburnia*, the merits of which had first been recognized after the success of the raids by Dalmatian pirates who had been using these swift little galleys in the Adriatic for years. There is almost no reliable evidence of their shape or form of construction except the relief of Palestrina in the Vatican, which has been subjected to every form of interpretation, even to the claim that it is Cleopatra's flagship anyway. We can be fairly sure only that these were biremes, that their speed and manoeuvrability brought about a radical change in Roman tactics which had previously relied on the slogging quality of skill in close combat of the

23

legionary. Estimates of their size vary from a length of 85 feet to over 100 feet, with a beam of around 16 feet including the outriggers.

The liburnian bireme galley formed the backbone of Roman naval strength for some four centuries when her maritime power and responsibilities were greatest. For this reason alone it must be considered the most important fighting ship of all time. With the shifting of the seat of power of Roman rule to Byzantium, the subsequent decline was marked by a reversion to a larger, heavier and less handy galley. A little more is known about the *dromon* than the liburnium. It is probable that, with its blunt ends and wall sides, the task of the oarsmen was eased by the wider use of wind power, that rigging became more elaborate and that there may have been more than a single mast. Anderson conjectures that by around AD 500 the dromon carried high-peaked fore and aft sails. The Emperor Leo VI gives us some guidance, in his directive written around AD 900:

> Your dromons should be well built and fit for battle. The bulwarks must not be too thick, for they would make the ship heavy; nor yet too thin, for they would be broken by collision with the enemy . . . . You will put a tube covered with bronze at the bow to throw flame at the enemy. Above the tube there will be a wooden platform with a solid parapet and soldiers will go there to fight and shoot arrows. On large dromons there will also be a wooden castle amidships, and upon it the soldiers will be stationed to hurl heavy stones against the enemy, or heavy pointed pieces of iron to break or smash, or else to throw fire.
>
> Every dromon should be long and of proportional breadth, with two ranks of oars, one above the other. Each rank should have twenty-five thwarts with two rowers on each, one to port and one to starboard – in all a hundred men, rowers or soldiers. Dromons may be built larger with as many as 200 rowers or more with fifty at the lower oars and the rest above . . . . The rowers of the upper rank and all on the upper deck will be fully armoured with helmets, breast plates, and arm and thigh pieces. They will fight with pikes, javelins and swords . . . .

Certainly by about AD 880, according to two manuscript drawings, the lateen sail, probably of Arab origin, had arrived; and this date may reasonably be taken as the starting point of the thousand-year-long dominance of wind as the main motive power of the fighting ship. But during these ten centuries the oar was never entirely displaced by the sail; the sail itself was to surrender unconditionally to steam power in less than half a century. There remained places and occasions where the muscle power of the oarsman continued to possess advantages over the vagaries of the wind, most notably in the Mediterranean and Baltic.

Detail of a naval battle between galleys

Overleaf: the port of Naples, by Strozzi, and (bottom) the Battle of Lepanto, 1572, by Micheli

# 3. THE VENETIANS

It says much for the early Mediterranean naval architects that their form of oar-driven fighting ship remained basically unchanged for another fifteen or more centuries after the birth of Christ. The power and speed varied with the size of the vessel and the number and disposition of the oarsmen, the introduction of the lateen sail made possible the more frequent use of the capricious Mediterranean winds, the cannon was introduced and influenced the design and destructive potential. But in overall concept there was little to choose between a dromon of the first century and a galley of the 1700s, in spite of all the ingenuity of the Venetian builders.

Venice was the most maritime-conscious nation in the Mediterranean for more than five hundred years, and for most of this period the Venetians led the way in the small variations in design of the fighting galley. Biremes following the basic pattern of the Roman galleys centuries earlier remained the most common vessel until the latter part of the fourteenth century. But there is evidence, in a painting in the Palazzo della Signoria in Siena of a Venetian sea battle, that a new, or perhaps revived, practice of grouping the oars close together on one level had become accepted, the distance between the thole-pins being about 10 inches. The oarsmen's benches were set obliquely, so that the rowing could be synchronized with the different length of oars. These, then, were the new triremes or biremes of the medieval period, with perhaps 120 oarsmen, separated longitudinally by two parallel webs – the corsia – which served to stiffen the vessel's structure, leaving room between them for the stowage of sails and gear, and

Detail of 'Portuguese carracks off a rocky coast', 1521, by Anthoniszoon, showing oars grouped in threes

providing a fore and aft passage. The corsia was often broken by a castle which offered a dominant position for archers and slingers, and when combat was imminent soldiers would stand between the groups of oars to repel boarders. The soldiers and oarsmen were protected by sections of wooden armour plate, and the sides of the hull were protected from the flame-thrower of the time – the 'Greek-fire' ejector – by leather or heavy felt. The ram had long ceased to be the galley's primary weapon, and this projection served, like the dromon's, as a boarding bridge and a means of breaking up the enemy's lines of oars if he had been tardy in shipping them. Besides the 'Greek fire', the Mediterranean galley of this period probably possessed a wide range of mechanical artillery at the bows – soon to be superseded by cannon. Rodgers has given us this informative picture of a Mediterranean combat before the advent of gunpowder wrought its slow revolution in tactics:

The galie subtile from the Anthony Anthony Roll, 1546

> The engagement commenced at a distance with flights of arrows, stones, and bolts from the machines. When attacking sailing ships, it was an object to tear the sails with arrows and cut the rigging with scythes. After ships collided the rowers left their oars to fight; divers tried to bore holes under water. Liquid soap was thrown on the hostile decks to make them slippery. Greek fire was thrown in pots and also quick lime, liquid pitch, and boiling oil and incendiary darts. Against all the incendiary devices the ships were protected by movable leather shields and felting which was wet with vinegar. . . .[6]

An early seventeenth century galley, which later developed into the réale, by Furttenbach

Although documentation on Mediterranean galleys, and Venetian galleys in particular, during the Middle Ages is complete by contrast with the dearth of information on fighting ships of the pre-Christian era, it is not known for certain when different arrangements of oars and oarsmen came into common usage. For a long period the old 'simple fashion' (*alla sensile*) was the only accepted method of oared propulsion. Anderson tells us that the 'simple' Mediterranean galley as a flagship grew to a length of $152\frac{1}{2}$ feet with a beam of 18 feet, with thirty groups of oars on either side, each individually manned.

But probably towards the end of the fifteenth century the greater efficiency to be obtained from having several oarsmen to each oar began to be appreciated. Two watercolour paintings by Raphael seemed to confirm this, and in Siena cathedral there is a painting by Pinturicchio which suggests single spacing of the oars again, and the manning of each by as many as five (quinquereme?) oarsmen.

Landström has given us a fine and probably accurate reconstruction of a typical Venetian fighting galley, based on reliefs on the tomb of a Venetian admiral in Padua cathedral, a model in the Museo Storico Navale, and the statistics included in a manuscript left by the Venetian galley-builder Pre Theodoro de Nicoló. It is a lean and graceful vessel, classically simple in line. There is a long prow, abaft of which there rises up a simple forecastle containing a single heavy gun, a bombard, on a fixed carriage. This was the natural development of the fixed ram it replaced. Down the length of the galley runs the corsia, protected by heavy planking, as much as 8 inches thick, and on each side sit the oarsmen, their oars resting on a long beam – the *apostis* – extending far out from the galley's side. The carved and gilded stern rises up slightly, and here in the traditional position and beneath a protective canopy sits the steersman. But the old twin side rudders have long since disappeared, to be replaced by a single rudder hung on the curved sternpost. Slightly forward of amidships the single pole mast rises up to support the lateen sail, which remained the galley's standard rig until its final demise.

The acceptance of gunpowder artillery as the fighting ship's most devastating weapon was a slow process. Like the later advent of steam power with all its accompanying early inefficiency and the retarding influence of suspicion and conservatism, the gun took a long time to influence warship design radically. Slings and mechanical artillery, after all, did work. They were predictable weapons which did not make a lot of noise and from time to time blow up in your face. The cannon's awful power could not be denied, however; and with the increasing skill of the gunsmith, room had to be found for more cannon. Flanking the big two- or three-ton bombard in the prow there appeared a pair of smaller guns, probably 12-pounders, on swivel mountings – then two more 3- or 6-pounders outboard of the first pair. So that the light *alla sensile* galley at the end of its life possessed a forward-firing armament of five guns, and a broadside – through a narrow arc – of two guns.

With the growing need for more powerful and more numerous guns, the Mediterranean galley began again to increase in size and complexity, just as the iron-clad and steel-clad battleships of the nineteenth and twentieth centuries became more elaborate and formidable with the increasing range and destructive power of contemporary artillery. And as the need for greater speed to meet the tactical demands of battle and the greater displacement of the hull caused the horsepower of the twentieth-century battleship to rise from 12,000 to 220,000, so more oarsmen had to be accommodated. Admiral Fincati draws on contemporary writers to give us a clear picture of the fighting galley as it had developed by about 1550. The displacement was about 170 tons and the overall length had increased to 165 feet from the tip of the prow to the extremity of the raised and carved poop, and the beam at the waterline was 18 feet. Within these dimensions there was housed a total complement of 225 men, the oarsmen working on askew benches in groups of three, each with a single oar weighing about 125 pounds. It is no wonder that the stroke was a slow one, no more than 26 a minute at racing speeds, which with a following wind, under the most favourable conditions and for a brief spurt only, might rise to 12 knots. All the oarsmen rose together from their seats, placing a foot on the bench ahead to gain leverage and inserting their blades as far forward as possible. Then they would all laboriously draw on the oar, falling back slowly into their seats as they did so. A gong, or perhaps a primitive band, would provide encouragement and the beat. Most Mediterranean states used captured Turkish slaves, and these were chained to their benches. The Venetians retained the old practice of using freemen, who were provided with arms, so that fewer permanent soldiers had to be carried. Whether Turkish, Genoese, Spanish or Venetian, the fighting galley was an evil-smelling vessel and conditions on board were fearful. Rodgers states that 'the odour of a galley could be perceived a mile or more to leeward,' and suggests that 'the habit of using very strong perfumes on the person, which still endures to a certain extent in Latin countries, established itself in galley times to overpower the ship's stench and became popular as a suggestion that a man had served his king and religion against the Turk.'[6] Normally, the oarsmen slept on deck under awnings, the officers being accommodated in a cabin aft, which grew with the size of the galley, and was used as an aftercastle in battle.

Besides the five forward-mounted guns, these highly-developed mid-sixteenth-century galleys carried perhaps half a dozen light 3-pounder guns on pivot mounts on each side, and the slow revolution gunpowder was bringing about in the whole nature of the fighting ship was further evidenced in the provision of arquebuses and muskets in place of bows and arrows for close-range action.

Before wind-power took over from the oar-driven vessel – with all its wretched human misery – there was a period of unsatisfactory compromise comparable with the era of mixed sail and steam motive power in the second half of the nineteenth century. Out of the need of the fighting seamen for more guns and bigger guns, and the need to flee or pursue or manoeuvre in battle, there grew the hybrid *galleass*. Its origins were again Mediterranean, a sea where the disparity between the development of the gun and the means to bring it to bear on the enemy was most marked because of the inadequacy of wind as motive power. The galleass was a greatly enlarged galley, carrying a very large number of guns and with its oar-power augmented normally by three lateen-rigged masts. It was the capital ship of its day. It grew out of the heavy merchantmen, the *galia grosa*, which plied its trade in the Mediterranean from the 1400s, protected against marauders by a small number of light guns. For its conversion to a

The réale, by Gueroult

fighting rôle the artillery of this merchantman was augmented with a heavy battery consisting perhaps of six 36-pounders firing forward and three 24-pounders to fire on the broadside. The broadside armament carried on each side would also normally be increased. These converted galleasses, with their additional weight of guns and fighting men, were even slower than they had been as merchantmen. Greater power from the oars was required, but to increase the number of banks would have entailed a longer, heavier and less handy vessel. Already by the 1540s the *alla sensile* – one man to one oar – system of rowing galleys was again coming to an end following experiments dating from 1534. Fifteen years later the multiplication of rowers to each oar was being introduced into galleass merchantmen. As in earlier times, this could be accomplished only by extending the length of the oars and the distance between the thole pins to allow for a greater distance of travel required by the inboard oarsmen. Conveniently, this did not call for an increase in beam, only the widening of the telaro. Experiments were tried with two men to an oar, with five men on two oars and four men to an oar. The most successful arrangement was five men to an oar, and this became standard in the big Venetian galleasses until their demise.

It was immediately evident from every angle that these big vessels were fighting ships. Forward, the high protected forecastle bristled with cannon, and there might be now as many as eight more pieces of artillery in the elaborate and substantial aftercastle. Nine more lighter pieces would be on each broadside, fixed just above or below or even between the oarsmen, who were protected by decking above, broken by gratings, used as a fore and aft gallery by soldiers firing small arms. Besides this small arms fire, the Venetian galleass in its

34

The Venetian galeass, by Gueroult

The Battle of Lepanto, 1571, by an anonymous sixteenth-century Venetian painter

ultimate form could fire a total weight of shot of some 325 pounds. The three lateen sails might carry as much as 8,000 square feet of sail area.

The galley and galleass were to survive actively in the Mediterranean into the 1700s, when at last the centuries of skill and experience which the northern nations had applied to the efficient application of wind-power made their influence felt. Before that time, the French, the English, the Swedes, the Danes and the Russians among others built galleys and galleasses either experimentally or in small numbers for use in northern waters. Many of these were even uneasier compromises than their southern counterparts because they had to contend with heavier weather for most of their time at sea, although they worked very well in the Baltic. Henry VIII's *Great Galley* represents both the

grandeur of conception to which the architects of the time aspired, and the failure of execution which doomed these hybrids. The Venetian influence was everywhere evident in her design, and the Venetian ambassador was actually present at her launching and wrote of her in his despatches home, describing her as a 'large galleass' with her fourteen heavy guns on a deck above the 160 oarsmen, and with four masts. She may have been the wonder of her day, but she was also a fiasco, and fourteen years after she first went to sea she was rebuilt as a 'pure' sailing ship.

The French had better reason to build great galleasses for they were constantly beset by troubles in the Mediterranean. It was, appropriately, left to that great navalist Louis XIV to build the most spectacular oared fighting ships of any age. These were the galleasses known as *les réales*, the navy's flagships and the largest, grandest, most decorated of them all. Landström has produced not only a beautiful reproduction of the carved stern, the original of which can be seen in the Musée de la Marine in Paris, but also a precise exploded drawing revealing the disposition of the armament – five bronze pieces under the forecastle and twelve swivel guns on the catwalks – and of the oarsmen, of which there were no less than seven to an oar and 427 in all. The splendours of Louis's Versailles were represented in miniature in the exquisite carving and decorative painting, from the long, delicate prow, to the intricately wrought brass cannon and the sumptuous gilded aftercastle and rudder. But the ostentatious réales, like the last of the Venetian galleys, could not sustain themselves by their brazen pretensions alone. They were poor sailers in a heavy sea, were unhandy, and were dreadfully vulnerable to a full broadside from a contemporary sailing ship.

The last great battle in which galleys or galleasses took part was off Cape Matapan in 1717, and only a handful were built in later years. The summit of their achievements occurred nearly a century and a half earlier. At Lepanto, fought off the coast of Greece in 1571, some 230 galleys, galleasses and other vessels of the combined fleets of Spain, Malta, Venice and the Vatican fought an even larger concourse of Turkish vessels, from dawn until just before midnight on 7 October. Maritime power at sea, in the finest hours of the oar-driven fighting ship, was fully to justify itself in the cause of Christianity, for a Turkish victory must have changed the course of history throughout Europe. On the *matériel* side it was also a marvellous justification of the galleass, for though only six Venetian vessels of this class were present, their firepower was to prove decisive in the later stages and to cause this

Two details from 'Battle in the Gu of Naples', by Breughel

λαδαναυτικόν. ταχέως έκελευεν άναχθῆναι· ὡς αν ποτων κατα ταραχ ταχαν τεξομερος προμλ τ
Και τομερ ναντικόμεν τιπ πλο κ σαι ταχέως άρετ ται· Και πεχωρισω προσορμί ζεται πρὸ β ρυ
δωρ. έκ τερ ῆ κορ τα και τρια κοσωρσωι γάμενον πλόι ων. πολεμικω π και σταφ θόν        οι
δε του βασιλ κόν φο λουκαταρ χοντες. τη τουτων μέτημ σ οκότεσ έλουσι. ρ υκ τος έ τ ι περ ται ραν
λοχ ωι τοισερ ν αν πολο. Οι πρ αι φυζι ωκα τα πλ ήξ αμχοι. πολλω μεραυ τα λδρ ωσεχορ
πω ν ιχ ων. Ηρα ω δε και πο σκ λα σ ωι π ρ πολ ω π υρί ·

τόλεμ ρωι και  π υ ρ πολ        τον τω νέ ναν τι φ λον.

Ολίγαι σαν τε λ αι ό σ ξ α γ νομ έ ν αυ του π άλοισ· Και προσ τ ον κόλ πον τ αι ο υβ λαι δ ρω ν κ α τ α ραλ ως |

FV FATTO L ANNO 1517 SOTTO MISIER ZACHARIA D'ANTONIO GASTALDO DE MARANGONI D'NAVE D'L ARSENAL
FV RINOVATO D'L ANNO 1753 SOTTO LA GASTALDIA DI FRANCESCO ZANOT TO GASTALDO E COMPAGNI

hybrid to remain in high esteem for many years. In spite of the galleass's reputation as the capital ship of the Mediterranean, like the twentieth-century battleship it saw little combat and its value was limited. And its life-span was a fraction of that of the galley from which it derived, and which was still being built – the very last of its kind – for the Sardinian Navy as late as 1814.

It was forty years before this that the oared fighting ship was to have its final *esprit de joie* in the Lake Campaign of the American War of Independence in 1775-6, when galleys and – of all things – gondolas were to play a crucial rôle in relieving pressure from General Sir William Howe on George Washington and preventing his army from being taken in the rear by Sir Guy Carleton. Some historians have contended that the American lake squadron, in which the oared fighting ship played a prominent part, succeeded not only in delaying for a vital period the British advance, but in the long term by limiting as well as delaying British successes, made possible General John Burgoyne's defeat at Saratoga in 1777, which brought France into the war on the side of the colonists. Perhaps this may exaggerate the claims made for Benedict Arnold's curious collection of vessels; but it is certainly true that the command of a narrow stretch of inland water fundamentally influenced the course of this land campaign.

Lake Champlain was of vital importance as the only possible advance route, between the impassable surrounding country, for the British army. Arnold had acquired by daring and enterprise a couple of sloops, with which, in the words of General Schuyler, commanding the Northern Department, 'we have happily such a naval superiority on Lake Champlain that I have a confident hope the enemy will not appear upon it this campaign.' But Arnold busied himself with the construction of reinforcements, knowing that it was only a matter of time before the British, who understood sea power, asserted their dominance of this lake. There was a vast amount of timber for the asking; the difficulty was to find enough carpenters. But, he emphasized, 'to augment our navy on the lake appears to me of the utmost importance. There is water between Crown Point and Pointe au Fer for vessels of the largest size. I am of the opinion that row-galleys are the best construction and cheapest for this lake . . . they are quick moving, which will give us a great advantage. . . .'

And so at last, 1,800 years after Actium and two oceans away from the scene of this great galley battle, the oarsman again came into his own. By August 1776 Arnold was still in control of the lake and had accumulated three schooners and a sloop, and had completed the construction of five gondolas – crude, flat-bottomed oared craft,

he use of 'Greek fire', from Juan
kylitzes 'Sinopsis Historiarum',
nd (bottom) a Venetian shipyard
1517

mounting perhaps a 12-pounder, a pair of 6-pounders and some swivel guns. By prodigious efforts from the carpenters, the galleys came along apace, and by October four of these craft had been added to the Lilliputian squadron. Their precise nature is uncertain, but they were probably keeled craft carrying sails, manned by some eighty oarsmen, and with an armament of two medium-weight guns in the bows, a pair of 9-pounders in the stern and half a dozen 4- or 6-pounders on the broadside. Arnold greatly preferred them to the gondolas.

The British were slow to react, and through that summer of 1776 – one of the most momentous in American history – Arnold's force held the key to the lake waters with a naval force of diminutive size but of immense strategical importance. The oarsmen of those galleys and gondolas could not hope to survive for long after the British strength was built up and commanded with adequate skill and determination. Two schooners armed with 6-pounders and a ship-rigged 180-ton fighting ship armed with 12-pounders, supported by smaller vessels, formed a British squadron which swept Lake Champlain clear of Arnold's revolutionary force during October, but not before the galley had given a clear demonstration of its prime advantage of manoeuvrability.

A model of the réale *Dauphine* from the end of the seventeenth century with twenty-six pairs of thwarts and five men to each oar. The most sumptuous réales were decorated with carving by Pierre Pugin; their most famous action was Matapan in 1717

40

# . THE VIKINGS

While the genesis of the Mediterranean galley lay in the primitive papyrus rafts of the Nile and the Tigris, the ancestors of the Viking longship were crudely hollowed-out tree trunks used on the lakes, rivers and fjords which are such marked geographical features of Scandinavia. Papyrus rafts of a design believed to be identical to those of the prehistoric age are built today on the Nile and other African rivers, and dugouts were still being hewn in the more remote regions of Finland in this century. But while the life-span of a papyrus raft must be measured in weeks, there is ample archaeological evidence of the design and construction of the various forms of ancient northern dugout. The climate of the north may have its drawbacks, but at least for the purpose of tracing the development of boat design it is not necessary to rely on fragments of carvings and the coloured accounts of contemporary poets. The preservative qualitites of the mud and clay of marshlands, river estuaries and poorly-drained fields have yielded up numerous examples of northern boat design, from the most simple hollowed-out tree trunk to near-complete Viking fighting ships, which were sometimes ceremonially buried and discovered centuries later by delighted archaeologists.

Until recent times, the characteristics of the fighting ship have been closely related to its local climate and geographical environment. The Viking longship, lean, robust, with fine seagoing and sailing qualities, was the ideal man-of-war for the northern warrior travelling on his long-distance raids in the storm-racked waters of the North Sea and Atlantic. The Viking's fighting ship never matched the

The Gotland pictorial stones of the seventh and eighth centuries, showing two types of ship: with curved and with angled stern and keel. It is thought the sharply-angled ships were for trade

fighting qualities of the contemporary Roman galley, but the fierce weather of the north with its long swells would soon have smashed the frail Mediterranean trireme; and no southern vessel could equal the sailing qualities of its northern counterpart. In the north, the wind was the prime motive power, and centuries before the coming of the Viking longship, the northern sailor had mastered the art of close-hauling and sailing into the wind. Julius Caesar has recorded how that Celtic tribe, the Veneti, as early as 56 BC were able to flee by sailing against the wind and hove-to in a gale.

Viking restlessness, the subsequent raiding and then massive colonization which spread throughout most of northern Europe, had its origins in the discovery in Scandinavia of great supplies of readily available iron ore. With the tools wrought from this new mineral, agriculture flourished and the population increased rapidly – so rapidly that efforts to feed the hungry began to fail. Fishing was one answer to the problem, and this led to the application of greater skills to the art of ship design. The need for new lands to colonize became critical, and by AD 700 the practice of raiding across the North Sea and beyond was firmly established. At first the vessels were fighting ships, and battle was the chief occupation of those who sailed in them. From these were developed the fierce and beautiful longships which sailed on those remarkable voyages of discovery to Iceland and Greenland and to the Continent of America. Only in the later Viking period were ships built primarily for transporting colonists with their families and tools. These vessels, the *knorrs*, were constructed with a wider beam and flatter bottom, and relied even more than the longships on the wind for propulsion.

Although so much is known from archaeological finds about the fighting ship and its ancestors during the Viking era of power from about AD 800, knowledge of the longship's sequence of derivation remains uncertain. From the mud of the River Humber at North Ferriby on the east coast of England, two boats were retrieved in 1937 which give us the shapes of the longship's ancestors. One of these was a flat-bottomed craft, apparently constructed from nine great oak planks – three forming the bottom – set edge to edge and secured by yew withes. There were battens over the seams and caulking appears to have been accomplished with moss. Being 45 feet long, it was necessary to reinforce the bottom with cross pieces. Another boat, about half the overall length of the Ferriby boat, and dated at about AD 100, was discovered at Björke in Sweden. The bottom board, hollowed out and tapering at stem and stern, acts also as a keel. A single plank overlapping and secured to the bottom board with iron

rivets forms the side, which is strengthened by six ribs stitched to cleats left in the planks and riveted at the gunwale. A similar form of overlapping clinker-built construction is found in the much larger and more complex Nydam boat, dated around AD 350 and dug up from a bog in Schleswig in 1863. The measurements are 76 feet overall, with a beam of $10\frac{1}{2}$ feet, and the timber is oak throughout. Thwarts are cut to secure to the upper ends of the ribs; and the gunwale plank, shaped to offer greater strength, has lashed to it fourteen thole-pins on each side for the oars, and carries on the starboard quarter a socket for the single steering paddle. There is no evidence that a sail was carried, even for emergency use, and this type of vessel probably limited its trading and fighting activities to fjords, estuaries and coastal waters.

It is the famous Gökstad ship on which we mainly rely for exact details of the construction of the Viking longship in its ultimate form, although it is known that vessels designed for extended seagoing trips were considerably larger. The almost completely preserved Gökstad ship of AD 900 was found in a 15-foot-high burial mound of blue clay on a farm near Sande Fjord in Norway in 1880, and today can be seen, fully restored, in Oslo. Again constructed entirely of oak, and skilfully fashioned by the new iron tools, it probably weighed 20 tons when fully laden for sea. The vessel would have been built on land and launched on rollers into shallow water. Three main classes of shipwrights would have been employed on her – the head-smiths, the

The Nydam ship, fourth century, is thought to have had stones for ballast and a bottom board rather than a keel. Tacitus described this type of ship: 'Clinker built, oak, riveted, V-shaped'

The Gökstad ship, tenth century, had sixteen oars a side

stem-smiths, who constructed the framework, and the strake-smiths, assisted by joiners, blacksmiths, nail-makers and others. The Gökstad ship is built up from a heavy external keel to a high stem and stern post, to which the ribbing is secured by the garboard strakes – the planking adjacent to the keel. The other seven lower planks up to the turn of the bilge are lashed through lugs to the ribs, while the upper ones are nailed direct by iron spikes. All the strakes overlap (clinker-built) and are bound together by clench-nail and rove as they are today, and caulked with tarred ropes. Two feet above the top of the keel and secured to the ribs on either side are the beams, which fill the dual purpose of supporting the decking and the whole hull structure in heavy weather. Piercing the strakes some 18 inches below the gunwale are the sixteen oar-ports on each side, each ingeniously contrived with a circular sealing cap for use when heeling over under sail in rough seas. There is no sign of thwarts for the oarsmen, and as it would not be possible to row standing up at this low level, Landström suggests that the oarsmen sat on loose benches, which were removed before this particular ship was ceremonially buried. The oars were probably 18 feet long. When it was dug up there were also sixteen overlapping shields hung on each side of the vessel, and this romantic but highly impractical aspect has been inaccurately per-petuated by imaginative artists ever since the ship's discovery at Gökstad farm. For those shields were probably hung in this way only

45

for identification in harbour, for ceremonial occasions, and possibly when under sail in calm weather off an enemy shore as a gesture of challenge and intimidation. They prohibited rowing and must soon have been swept away in high seas. The single pine mast of some 40 feet is stepped amidships and very substantially formed, and like its Mediterranean counterpart, can be lowered when the boat is being rowed or is in close action. Steering is by a single paddle on the starboard quarter, having an athwartship tiller at its upper end. The overall length of the Gökstad ship is 79 feet, its beam about 16½ feet.

Chatterton has some informative comments on the sail of a Viking longship, which can as well be applied specifically to the Gökstad ship. It was made from flax, he writes, 'was strengthened with a hem of rope, and was frequently striped. Sometimes it was embroidered or decked with a pall . . . . The portions of the sail were sewed together with thread, rings being attached to the leach in such a place that the sheets could conveniently be made fast when the vessel had need to shorten sail. Small ropes or reefing points were also affixed to the sail. . . . Gorgeous sails were worked by their women-folk, with cunning designs and beautiful embroidery, even historic incidents being included. White sails were sometimes striped with red and with blue, whilst others of double velvet were made gay with exquisitely woven patterns in red, purple and gold.'[7]

That the Gökstad ship was a modest-sized fighting ship for its time is borne out by the fact that the more common Viking longship was pulled by twenty or thirty pairs of oars. And gigantism, that perennial temptation to which the naval architect of every age seems inevitably to fall victim, appears to have been indulged in. There is a record, factual or fanciful, the King Olaf Tryggvesson built the largest vessel of her day, the *Long Serpent*, which was pulled by sixty-eight oars and may have been as long as 165 feet overall. Rodgers gives her a displacement of 220–30 tons and a complement – equipped for battle – of 400 men. There is also evidence that as a fighting ship she

The figurehead of a Viking ship. It is interesting to compare this with the carved Norman prows

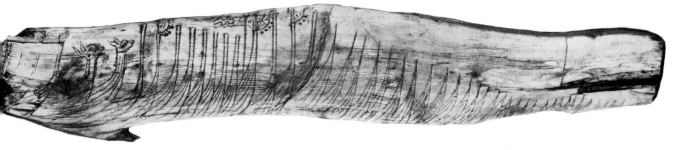

A thirteenth-century wood carving of a fleet of Viking-type ships in battle order

was a failure, but this did not deter other grandiose schemes in later years, notably King Sverre's mammoth *Marasuden*, which could so easily be out-manoeuvred in combat.

As proof of the seagoing qualities of the more modest-sized longship, a replica of the Gökstad ship was built in 1893 and sailed across the Atlantic for the World's Fair at Chicago and the four hundredth anniversary of the 'discovery' of America. She made the passage without mishap, proving herself capable of a speed of 11 knots under sail.

Sea fighting among the Norsemen was a fierce and brutish business, with little skill or subtlety. As in the early days of Roman power, it was nothing more than land combat transferred to the precarious uncertainty of narrow vessels of war, and conducted wherever possible in sheltered waters. It was fought with swords and spears and fearful great axes. As in the Mediterranean, an action was opened at a distance with volleys of stones and arrows – the Viking was a specially fine bowman. But the elaborate tactical evolution on which the Mediterranean sailor prided himself, and the ram which governed these manoeuvrings, were unknown in the north. The longships were sometimes lashed together for mutual protection; from that point in any combat the situation, it would seem, from this account in *Heimskringla*, Saga VII, became nothing more than a furious mêlée:

They fought at the bows [at the battle of Aarhus, 1044] so that only the men on the bows could strike; the men on the forecastle thrust with spears and all who were farther off shot with light spears or javelins or war arrows. Some fought with stones or short stakes and those who were abaft the mast shot with the bow. The battle was hot with casting weapons. King Magnus [of Norway and Denmark] stood in the beginning of the battle with a shield rampart but as it appeared to him that matters were going too slowly, he leaped over the shields and rushed forward in the ship, encouraging his men with a loud cheer and springing to the bows where the battle was going on hand-to-hand. When his men saw this they urged each other on with mutual cheering and there was one great hurra through all the ships. And now the battle was exceedingly sharp and in the assault Swend's [a claimant to the throne of Denmark] ship was cleared of all forecastle men on both sides of the forecastle. Then Magnus boarded Swend's ship followed by his men and one after the other came up and made so stout an assault that Swend's men gave way and King Magnus cleared first that ship and then the rest one after the other. . . .

It is fortunate that the enduring nature of oak timber and the pre-serving nature of certain damp soil have provided us with all the authentic information we need of the Viking fighting ship of about one thousand years after Christ. There is no record of any other effective type of northern fighting ship at this time, but there is plenty of evidence, above all from the Bayeux tapestry, that this graceful, single-masted, clinker-built Gökstad-style vessel, with its sharp sheer forward and aft leading up to a high stem and stern-post, spread to all northern regions washed by the Atlantic, the North Sea and the Baltic. Its effectiveness is undeniable considering that its outward shape has been retained for another thousand years along the northern coasts of Norway and among the Shetland Islands. William the Conqueror's ship in which he landed in England in 1066 is under its single sail, and the oar-ports are not shown. It is also properly gaudy for the occasion, with brightly painted and decorated sail and fearful carved figurehead at the prow, as well as a cross at the masthead indicating the Pope's approval of the invasion. In King Harold's ship, and others, the lady embroiderers have included the oar-ports – sixteen a side as in the Gökstad ship. Everything points to the enduring dominance of this style and form of construction in northern Europe until perhaps a hundred years after the Norman Conquest, when – as in the Mediterranean – an increasing reliance on the power of the wind and skill in taming it relegated the oarsman to a secondary and occasional rôle.

The French fleet from the Bayeux tapestry

The English fleet from the Bayeux tapestry

# 5. PRELUDE TO THE THREE-MASTER

> Whither, O splendid ship, thy white sails crowding,
> Leaning across the bosom of the urgent West,
> That fearest nor sea rising, nor sky clouding,
> Whither away, fair rover, and what thy quest?
>
> Robert Bridges

Until recently, the oceans of the world have been thought hostile and mysterious, and at best the relationship between man and the sea has been an uneasy one, in which anxiety and superstition have thrived. It is no wonder that the development of the fighting ship from its earliest days has been retarded by caution and traditionalism. The sailor has always hated change of any kind; and the taming of the wind to the needs of the long-distance mariner was therefore a long and arduous process. But at length the means by which a ship could be sailed efficiently close to and into the wind was discovered, and accepted by the sailor. Thus the inception of the three-master was brought about. It was a slow business, and it was not achieved until Western man had emerged from the Dark Ages, and had begun to enjoy the security at home which, paradoxically, has always sent him off in fighting ships to conquer and then to colonize. The three-masted ship opened up the world and brought about the great age of discovery and exploration. It also revolutionized the fighting ship and sea warfare. Until the fighting sailor, with the three-master, was able to sail in all weathers and to all places, and the gunsmith had mastered his craft, sea fighting remained essentially a matter of hand-to-hand combat carried out in quiet waters close to shore. Among the weapons used, only the ram brought about any degree of tactical elaboration, for the purpose of missiles, arrows and spears, and even molten lead and liquid fire, was to strike fear and injury among the foe before sword, muscle, and courage brought about a decision. In sea fighting the quality of the man always counted above the quality of the

*matériel*, but never more so than during the two thousand years that separated the period of Phoenician maritime power from the Battle of Sluys.

By the standards of later progress, little happened to the fighting ship between the arrival of the Duke of Normandy in Pevensey Bay for the conquest of England in 1066 and the departure of Christopher Columbus from Palos for America in 1492. But the fact the Columbus could even contemplate such a long and hazardous journey – and without oars – is evidence that the ship had become an ocean-going means of transport. For fighting, the ship had also acquired cannon. By the late 1400s, then, a new age of battle at sea had opened. Suddenly, the fighting ship could sail for thousands of miles, hover off an enemy coast, blockade, strike at targets ashore, manoeuvre freely and engage an enemy in the open sea. The fighting ship, and sea warfare, had grown up, and neither were to change fundamentally for another 400 years.

Paganism has been a blessing to the marine archaeologist. We know less about the shape of the northern fighting ship during the Christian period between the Norman Conquest and the opening up of the world in the 1400s and 1500s by the three-masted sailing ship than we know, from burial mounds, about the ships of the Norsemen. There was a lot of informal exchange of knowledge and experience between the northern and the southern shipbuilders. As trade flourished in the north and the sailor gained increasing confidence with his sail, the design of his ship began to develop to meet his needs.

William of Normandy may or may not have had oars in his ships. But he *sailed* to conquer England. The single-masted warship continued to dominate northern waters for many years after the invasion, and the heavy oars carried aboard were resorted to only in a rare calm. Evidence of the shape and form of ships of the 1100s and 1200s is derived almost entirely from the contemporary seals of the northern ports. The artists had a hard time portraying a long ship on a small, round piece of metal; and, while it is certain that seagoing vessels were constructed more stubbily as the sail took over from the oar, they still owed much to the Viking longship, and the seals show a deceptively foreshortened hull. These seals of Continental ports, and of the Cinque ports* in England – originally Hythe, Dover, Romney, Sandwich and Hastings – offer evidence that may not always be reliable, but it is about all we have. A seal of La Rochelle of the 1100s, for instance, suggests that reef points to reduce sail area in stormy weather had been introduced – a notable advance in sail-craft. The Sandwich seal

struck in 1238 shows that Viking principles were still being followed – clinker construction, a heavy sheer fore and aft, high stem and sternposts, a single pole mast stepped amidships with a square sail. But this seal also seems to confirm that sailors who had fought their way through the Mediterranean had passed on to the shipwrights at home valuable lessons from the southern sea. The deck beams appear to project through the sides of the vessel, where they are secured with pegs as in some Mediterranean ships. Wooden castles built up on stout pillars rise fore and aft, giving the bowmen the benefit of superior height. It was to the crusading spirit of Richard I that the English shipwright owed this fundamental advance in the fighting power of his vessels, which decreed the shape of the sailing fighting ship for so many centuries. And no event could have more strongly persuaded the English sailor of the superiority in design of the big Mediterranean warship than Richard I's famous engagement with the Saracen galley off Beirut, described here by Chatterton.

'The English espied in the distance a great ship with three tapering masts, strongly built, painted green and yellow. . . . On being hailed she pretended at first to belong to Richard's colleague in the Crusade, the King of France, whose flag indeed she was flying, but she was soon discovered to be a Saracen ship, and after some difficulty was rammed and sunk by the English Viking-shaped and smaller vessels.'[1] Hakluyt describes her as 'a great carak fraught with souldiers and men of warre to a number of a thousand and five hundred.'

Chatterton continues: 'The three tapering masts which astounded the Englishmen in their one-masted Viking-type ships and the tall sides of the carak which gave Richard's men so much difficulty in

The seal of Hythe, Kent, showing a late twelfth- or early thirteenth century ship and (right) the seal of Sandwich showing a late thirteenth- or early fourteenth century ship.

The Seal of Dover of 1305 and (right) an impression of the seal of John, Duke of Bedford, warden of the Cinque Ports, of about 1426

assault from their comparatively small vessels of low freeboard, would not fail to bring forth changes in English shipbuilding as soon as internal and external peace was assured and sufficient technical skill had been acquired. This big ship . . . marks a determined stand in naval architecture to build real ships as distinct from big boats. From her evolved the vessels that sailed across the Atlantic with Columbus, that carried Elizabethan explorers to all points of the compass, that fought the Armada and the Dutch. . . . What seems to have had an almost immediate effect were the castles on the Mediterranean galley at both bow and stern.'[1]

In the English fighting ship, these forecastles and aftercastles soon became higher and stronger. Other English seals suggest that old Roman (and contemporary Mediterranean) practice was followed with a primitive form of bowsprit which served both the grapnel and for securing the bowlines to allow the ship to sail more closely to the wind. (The Romans had not recognized the value of their artemon for this second purpose.)

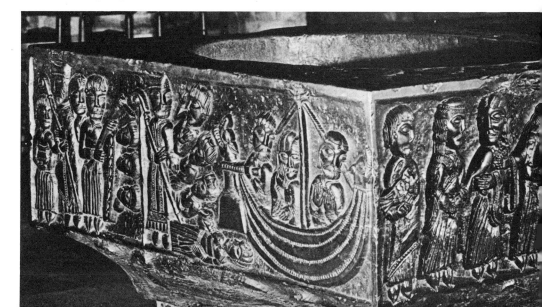

The Belgian font of Winchester Cathedral showing a ship with a mid-twelfth-century rudder in a scene from the life of St Nicholas

Fifty years later than the Sandwich seal, the seal of Dover struck in 1284 shows that the typical English fighting ship has heavier and more elaborate castles, and there is a top-castle for the look-out to sight the enemy and the archers and slingers to use in battle. The fact that the steersman's oar is shown on the port side is evidently artistic licence: the ship was always secured in port with the less vulnerable ('port') side to the quay. By the early 1200s it seems likely that the Flemish and Hanseatic vessels were already being steered by a stern rudder. It was not only in their steering arrangements that English warships of the 1100s and 1200s were behind Mediterranean and north European practice.

The early thirteenth-century north European warship had acquired small but significant advantages over the old Viking longship. The cannon had not yet arrived to revolutionize the fighting power of the warship, but the castles offered real advantages in close combat. A higher freeboard, a wider beam, now about a third instead of a fifth of the overall length, and an improved comprehension of the use of sail, offered greater seaworthiness and manoeuvrability, so that fighting was no longer limited entirely to coastal waters. But the final break with the earliest and most primitive fighting ships still remained to be taken. Now that the wind was the common means of propulsion, the drawbacks of the starboard-projecting oar or paddle were being shown up more than ever before. Especially in the rougher northern seas, a ship heeled over for most of the time when under sail. It did not have to heel far to port before the steering paddle lifted out of the water – and steering control ceased. Ship designers began to meet this rather fundamental failing by moving the paddle towards the sternpost: ship by ship taking it perhaps a few feet farther. Just when it slipped round, neatly and obviously, into the sternpost itself, is only conjectural, but probably around the end of the 1100s. On one of the decorative panels of the font at Winchester Cathedral there is a relief of a ship, believed to be by a Belgian artist and dated at about 1180, which shows the rudder at the stern. Several historians argue that this is only a quarter-rudder and that the artist has taken liberties, but this is not very important, because if it is not a stern-rudder it is very nearly one, and at least suggests that very soon the ship's designer is going to take the plunge. Experts have dated a carving on the wall of a church in Gotland in the early 1200s, and there is no doubt that the rudder of this ship is at the stern. What is more, the vessel has a straight stern, for the convenience both of operation and of the carpenter who made it.

The carved prow of the Oseberg ship, an oak-built, ninth-century vessel

This pictorial evidence marks a double revolution. For not only will the fighting ship – except those simple craft that endured for centuries among primitive peoples – always now be steered by a stern rudder, but for the first time in northern ships the straight formation of the sternpost is in marked contrast with the curved stem. Gone now is the graceful symmetry of the longships, and there is no doubt which end is the stern. However you choose to interpret the Winchester font decoration, by the early 1300s the stern rudder was probably commonplace among larger English men-of-war.

At this period, immediately before the introduction of the cannon, there were fewer points of distinction between the northern man-of-war and large merchantman than at any time before or since. There did not need to be. The castles fore and aft, which had been inherited from the Mediterranean and were incorporated in the fighting ship, were found to have real benefits for the merchantman too. Not only did they give the crew a marked advantage when they were attacked by the small pirate vessels that ravaged the Channel and North Sea, but they added to the comfort and safety of the ship, the forecastle helping to break the force of the waves and the aftercastle providing shelter and accommodation. This duality of operation was extremely convenient and economical for a king who could not afford to keep a large standing navy. Instead, he possessed a few large ships – of around 200 or 300 tons – which he hired out to traders when he did not need them. In time of war he withdrew these, hired or commandeered all the other merchantmen he needed, filled them with soldiers, and set sail for the enemy. So King Edward III of England, who has since been called the father of the British navy (so has King Alfred) never really possessed a navy at all. The Battle of Sluys was not only one of the last decisive major sea battles in the north before the introduction of cannon. It was also the last occasion when the respective fleets were nothing more than troop- and boarding-ships. It was a land battle conducted at great inconvenience to both sides on the decks of merchantmen.

In 1340 the Hundred Years War began with the collection by both King Edward and King Philip of France of all the merchantmen they could lay their hands on. In addition, Philip of Valois succeeded in hiring some Genoese ships, complete with sailors and commander, who were to have good cause for regretting their decision. Soon the French King had around 190 ships in all, which he assembled off the Flanders coast at Sluys. King Edward called on the Cinque Ports for their contribution, and drew on more ships from other seaports from the Tyne to the Severn, many of them only small undecked sailing

orman soldiers crossing the hannel

57

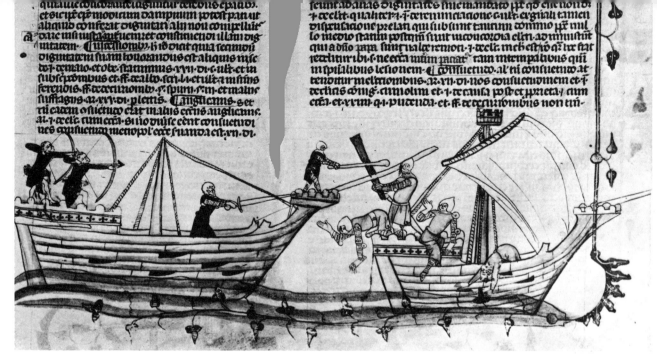

boats. This took a long time but by June the King's army, from knights in full armour complete with their great steeds to light infantry armed with long-bows, began to embark. Very slowly and very uncomfortably this mixed armada set sail down the coast from the Stour and the Orwell and made the hazardous crossing. Then all the ships that could be dragged ashore were beached and camp was set up. A party of knights was despatched by land – rather as frigates and cruisers scouted in later sea battles – to reconnoitre the enemy. The French disposition was entirely defensive, with the two French divisions and one Genoese division ranged side by side in the estuary of the River Eede. Their prows were pointing towards the direction of attack, lashed together Viking-style, and they had makeshift wooden barriers secured across the bows as defence against boarding.

Hale has vividly reconstructed the moments before the clash of arms – the 'murderous and horrible' battle, as Froissart called it – on 24 June:

The wind was blowing fair into the mouth of the Eede, but the tide was ebbing, and the attack could not be driven home till it turned, and gave deep water everywhere between the banks of the inlet. King Edward used the interval to array his fleet and get it into position for the dash into the river. His ships stood out to sea on the starboard tack, a brave sight with midsummer sun shining on the white sails, the hundreds of banners glowing with red, blue, white, and gold, the painted shields hanging on poop and bulwark. On the raised bows and sterns of the larger ships, barons and knights and men-at-arms stood arrayed in complete armour. The archers were ranged along the bulwarks, or looked out from the crow's-nest-tops over the swelling sails . . . . King Edward's trumpets gave the expected signal for action. As their notes rang over the sea the shouting sailors squared the yards and the fleet began to scud before the wind for the river-mouth, where beyond the green dykes a forest of masts bristled along the bank towards Sluys . . . . At some 60 yards, when men could see each other's faces across the gap, the English archers drew their bows, and their cloth-yard arrows began to fly . . . . Two English ships crashed into the bows and the port side of the *Christopher*, and with the cry of 'St George for England!' a score of knights vied with each other for the honour of being first to board the enemy.[2]

'Sovereign of the seas', the title claimed by Edward after the massacre of the French at Sluys, was not really so pretentious as it may seem. The same long-bow and pike won the day at the sea battle of Sluys as at Crécy six years later. But although that fierce clash of arms off Flanders (some 30,000 French are said to have died) was in all but name and location a land battle, the maritime results were profound. As in the great wars of this century, safe passage of the Channel was thereby assured to the British Army. And the ships which annihilated the squadrons of Sieur de Kiriet and Sieur de Bahuchet were soon engaged in transporting men and supplies to the English armies in France. The control of the sea between England and France remained in English hands until their defeat off La Rochelle in 1372.

The Battle of Zonchio, 1499, an anonymous sixteenth-century Venetian school woodcut, which is probably the earliest extant print of a definite historical sea fight

The shape of the fighting ship at Sluys is depicted on the seal struck at Poole in 1325, and better still on 'the golden nobles' struck by Edward III to celebrate his first great naval victory and the siege of Calais in 1346–7. It might appear that even more than a hundred years later still no profound change had taken place. It seems as if the fighting ship is set in frozen expectation of the momentous advances in sails and weapons that were to change its shape for ever. In the Science Museum in London there is a model of a ship of about 1426. Eighty-six years had passed since Sluys was fought and her appearance in the English line might have been unnoticed. If this ship is almost an evolutionary throw-back, it does also reveal the progress that has been made since King Harold's fleet waited off the Isle of Wight for the invasion force of the Duke of Normandy. The model is based on the crude representation of a ship on the seal of John, Duke of Bedford, then Lord High Admiral* of England. Except for its clinker form of construction, the stem post which still rises up gracefully enough, and the single mast with its square sail stepped almost amidships, the longship influence has almost disappeared, and the hull formation appears bluff, almost ungainly. The heavy fighting forward castle is built into the ship and from it there thrusts outwards threateningly the short bowsprit from which is slung the grappling iron, in the old Roman manner. The mast is surmounted by a small circular fighting top for perhaps half a dozen bold warriors; and in action there will be many more with their bows and slings on the big aftercastle, which now forms the roof of a substantial cabin. Here when the Lord High Admiral is on board – and his coat-of-arms is emblazoned on the sail – the fittings will be luxurious, and he will live in a degree of comfort and splendour unknown by any Viking chieftain. Now the heavy sternpost is almost vertical and of course the median rudder is well-established in its appropriate place at the stern.

This 60-foot-long heavy fighting ship will be slow and unhandy by contrast with the longships. But it will be capable of staying at sea for long periods – accompanied by supply ships – and of riding out almost any gale.

Shakespeare's 'villainous saltpetre' had by this time been 'digg'd out of the bowels of the harmless earth', and cannon had been fired at sea. But they had not yet appeared in serious numbers to clutter the decks and relieve from the fighting men aboard much of their responsibility for killing the foe with their own muscles and hand-weapons. Combat continued to be conducted mainly at a range of a few feet until some time after this stout but pretty little fighting ship had been broken up.

*The date when this rank was formal introduced remains doubtful.

While King Edward III had given Europe an early demonstration of English prowess in sea warfare at Sluys, it was a long time before English designers and shipwrights caught up with their Continental and Mediterranean counterparts. Even in the 1300s England was not a great trading country, and as always it was those who sailed most and farthest who had the best ships. After the breakdown of the stabilizing influence of Roman power, trade throughout the western world greatly diminished, and with it the pace of development of the trading ship. By the 1100s, trade between the northern ports and in the Mediterranean was again increasing year by year. From the East came the silks and scents, the cargoes of 'ivory, and apes and peacocks, sandalwood, cedarwood, and sweet white wine' for the countries of the Mediterranean, and over the Alps to Germany, and thence by sea to the northern countries. The minerals, wax and furs of Russia, the wines of Gascony, the salted fish of Scandinavia, the wool of southern England and coal of the north, all relied mainly on the pirate-ridden routes of the northern seas for their trade and transport. The ports of Europe became ever more powerful and important, and moved from up-river to estuaries as ships increased in size.

The greatest traders were the Germans, and in the last decades of the twelfth century the north German ports began to form groups for mutual protection and the creation of an all-powerful monopoly in the north. Although over the centuries, the monopolistic Hanseatic League used all sizes and kinds of vessels for different forms of trade, it is the *cog*, if only because it is the largest and most often portrayed on the ports' seals, that is always most closely associated with Hanseatic trade – and, inevitably, the occasional combat that was a perennial risk.

The Hansa cog was a deep-draught vessel with a great load-carrying capacity, clinker-built, with a high freeboard and a long keel for stability and seaworthiness in the unpredictable northern weather. Although its development from the Viking longships can be presumed, by the 1300s it showed little evidence of its ancestry. The end-posts ran straight down to the long keel giving a characteristic sharp-ended silhouette, and as further evidence of its advanced conception, by this time the forecastle has already been greatly reduced in size by contrast with English and French ships at Sluys, while the aftercastle has been formed into an integral part of the hull and become long enough to be called a poop deck. From Landström's beautiful reconstructions, based mainly on contemporary seals and a manuscript drawing, the elaboration of the cog's rig is clearly shown, with bowlines, topping lifts, and bonnets or reef-points for shortening sail in rough weather. Here, then, was a sturdy, useful vessel that dominated the trade routes of the North Sea and the Baltic for at least a century, that could carry a well-armed crew of some twenty men to sail the ship and successfully ward off attacks, and a cargo of perhaps 30 tons. When well-handled, it could probably ride out the worst storm. In the north there was nothing to match it in the 1200s and 1300s.

While the Hanseatics dominated northern trade from Germany, and the Flemish ports (which soon began to rival the power of their German neighbours) monopolized the Channel and Atlantic routes, in the south maritime power rested mainly in the hands of the Genoese and Venetians. While the Mediterranean galley had revealed few indications of development since the days of Roman power, the southern sailing ship, under the ever-growing demands of trade, became much more robust and versatile. As in the north, the story of

A Mediterranean carrack of the late fifteenth century

Mediterranean ship development from the 1100s to the 1400s shows a curious mixture of enterprise and conservatism. The element of enterprise, as so often happens, had its roots in geography. As Charnock put it so nicely:

> Experiment, generally speaking, takes place in quarters, and on occasions, where the least danger is to be apprehended from it. The boisterous billows of a northern ocean appeared to militate very strongly against any attempt at innovation; there the greatest risk of misfortune existed, and the smallest deviation from principles, the result of which had not been experimentally proved, appeared to be, with great prudence, most studiously avoided. In the more southern climes, such experiments were naturally considered far less dangerous.[3]

Even the apparent conservatism of southern shipbuilders in the matter of steering had climatic origins. The art of sailing close to the wind in the Mediterranean was slower to develop because wind still remained of less importance as a source of power. For the same reason it took longer for the stern rudder to become accepted. Side steering did not develop into the rudder because of any advantage of either in windward sailing. For a long time the southern mariner made do with a steering paddle on both the port and starboard quarters, making it possible for the ship to be steered even when heeling over. It was not very satisfactory, but it worked well enough for Mediterranean-strength winds. In the course of time and experience, the northern stern rudder was accepted in the south – an instance of the southern ship benefiting from northern practice.

The southern equivalent of the cog, and its successor the hulk, was the carrack, a vessel of both trade and war, and of which little is known for sure. In the early 1300s it was probably no more than a dumpy, round-ended merchantman – a 'round ship' – with a single mast raked forward, and carrying a single lateen sail. Carvel construction was used, as always in the Mediterranean, and horizontal wales appear to have been incorporated in the hull for additional strength. As the southern traders became more adventurous in their voyages, and the journey through the Straits of Gibraltar and across the Bay of Biscay to the Channel became commonplace, European influence was absorbed – as it needed to be in these less predictable and angrier seas. The lateen sail was dropped in favour of the square sail, and – we will now have to surmise – the southern seamen demanded a small mizzen mast carrying a lateen sail because they found the square sail at first difficult to manage. As ships with two and even three masts had been used in the Mediterranean for many generations, this step would not here be regarded with the wonder and caution of the northern sailor.

Apart from this second mast, the configuration of the southern carrack of the first half of the fifteenth century was very similar to that of its northern equivalent. This is not surprising. Regional characteristics stemming from local traditions and weather conditions diminished as the ships of the western world grew larger and more seaworthy; and as they met the ships of other peoples, influences must have brushed off one against the other. From this point in history the shape and the design of the ship (it is soon to become a distinctive class, a fighting ship again) becomes more uniform.

Detail of 'Portuguese carracks off a rocky coast', 1521, by Anthoniszoon

Overleaf: 'Equipping the Argo', (top right) 'The Argonauts land at Colchis', from a fifteenth-century French manuscript; (bottom left) a sixteenth-century manuscript picture thought to show a contemporary English ship; (bottom right) 'Henry I's nightmare', from a twelfth-century English manuscript

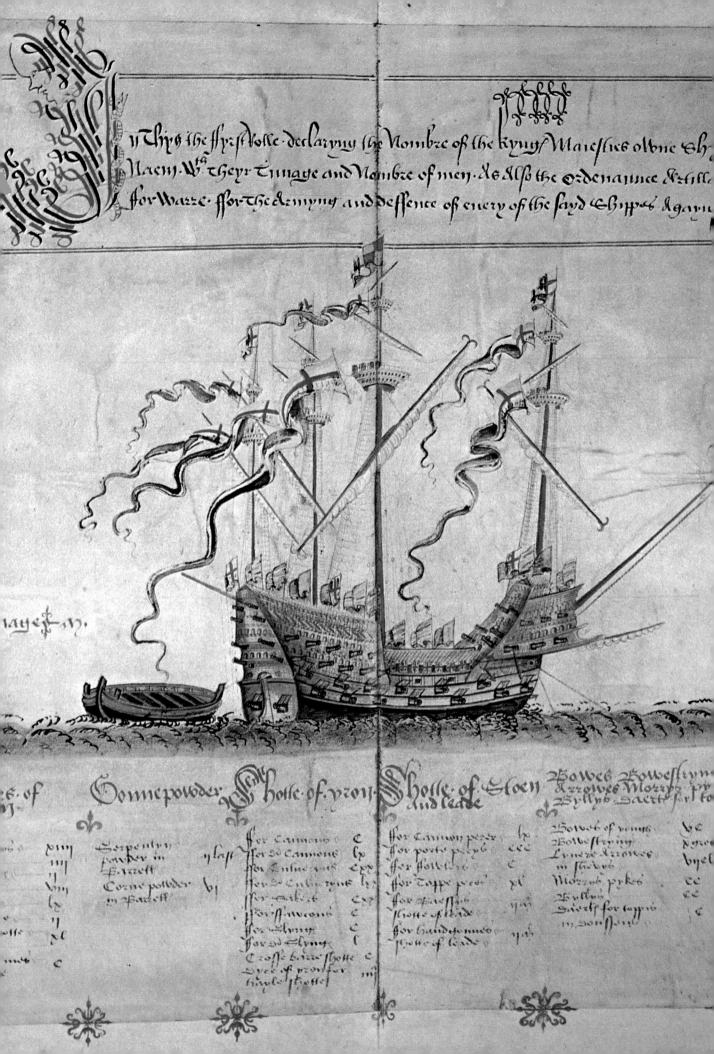

Iy This the ffyrst Rolle declaryng the Nombre of the kyngs Maiesties olde Shy
Naem Wth theyr Tunage and Nombre of men As Alfo the Ordenaunce Artill
for Warre ffor the armyng and deffence of every of the sayd Shipps Agayn

Gonnepowder    Shotte of yron  Shotte of Yron    Bowes Bowestryng
                               and leade          Arrowes Morryſh p
                                                  Byllys Dartys for to

Serpentyn      for cannons  c      for cannon peces  lx    Bowes of yewgh
powder in   ij laſt  for so cannons  lx   for porte peces  ccc   Bowestryng
Barrell           for culueryns  cxx  for sowlers  c      Lyuere Arrowes
Corne powder  vj  for so culueryns  lx   for Toppe peces  xl   in sheffis
in Barrell         for sakers  cxx   for fawcons      Morryſh pykes
                   for fawcons   for flytes  yiij  Byllys
                   for slyng            Shotte of leade       Dartys for toppis
                   for so slyng  c      for handgonnes  yiij   in dossen
                   Crosse barre shotte  c
                   Dyce of yron  iiij
                   Hayle shotte

# THE FIGHTING SHIP AS A GUN-PLATFORM

Like every evolution throughout history, it was the needs of man which shaped the form and nature of the sailing fighting ship. From around 1400, widening curiosity about the world – and the subsequent conflicts of interest – brought about notable advances in the science of navigation and exploration, and of combat at sea. As the ship grew to meet the mariners' needs, a true comprehension of the means to propel it more safely and efficiently on any desired course spread among all the European ship designers. This was the century of the three-master, the compass, and the gun. America was rediscovered, the world was circumnavigated, and the shape of the ship was changed for ever. Moreover, the fighting ship began again to take on an exclusive warlike rôle and characteristics of its own. No longer could those bent on war rely entirely on recalling the vessels from peaceful trade and fit them out with soldiers and a handful of primitive missile-throwers. Henceforward, naval power was to be wielded more and more by standing fleets of fighting ships, which were to prove at once one of the more distressing extravagances and noble creations of modern man.

'In the naval accounts between 1377 and 1422,' wrote one naval historian more than a century ago, 'the only instances which have been found of ships having two masts are in the statement of the Monk of St Denys, that some of the French vessels in the expedition against England in 1386 had two sails; and in the list of the stores of the King's carrack about 1410, among which were "one large mast" and "one small mast"; but she seems to have had only "one sail-yard of two

The *Great Harry*, 1546, pride of Henry VIII's Navy, from the Anthony Anthony Rolls. Woolwich Dockyard grew around her building; this picture shows her after her complete rebuild

pieces", and "one tref with two bonnets", which are the only notices of a yard or sail belonging to her. In every other instance vessels had only one mast, one yard, and one sail.'[4]

Since this was written, no fresh evidence has come to light to suggest that among the northern seafarers the two- and three-master was known before the opening of the new century. Gibson considers it possible that the Hanseatic League's largest ship of around 1400, the *Brindled Cow* – a tame name for a great ship that was said to have put down the fiercest band of Baltic pirates of its time – possessed three masts. Certainly it was an increase in size and the resulting need for better sailing and steering qualities that at last forced the northern shipbuilders to introduce the short-lived two-master. The sequence of events probably followed this pattern:

Influence from the Mediterranean, where the two-masted carrack, with square mainsail derived from northern practice and lateen-rigged mizzen mast, had become commonplace in the late 1300s, spread first westwards to Spain and Portugal and then northwards. In 1416 or 1417 several Genoese carracks, either two- or three-masters, had been captured and brought north. Their exceptional sailing qualities impressed their captors. Perhaps those great early colonists, the Portuguese, were among the first to learn from the Venetians and Genoese. In the Victoria and Albert Museum in London there is a beautiful Hispano-Moresque vase, dated at the beginning of the new century, on which there is depicted in great detail a Portuguese three-master, even though both fore and mizzen masts are diminutive. The forecastle is small and triangular to fit on and overlap the stem; above the quarter deck and abaft the mizzen mast a small half deck has already made its appearance. Among other notable characteristics are the prominent vertical fender cleats, designed to reinforce the carvel-planked hull and protect it from damage against quays.

From this point the shreds of evidence begin to multiply. As early as 1419, years before the Duke of Bedford was appointed Lord High Admiral, Henry V ordered to be laid down at Bayonne a fighting ship 186 feet long overall. 'It is difficult to believe,' wrote Clowes, 'that such a vessel . . . could have been successfully navigated even with two masts.'[5] For a brief period in the North – no one knows for how long – two masts with square sails became common practice. This arrangement had very unhappy results, for now the ship lost almost all its limited ability to sail close-hauled. Even poorer steering qualities resulted from lateen-rigging the mizzen mast. It is pleasant to imagine the exasperation of conservative-minded shipwrights after being upbraided by angry seamen on their return to port – and their

Portuguese ship painted on an early fifteenth-century Hispano-Moresque bowl

temptation to return to the single mast and square sail that had proved its worth for centuries. Then perhaps a tip from Venice or Portugal put them on the right track at last. There will be a *third* mast! With this, set well forward and carrying a single square sail acting as a head-sail (to keep the ship's head off the wind), an entirely new sense of balance became evident. Enterprise was rewarded. The classic sail arrangement of three masts, fore and main square-rigged, mizzen fore-and-aft-rigged, had been set, and would endure for centuries.

It is exasperating that we have to rely mostly on our imagination for a picture of development from one to two to three masts. Uncertainty over language and interpretation of terms further confuses the

71

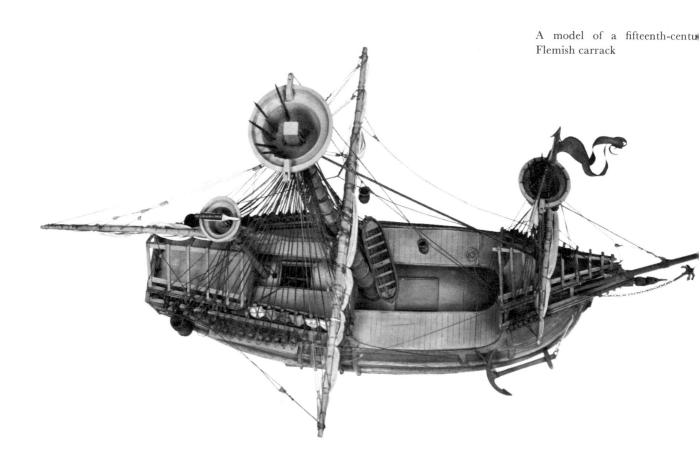

situation. What was the 'mesan' of Henry V's *Grace Dieu* of 1418? With an overall length of some 200 feet, she must certainly have been in need of a second mast. But it could be an English mizzen or after-mast, or a French *misaine* or foremast! Clowes considers that: 'On the whole, the trend of available evidence seems to indicate that the fore-mast, long established in the Mediterranean, came north in the first instance as the "mesan", and this view is strengthened by the discovery of a fifteenth-century fresco in Canterbury Cathedral, which shows two vessels, both square-rigged two-masters, with definite mainmast and foremast.'[5]

The seal of Southampton

Pictorial evidence of the advent of the three-master in the north has been discovered in a manuscript dated around 1450: and a three-masted ship is clearly depicted on a seal struck for Louis XI in 1466. There can be no doubt that by the second half of the century all large sea-going vessels constructed in northern Europe, in Spain, Portugal, and the Mediterranean, carried three masts. With its fundamental advantages now recognized everywhere in Europe, development went ahead apace, and before the end of the century numerous refinements had been introduced. The most important was the spritsail. The bowsprit had not been used as a spar since the days of the Roman artemon. Now that – at last – the benefits to be derived from a sail far forward were again becoming appreciated, the next step was simple. The spritsail was rigged *under* the bowsprit, where it proved its worth as a headsail more effectively than the earlier foresail. What was more, the foremast could now be used to carry a driving sail – at first a small one because of the mast's inadequate support in its forward position, but soon to grow larger as its mast was stepped farther aft. By 1498 Vasco da Gama was actually able to hoist a small fore-topsail.

So much for the influence on the shape and sailing efficiency of the fighting ship of the belated discovery by the northern shipwright of this new mast and sail arrangement.

Holland's seventeenth-century man of war

The gunsmith, too, had been busy throughout the century. The influence of his works was to be profound and long-lasting. Until the 1300s, the means of destroying the enemy in sea warfare were limited, at a distance, to various forms of missile and – much more rarely – to fire; at close quarters to the common hand-weapons of the time. Only the ancient ram and, again very rarely, fire had served as ship destroyers. All this was to be changed by the discovery of a diabolical compound of charcoal, saltpetre and sulphur, and the means of harnessing its ignition through the medium of a cylinder. It was not a neat, quick revolution; like all great developments in the fighting ship up to the 1900s, the refinement and acceptance of the gun, even from a sort of cast bowl to a cylinder, took a long time. From what we know about the operation and effect of the earliest guns, the fighting sailor's preference for the bow or sling, *trébuchet* or ballista can be understood. The gun was a clumsy, heavy, inefficient, highly dangerous weapon, and it says much for the courage of the mariner of the 1300s and 1400s that he allowed it on board his ship at all.

It is not possible to date for sure within ten or twenty years when the first gun was taken on board. There is some evidence that the French, Genoese and English used them to add to the holocaust at Sluys. It is possible that the Venetians and Genoese – the most far-sighted seamen – used them before the 1340s; certainly they fought each other with them in the 1370s. There is documentary evidence, in the Public Record Office, that English ships carried a modest armament of guns in 1411. But long before that, in 1345, King Henry IV's ship *Christopher* sported '*iii cannons de ferr ove v. chambres, un handgone, un petit barrell de gonpouder, le quart plein*', and the Keeper of the King's Wardrobe was honoured – surely to his surprise and alarm – with the

Model of a carronade in the Musé de la Marine, Paris

task of looking after ships' guns and keeping them supplied with powder and shot.

These early ship guns, employed in combat by all the European maritime nations by the middle 1400s, were only man-destroyers. They were small, light, few in number, and probably regarded as rather novel and dashing, if only because it called for exceptional courage to fire the charge. No doubt, however, they provided the moral reinforcement in the man behind the breech and the fear in the man facing the muzzle that the naval gun has instilled right down to the 16- and 18-inch weapons of the 1940s. These early ship-borne cannon, unlike the cast pieces used in land warfare in the 1300s, were built up from a number of forged iron strips welded together longitudinally about a cylindrical tube and reinforced at first with a wood case or a wound rope, and later with shrunk-on iron hoops. A typical light *petarara* of the 1470s was some 3 feet long and weighed around 120 pounds. A trunnion secured to the barrel could be locked into a swivel post by fork extensions curving up each side of the breech, drilled to carry a horizontal securing pin, which provided the gunner with the means to adjust the elevation for range. The breech piece was hollowed out to slide over the rear end of the barrel and to receive the separate chamber which had been pre-loaded with powder and ball shot and was dropped in by a fixed handle. A wedge through the breech piece was driven home and forced the chamber up against the barrel. A light at the end of a long stick was then applied to the touch-hole, accompanied at first by prayers but soon by a show of self-confidence. The calibre of this light gun might be 2 or 3 inches, the weight of the ball little more than a pound, and the effective range no more than that of an arrow. It would make no effect on the structure of a ship, but fired into a crowd could kill one or more of the enemy and frighten the rest. With reserve chambers ready charged, the rate of fire was quite rapid, until the barrel became too hot.

As these light pieces of artillery increasingly proved their effectiveness during the late 1400s, the natural prejudice against them diminished and the fighting seamen demanded more. At first these

The Turkish gun at the Tower of London

were sited on each side of the two castles, the traditional station of the missile thrower, and also to fire down into the low waist of their own ship where boarders were likely to secure their first foothold – for, until the perfection of ship-destroying artillery, combat at sea remained essentially a man-to-man business with the capture of the enemy vessel the main target, and no ship could be taken as a prize until the castles had been stormed and the men overcome. Later, a few guns were disposed low down in the waist, and were protected by an additional heavy plank which became known as the gunwale; but the castles, with their commanding situation, made much the best sites. More and more of these light railing-pieces were added until they jammed both castles, which in turn had to be extended towards the centre of the ship. When even this proved inadequate accommodation, a second deck was added above the first, and filled with more guns, the spaces between the lower guns being planked in for protection of the gunners, thus forming the first gun embrasures. Then a third deck to each castle was added, and now it could truly be said that the gun – even the light man-destroying gun – had proved itself. By the end of the 1400s it must have shown itself to be a real killer and reasonably reliable. Although no ship had yet been sunk as a result of the introduction of gunpowder, in its design and shape the fighting ship was already bending to the needs of its own gunpower.

For the next four centuries the man-of-war, which until so recently had been just a troop transport, became more and more a floating gun platform. Speed, manoeuvrability and power to resist the elements had figured largely in the minds of naval architects since the Phoenicians. All these characteristics would continue to be important; but henceforward the fighting prowess of the warship would rest on the guns – their number, their reliability, their accuracy and rate of fire. The gun had won over all the missiles, and its fearful thunder would shape the form and character of the fighting ship until the new underwater weapons of modern times threatened its dominance.

The fighting ship at the turn of the 1400s to the 1500s is well represented by Henry VII's great ship, the *Regent*. Many years earlier, in 1436, there was published *The Libelle of Englyshe Policie*, credited to Adam de Moleyns, Bishop of Chichester. 'Cherish merchandise, kepe the Admiraltie,' ran one significant passage, 'Kepe then the sea that is the wall of England, and then is England kept by Goddes hand.' The real achievement of the first of the Tudor monarchs was to comprehend the implications of this Bishop's words of wisdom and to instil into the English people a maritime consciousness rather than to provide them with a large – and expensive – standing navy. As Michael Lewis succinctly puts it, Henry VII 'wanted to make his people sea-minded like himself and to help them to greater affluence as he had helped himself. In affirming this we need not ascribe to him too modern a set of motives. He still held, no doubt, the strictly medieval view that he was the owner of his country's wealth, or at least that he was the principal legatee of his country's prosperity. And he probably had at the back of his mind another motive, still more medieval, for encouraging his people to build larger and stronger ships. He had no intention of maintaining a big fighting fleet of his own, but he may well have wanted a reserve of potential fighters to fall back upon.'[6]

The economy of compromise perfectly suited this shrewd and parsimonious King; and it was fortunate and convenient that the fighting ship at this time was in a stage of transition from a merchant-man readily converted into a fighting rôle to a vessel designed exclusively for combat. The *Regent* was the *Dreadnought* of her day, not a three-master but a four-master – fore, main, mizzen and bona-venture, the mizzen carrying a lateen sail, and there was a spritsail under the bowsprit, as well as topsails, and even a topgallant sail on her mainmast. By contrast with this enterprising rig, the *Regent* was still a medieval ship in her construction. In spite of her displacement of around 1,000 tons, she was still a 'round ship', she was still clinker-built and carrack in form with a very high, very projecting forecastle, and even more massive poop and poop royal. She was reputed to have carried, on occasion, no less than 225 guns. These were still only man-destroyers, little 'serpentines', but the total of their weight and the weight of their powder and shot was considerable, and most of it was above the centre of gravity. Not only were the guns seriously upsetting the balance of the warship; but the castles – lightly-built though they might be – in which they were housed were becoming so tall that they were acting as permanent sails that could never be furled and were compromising the ship's handling and seaworthiness.

Here, then, was a fighting ship of formidable size and threatening demeanour, bristling like a porcupine with light cannon. Yet she was primarily a merchantman and lived out most of her life in this capacity, earning her keep and paying off her original cost, no doubt to the satisfaction of the King. Yet, by the standards of less than a century later, she was a clumsy old tub, neither one thing nor the other, a satisfactory merchantman and a satisfactory boarding warship, but essentially an interim vessel. At the end of the 1400s we are close to a revolution in the fighting ship. She has learned to sail, she has acquired gunpower. Yet her configuration is the same as 200 years earlier. So

The French fleet attacking Portsmouth in 1545, engraved by Basi̇

is her method of construction. And in spite of perhaps 200 guns, her tactics in battle are as primitive as ever – kill as many as you can at short range, lay alongside and board, then hand-to-hand combat and a storming operation against the castles.

All this was before the advent of the big gun. With its arrival, the artillery again takes command of events and shapes the future of the fighting ship. At the beginning of the 1500s the sailor, greatly daring, started to bring on board pieces of cannon which had proved for years their ability to tear through the walls of a castle on land. Perhaps they would tear through not only a castle at sea, but even through the hull on which the castle was built? Perhaps they could *sink* ships? Some 150 years had passed since gunpowder had first been used to destroy men at sea. The heady idea of extending this destruction to the ship itself– the first ship-destroyer since the ancient ram – opened up unprecedented new prospects to the fighting seaman. As a result, the fighting ship again became a vessel in its own right, progressively less suitable for fulfilling its secondary trading rôle. And sea fighting became an art for the first time since the Mediterranean galley battles. In the 1500s the fighting ship was growing up, with some growing pains.

In 1509, the first year of the reign of Henry VIII, the *Mary Rose* was completed, and she carried amongst her armament five brass cannon – called *curtalls* – each of which weighed about 3,000 pounds, or some ten times the weight of a serpentine. Later in her life her armament was greatly increased with more brass cannon – cannon-royal, demi-cannon and the culverine-bastard, the first of which could hurl a shot

of 50 pounds. This was too much for the poor *Mary Rose*. In the summer of 1545 the French fleet, under the Admiral M. de Annebault, attacked the Isle of Wight, and made landings there and on the coast of Sussex.

King Henry VIII, greatly irritated and perturbed, came to Portsmouth to supervise counter-action. He dined aboard the *Henry Grace à Dieu* 'and was there served [according to Hakluyt] by the Lord High Admiral, Sir George Carew, this gentleman, Peter Carew, and their uncle Sir Gawen Carew, with such others as were appointed to that voyage and service. The King being at dinner, willed some one to go up to the top of the ship, and see whether he could see anything at the seas . . . it was not long but he had espied a great number. . . . The King supposing them to be the French men-of-war, as they were indeed, willed the board to be taken up, and every man to go to his ship, as also a long boat to come and carry him on land. . . . Sir George Carew being entered into his ship, he commanded every man to take his place, and the sails to be hoisted; but the same was no sooner done, but that the *Mary Rose* began to heel, that is to say, lean on one side. Sir Gawen Carew being then in his own ship, and seeing the same, called for the master of his ship, and told him thereof, and asked him what it meant, who answered that if she did heel she was liked to be cast away. Then the said Sir Gawen passing by the *Mary Rose*, called out to Sir George Carew, asking him how he did, who answered that he had a set of knaves whom he could not rule. And it was not long after but that the said *Mary Rose*, thus heeling more and more, was drowned with 700 men which were in her, whereof very few escaped.'[7]

In 1836 a number of the *Mary Rose*'s guns, many of them loaded for action, were recovered from Portsmouth harbour, and can now be seen at the Tower of London. At this point in history, the cannon had outgrown its platform. Everybody was having the same trouble. The French lost one of their best men-of-war for the same reason during this campaign. The shipwright would have radically to redesign the fighting ship to match the needs of the fighting sailor for even more and even heavier ordnance.

Much progress had already been made at the time of the tragedy to the aged *Mary Rose*. The origin of the gunport is shrouded in obscurity, but it almost certainly began as an entry-port in a large merchantman to facilitate hoisting large cargoes over the bulwark. According to tradition, a shipwright of Brest named Descharges cut the first entry-port in 1501. But there is good reason for believing that the Spaniards and Portuguese were quicker off the mark. The adoption of this simple, but epochal, device for military needs quickly followed. Loading the tall castles with artillery had never been very satisfactory. With the arrival of ship-destroying cannon, it became not only hazardous but unnecessary. The importance of close-action and boarding diminished as the ordnance became heavier. When it was learned that cannon could do better execution to ships as well as men from a distance, the importance of the boarding party began to diminish, although right to the end of the sailing fighting ship's life, boarding the enemy continued to figure as an accepted part of naval warfare (pikes were still carried on British men-of-war in the 1890s).

Ironically, it was in the *Mary Rose* herself (which capsized from having too great a weight of armament 'upstairs' and her lower guns too near the waterline) that gunports were first introduced into the British navy, and the man who was said to have been responsible for this was a shipwright named James Baker. There had been light, and perhaps heavier, guns in the waist of ships for years, with the gunwale built up round them. But a series of holes pierced in the side of the ship at the cargo deck level, and with large cannon and their mountings occupying the cargo space behind these ports – all this was a very different thing. In no more than a decade the fighting ship had taken its most decisive step away from its old dual rôle. James Baker's rows of holes resulted in the broadside, in the calculation of a ship's power by the weight of its broadside, in the creation of the line of battle and the line-of-battle ship which endured effectively to the 1940s, in the re-development – after centuries of primitive hand-to-hand combat at sea – of tactical evolutions, and in the final maturing of the sailing fighting ship.

Now guns in ever greater numbers and ever greater size could be brought on board, and their muzzles inserted through the gun ports, their weight close to the centre of gravity of the ship. Soon there was not just one row of gunports, but two, and then three. These bristling batteries inevitably brought with them more changes in the shape of the fighting ship. The light man-destroying gun was no longer needed, or certainly not in large numbers. Castles would no longer be assaulted by soldiers because the cannon ball would have destroyed their ship first. Of what use, then, were the castles? They were vulnerable, they were a fire risk as well as a fair target, they spoilt the handling of the ship; in fact they diminished the ship-destroying qualities of the fighting ship – and they therefore had to go. The forecastle went entirely and within the century. The after castle was slower to disappear, and a vestigial raised poop was still there more than two hundred years later as an aid to the steersman and to allow the commander a view forward over the length of his vessel.

The gunports and their guns also brought new strains and stresses to the hull of the fighting ship, and new constructional problems for the shipwright. It was not possible to cut a series of holes in the side of a ship without weakening the structure, or to introduce several rows of guns each weighing a ton or more plus their ammunition without creating an adverse effect on the balance of the vessel. To meet the demands of these new weights and stresses, the northern shipbuilder was forced at last to conform with ancient Mediterranean practice and to resort to flush planking, or carvel construction, with each plank butting up against those above and below it. This was not only much stronger but made the cutting of the gunports a simpler operation for the carpenter. Clinker building of heavy ships had all but ceased by 1525. With the introduction of more than a single line of gunports, it also became necessary to bring the upper line as close to the centre of the ship as possible in order to reduce the effect of excessive top weight. The shipwright accomplished this by curving in the side of the vessel at a distance above the waterline – a convex form as seen in the cross-section that came to be known as *the tumble-home* – so that the upper line of guns was set back from the lower line. The greatest beam of the ship was therefore just below the lower gun deck.

Of even greater importance, the heavy gun and its port signalled the end of the medieval round ship. While the merchantman continued to act the occasional rôle of fighting ship between its customary peaceful duties of cargo-carrying, and while ships were boarded in battle rather than battered from a distance, it seemed sensible to construct them for maximum capacity. By the early 1500s, with the final disappearance of the merchantman's double function (though of course right up to the Napoleonic wars and even to the great wars of the 1900s merchantmen were pressed into combat service with the addition of a few guns) the dimensions of the fighting ship could be made solely to meet the needs of the battle.

At the beginning of the reign of Henry VIII the ratio of length to beam of his ships was about two to one; before his death it had increased to more than three to one. Both speed and handiness were thus gained by this reversion to hull proportions more closely comparable to those of the Viking longship and the Mediterranean galley. But the sterns of these new vessels bore no resemblance to those earlier fighting ships. They were cut off squarely by a wide athwartships transom, and the fighting power, especially in the event of a stern chase, was further increased by the addition of a stern armament of several heavy cannon.

It is one of the happy coincidences of history that the reign of Henry VIII spanned a dramatically important phase in the history of the fighting ship, for this English monarch was at once an enthusiastic navalist and an advocate of the heavy gun. Not for another 300 years was there to be a comparable period of advancement in the fighting ship and its gunpower, and his influence on this, by building up a navy of great power and by his enthusiastic interest in all maritime matters, was long-lasting. At the beginning of his reign there was constructed the appropriately named and famous *Henry Grace à Dieu*; before he died he had created the prototype of the ship-of-the-line which was to save England from Spanish rule and endure in developed form until the coming of iron and steam in the 1850s. The startling progress made in less than forty years is revealed in the modifications made to the first of these fighting ships and the hull form, rig and armament of the second.

The Spanish, Portuguese and French especially were building very large carrack-like men-of-war early in the 1500s, and one of the most formidable of these was the *Great Michael*, built in France for the King of Scotland. The existence of this ship, built by one of the Franco-Scottish alliance for the other, was alone enough to spur on the new King of England to go one better. The *Henry Grace à Dieu* was probably designed and built by the Clerk of the Ships, Robert Brygandine, under the supervision of the naval architect, William Bond. She was a four-master of 1,000 tons, with topmasts and topgallant masts on the forward three masts and a topmast only on the bonaventure. Massive castles rose fore and aft from the waist, and although her few big guns, including a pair of 4,500-pound culverins and a great brass mortar, were no doubt disposed in the waist, her man-destroyers including

An engraving of the *Henry Grace à Dieu* of 1514. It is interesting to compare this eighteenth-century reconstruction with Anthony Anthony's contemporary drawing on page 68

122 serpentines were probably all placed in these castles. Their fire, directed with gravitational assistance down onto the decks of the enemy, or perhaps at the rigging, would have cast a veritable storm of light shot. Built between 1512 and 1514, she was indeed the *ultima thule* of the northern round ship, clinker-built, un-handy, a close-action 'boarder', but a fearsome and even awe-inspiring opponent. At the time of her launching there was laid down for her a schedule which included a complement of 700, made up of 400 sailors, 260 soldiers and 40 gunners. Besides the soldiers – for boarding and capturing – there is further evidence that she was intended primarily for sea combat in medieval style in the proposed provision of 5,000 bowstrings, 4,000 sheaves of arrows, 2,000 bows and 500 suits of armour.

83

The *Henry Grace à Dieu* was obsolete almost as quickly as a battleship of the 1900s, and by 1536 was called in for a complete re-build. She emerged from this three years later, and was depicted in detail by the artist Anthony Anthony in 1546. Only her rig is unchanged. Now her stern is square cut and there are stern chase guns. There are two tiers of gunports below the waist, more heavy pieces of artillery low in the fore and after castles, while above there are ranged more tiers of man-destroyers. Now she is carrying in all 21 heavy bronze guns, 130 iron guns and 100 hand guns. This is a smaller total than before; but the ship-destroying power has multiplied many times over, while the *Henry Grace à Dieu* can still spray the decks of any vessel whose crew are old-fashioned and foolhardy enough to contemplate boarding.

Landström in his reconstruction based largely on Volpe's rather suspect painting of the ship clearing Dover with the king aboard and on Anthony Anthony's painting, gives the ship no less than six decks abaft the mainmast, the two above the orlop carrying the heaviest guns; light cannon and railing pieces on the next two; while on the upper deck, still covered with a boarding net, soldiers fire their hand weapons through small gunports.

The sinking of the *Mary Rose* before King Henry's eyes and the inadequate performance of the Navy during the operations of 1545 caused him to doubt the value in battle of giant vessels like the *Henry Grace à Dieu*, and to turn his eye towards much smaller fighting ships, with low freeboard, greatly reduced castles, and a ratio of length to beam close to four to one. In the last years of his reign a number of narrower, fleeter ships of this type were built. The one flaw in his reasoning was his proposal, after the clumsy handling of his ships off Portsmouth harbour against the French, that oars should supplement sail power. They were rarely used except in harbour or calm coastal waters. But the low freeboard introduced to facilitate the use of oars proved of inestimable value in the formulation of the English galleons of the late 1500s, the most advanced fighting ships of their day.

A TECHNICAL NOTE ON EARLY GUNS

Ship-destroying guns were slow to make their appearance on board because their weight and size and unpredictable performance made them a poor risk. The formidable recoil of a land gun that could destroy the wall of a castle might well, it was calculated, fatally injure the structure of a ship. Light man-destroyers came to be increasingly well-regarded but for some 150 years after their introduction had no fundamental influence on naval tactics. The development of heavy artillery, for use on land as well as at sea, depended on securing the breech block against the pressure of the explosion which was intended to thrust the projectile down the barrel. While the charge – and therefore the projectile – was a small one this could be accomplished without any great difficulty. Many ingenious methods of holding the breech block against the pressure of a greater explosion were tried, often with fatal results. The early gunsmiths got within an ace of success with a screw thread in the breech block mating with a similar screw thread in the barrel. Large and effective siege guns were constructed on this principle. But the understanding of metallurgy and expansion coefficients was still very primitive. The explosion of one great charge made the gun so hot that it was many hours before the breech could be unscrewed. Guns like these on shipboard would clearly be limited to one shot in any action. Centuries were to pass before someone chanced on the clever ruse of using an interrupted thread – the thread in the barrel and the breech block being broken by corresponding regular gaps – so that the block could be swung in and secured with one small twist. Instead, the early gunsmith was forced to take a step backwards and resort again to the single-piece gun – the muzzle-loader, which was to endure into the mid-1800s.

The cast muzzle-loader first began to supplement the light, built-up, breech-loading man-destroyer on shipboard in the early 1500s. The heathen Turk taught the Western Christian a lot about casting, and the evidence can be seen in the enormous Dardanelles Gun at the Tower of London. It is recorded that guns of this size (nearly 20 tons and almost unmoveable) were cast *in situ*, probably facing some troublesome wall. The material of these early cast guns was loosely termed 'brass', a compound at that time of 100 parts of copper, 10 parts of copper and zinc, and 8 parts of tin. The cast iron gun came later.

The casting of guns in one piece was a retrograde step because loading them from the muzzle was a clumsy business. But they were much safer for the ship, and especially for the gunner who lit the fuse. The trunnions securing the gun to its mounting, and later even the ring for the breech-rope to hold the recoil, were all cast in one piece.

The best-known, if not the first, Western gun-founder to perfect an effective cast brass big gun was Hans Poppenruyter of Malines. The art rapidly spread throughout Europe. There was no more enthusiastic advocate than Henry VIII, and in the early years of his reign he was encouraging English gun-founders to cast brass cannon and his shipwrights to instal them in his new great fighting ships. During the later years of Henry's reign these were the chief weapons in common use in his navy:

*Cannon* The heaviest piece of artillery throwing an iron shot weighing about 50 pounds, the ultimate ship destroyer. Length of bore about 20 calibres. Maximum range about a mile.

*Demi-cannon* A similar cast piece throwing a 32-pound shot.

*Culverin* A very long and efficient piece much favoured in the English Navy. Weight of shot about 18 pounds, length 32 calibres. Maximum range about $1\frac{1}{4}$ miles.

*Demi-culverin* Similar, but with weight of ball half of the Culverin.

Smaller pieces including the *Saker, Minion, Falcon, Falconet* and *Robinet*, throwing shot weighing from 5 pounds to less than a pound: man- and rigging-destroyers all.

### SHIP DECORATION AND ORNAMENT

> In the year 1400 one of the King's barges and her mast were painted red, and the vessel was adorned with collars and garters of gold, each collar containing a fleur-de-lys, and each garter a leopard; together with gold 'lyames', having within each of them a white greyhound and a gold collar. The ship called the *Good Pace of the Tower* was likewise painted red, but her bulwarks, cabin and stern were of other colours; and a large gold eagle, with a crown in its mouth, was placed on the bowsprit. The *Trinity of the Tower* was also red; four effigies, namely, St George, St Anthony, St Katherine, and St Margaret, stood in the stern, together with four shields of the King's arms within a collar of gold, and two with the arms of St George within the Garter. Two large eagles were painted in the cabin on a diapered ground. The King's barge the *Nicholas of the Tower* represented the badge of the Prince of Wales, and must have had a singular, and perhaps beautiful appearance, as she was painted black, and covered . . . with white ostrich feathers, the stems and escrols being of gold. . . .[4]

This brief extract from Nicolas's *History* underlines the great attention that was again being given to ship decoration by 1400.

Carving and decoration were an expression of the artistry of the shipwright and proof of his ability to match the skills of the craftsmen ashore. The gilding, the painting and the carving added a measure of cheer and reassurance to the hard and monotonous life of the sailor. They also served to frighten the enemy. The detachable dragon or snake heads on Viking longships which struck such fear among those who saw them driving towards their shore had, by law, to be removed when the ship neared its home port. The aspect of William the Conqueror's ships in 1066 was intended to impress and intimidate Harold's defending forces. The sides of his ships were brightly painted in patterns, the sails were heavily decorated and even embroidered, fierce and fearful beasts were represented in the stemheads.

The erection of castles fore and aft offered new opportunities for carving, and it was natural that the simple scaffolding should develop into arches carved in the medieval Gothic style. With the development and elaboration of the castle, the arches multiplied and the patterned carving sometimes blossomed out into representations of saints, although heraldic badges, coats-of-arms and animals were more common. Colour came to be used on the hull, for pride of ownership and ready identification, and extended to the fighting tops which were wrapped in coloured cloth. The colouring of sails which had been practised from earliest times and by the Vikings to a special degree, was revived in the 1400s, and streamers, pennants and standards of elaborate design and brilliant colour provided a new means of expression of the owner's style and extravagance. Religious emblems predominated in Spanish and Portuguese ships, and these were to be seen even at the mastheads in the 1500s.

The French were early and enthusiastic exponents of decorative skill in their fighting ships. Nicolas gives a vivid picture of the preparations for the massive invasion of England in 1386, when 'all the great lords vied with each other in the equipment and ornaments of their ships, which were gaily painted and gilt, having their arms depicted upon them and upon their banners. The masts were painted from top to bottom, some being even covered with sheets of goldleaf, and were surmounted with the arms of the owner of the vessel. One knight, Sir Guy de Trémouille, expended no less than 10,000 francs in adorning his ship. Rich banners, pennons, and standards floated everywhere. . . .'[4]

Drawing on Jehan Bytharne's *Book of War by Sea and by Land* (1543), Chatterton outlines the required decoration of the English contemporary fighting ship:

> The external ornamentation from the mainwale to the top of the castles ought to be painted with the colours and devices of the admiral. Likewise the forecastle and after-castle were to be decorated as splendidly as possible. All the shields . . . round the upper part of the castles were to be emblazoned with the admiral's arms and devices also. Above the forecastle on a staff inclining forwards was to be a [pennon] of the admiral's colours and devices, as also at the two corners of the castle. Amidships there should be two square banners, emblazoned with the admiral's arms, and on the after-castle high above the rudder he was to have a large square banner larger than any of the others. From the maintop a broad swallow-tailed standard was to be flown, of such a length as to reach to the water, and emblazoned with the admiral's arms and devices also.
>
> For celebrating a triumph the ship was to be covered in and curtained with rich cloth. 'You may also paint your sails with such devices and colours as you choose, or with the representation of a saint if you prefer it.'[1]

The four main streamers of the *Henry Grace à Dieu* fluttered out from 90 to 150 feet, and this ship sported twenty-eight banners wrought with gold and silver and with silken fringes, and no fewer than ten flags of St George.

But the carving on this great ship was comparatively modest. Another century was to pass before carving and gilding achieved a riot of detail and became a heavy item in the overall construction costs. All the same, as Laughton makes clear, 'the shipwrights of this period . . . thought much of the appearance of their ships, which they set themselves to improve both in their technical design, and use with ornament. They spoke of the "countenance" of their ships; of their "goodly port"; and in minor matters, such as the finishing of the upper works, were careful "to fit the ship with comeliness". They wished their ships to carry an impression of their "terror and majesty" to their enemies, and indeed to all beholders; and they were careful to examine any suggested innovation lest, in the literal sense, it should prove "disgraceful".'[8]

The figurehead, which had had such a long and varied history, from Phoenicia – when it might have represented the ship as a galloping horse – to the lion at the prow of Duke William's flagship, suffered a decline in England in the 1500s, and at the end of Henry VIII's reign the only two ships in his navy (according to contemporary artists) with figureheads were prizes captured from the Scots and the French and probably built in France. In the *Grande Françoise* of 1527 the figurehead was an effigy of St Francis with the royal badge of the salamander beneath it.

'The fall of Phaeton', by Breughel, showing the large gun-platform ship between two lateen-sailed craft

# . THE SPANISH ARMADA:
# THE IMPORTANCE OF MATÉRIEL

God has seen good to direct matters otherwise than we expected.

Alfonso Perez de Gusmán Medina Sidonia

That ripe old phrase 'conflict of maritime interests' has been used in many ways to justify combat at sea, varying in scale from petty raids to world wars. For almost its whole history, sea warfare has been marked by acts of piracy, itself a word that has been subjected to every form of interpretation. German submarines in this century, the seamen of the Barbary coasts up to the 1800s, the Vikings of a thousand years earlier, have all been termed pirates at some time. Nor is it always a pejorative word. For most of us in childhood the pirate is presented as a good-natured dare-devil, in spite of the efforts of J. M. Barrie and R. L. Stevenson. By present day standards, anyone who sailed west in the 1500s was a pirate – the Spanish and Portuguese who grasped the riches of both the Indies and the Incas, and the English who intercepted it on its way home. But however we interpret 'piracy' and 'conflict of maritime interests', they were the chief cause of the war between Spain and England, which endured for many years after the Armada, but culminated in that epochal event of 1588.

To catch a brief and vivid glimpse of what piracy meant in that century, it is worth reading a passage from 'An Accidence or The Pathway to Experience necessary for all young sea-men . . . written by Captain John Smith sometimes Governor of Virginia and Admirall of New England', which was printed in London in 1626:

A sail! How stands she? To windward, or leeward? Set him by the compass. He stands right ahead, or on the weather bow, or lee bow. Out with all your sails: a steady man to the helm. Sit close to keep her steady. Give chase or fetch him up. He holds his own. No: we gather on him. Out goeth his flag and pennants or streamers, also his colours, his waist-cloths and top-armings. He furles and slings his mainsail. In goes his spirit sail and mizzen. He makes ready his close fights fore and after: well, we shall reach him by and by. What? Is all ready? Yea, yea. Every man to his charge. Dowse your topsail. Salute him for the sea – hail him. 'Whence your ship?' 'Of Spain: whence is yours?' 'Of England.' 'Are you merchants or men of war?' 'We are of the sea.' He waves us to leeward for the King of Spain and keeps his luff. Give him a chase piece, a broad side and run ahead. Make ready to tack about, give him your stern pieces. Be yare [dexterous] at helm; hail him with a noise of trumpets.

We are shot through and through, and between wind and water. Try the pumps. Master, let us breathe and refresh a little. Sling a man overboard to stop the leak. Done, done! Is all ready again? Yea, yea. Bear up close with him. With all your great and small shot charge him. Board him on his weather quarter. Lash fast your grappling irons and sheer off. Then run stemlines the midships. Board and board or thwart the hawse.

Northern carrack and galley, b
Breughel

Spanish galleons fighting Turkish galleys, by Vroom. The galley slaves are clearly shown. They usually sank with the galley, as it was not safe to unchain them from their benches

We are foul on each other. The ship's on fire. Cut anything to get clear, and smother the fire with wet cloths. We are clear, and the fire out. God be thanked. The day is spent, let us consult. Surgeon, look to the wounded, wind up the slain. With each a weight or bullet at his head and feet. Give three pieces for their funerals. Swabber, make clean the ship. Purser, record their names. Watch, be vigilant to keep your berth to windward, and that we lose him not in the night. Gunners, spunge your ordinances. Soldiers, scour your pieces. Carpenters, about your leaks. Boatswain and the rest, repair the sails and shrouds. Cook, see you observe your directions against the morning watch. Boy! Hulloa, master, hulloa! Is the kettle boiled? Yea. Boatswain, call up the men to prayer and breakfast.

Boy, fetch my cellar of bottles. A health to you all fore and aft. Courage, my hearts, for a fresh charge. Master, lay him aboard luff for luff. Midshipmen, see the tops and yards well manned with stones and brass balls. To enter them at shrouds and every squadron else at their best advantage, sound drums and trumpets and St George for England. They hang out a flag of truce. Stand in with him, haul him amain, abaft, or take in his flag.

91

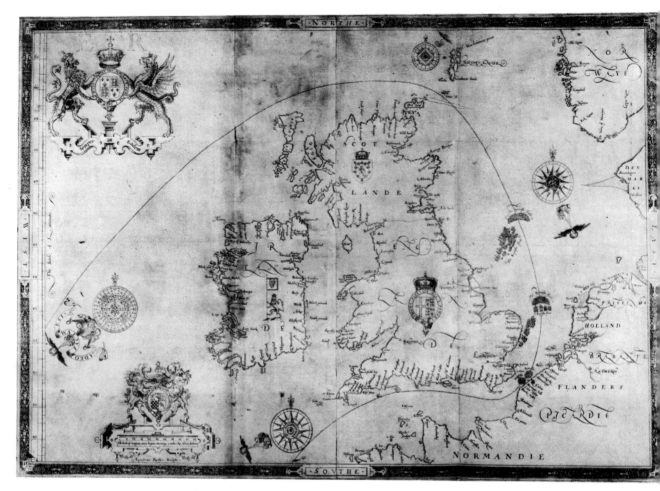

Strike their sails and come aboard, with the captain, purser and gunner, with your commission, cocket or bills of loading. Out goes their boat. They are launched from the ship side. Entertain them with a general cry. God save the captain, and all the company, with the trumpets sounding. Examine them in particular, and then conclude your conditions with feasting, freedom or punishment, as you find occasion. Otherwise if you surprise him or enter perforce, you may stow the men, rifle, pillage or sack and cry a prize.

Two of a set of maps of the Spanis[h] fleet invading England in 1588 from Ryther's 1590 translation o[f] Ubaldini's 'Vera Descriptio'. I[n] the detail map Sir Francis Drak[e] would have just finished his gam[e] of bowls

The mightiest naval and colonial power in the world was defeated in 1588 because it continued, long after it should have done, to treat sea warfare as an extension of land warfare, with the infantryman as the first weapon, and man rather than his ship as the first target. Also its men-of-war were inferior to those of the enemy in the waters on which they fought. Spain had created her vast empire largely through her maritime power and prowess. But the fighting had been conducted on land, by the best foot soldiers of their time. Spain's last massive and decisive victory at sea, at Lepanto, had similarly been achieved by the infantryman in close combat. It therefore seemed eminently reasonable that the Great Armada should number 19,000 soldiers and only 8,000 sailors; after all, England itself had to be conquered when the fleet had been dealt with. By contrast, the English flagship carried 270 seamen and 34 gunners, and only 126 soldiers to cope with the enemy soldiers in the unfortunate event of a boarding. The Spanish tactics were to pound the enemy ship with heavy short-range cannon, bear down on her while pouring from her fighting tops and high bulwarks and castles a rain of man-destroying projectiles, and then board with a fierce, self-confident body of men armed with pikes and swords. If everything worked out like this, the Spaniards were unbeatable. But in an era when the gunsmith could provide the fighting seaman with the means to destroy his enemy ship at a range of several hundred yards, the boarding and capturing of ships was great sport but tactically obsolete. It also required speed and handiness superior to the enemy's.

Since the Spring of 1586, when the Marquis of Santa Cruz had submitted to King Philip II of Spain his plan for the invasion of

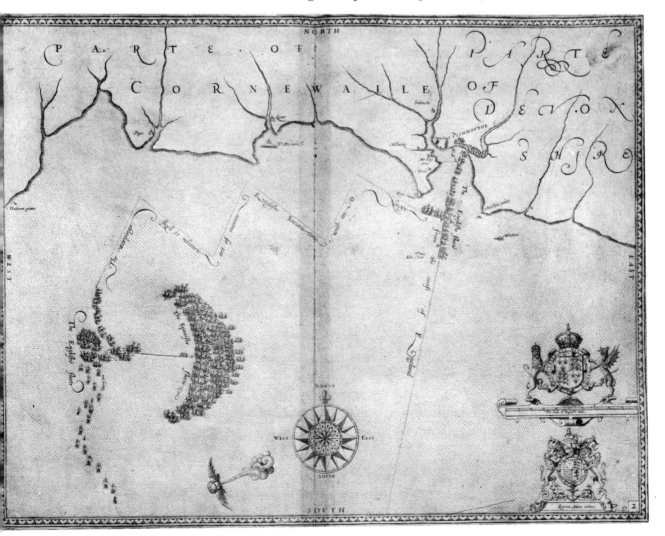

England, preparations had been going ahead for the construction and collection of the Great Armada, that 'long looked-for Fleete' (as James Aske described it) of

> . . . Spanyards Shippes on heapes,
> In al things like a huge and pop'ler towne:
> Their bigge-made Barkes with huge and mightie Mastes,
> Like Churches are with Steeples very high:
> Their lesser Shippes like Stately Pallaces. . . .

Hakluyt tells us: 'The king Catholique had given commandment long before in Italy and Spaine, that a great quantitie of timber should be felled for the building of shippes; and had besides made great preparation of things and furniture requisite for such an expedition; as namely in founding of brasen Ordinance, in storing up of corne and victuals, in trayning of men to use warlike weapons.' By the beginning of 1588 'he had finished such a mightie Navie, and brought it into Lisbon haven, as never the like had before that time sailed upon the Ocean sea. . . . The Galeons were 64 in number, being of an huge bignesse, and very stately built, being of marveilous force also, and so high, that they resembled great castles, most fit to defend themselves and to withstand any assault. . . . The upperworke of the said Galeons was of thicknesse and strength sufficient to beare off musket-shot. The lower worke and the timbers thereof were out of measure strong, being framed of plankes and ribs foure or five foote in thicknesse, insomuch that no bullets could pierce them. . . .'[7] The 'king Catholique' was also misguided enough to order the inclusion of four Mediterranean galleys, all of which were forced back at the first meeting with rough weather; and four galleasses 'of such bignesse', Hakluyt reported, 'that they contained within them chambers, chapels, turrets, pulpits, and other commodities of great houses' together with 300 slave oarsmen each. There was rather more sense in the inclusion of these, the most spectacular and intimidating fighting ships of their day and with a really formidable armament, because, while they did little damage, they succeeded in engaging the anxious attention of the English for much of the way up-Channel.

To get the Armada fighting into perspective, several neat legends, stemming from contemporary English poets, the writings of G. A. Henty and even quite recent history primers, have to be disposed of. A number of Medina Sidonia's galleons, while not vast floating castles, were of an impressive stature – which made them all the more difficult to handle. But most of them were merchantmen converted to troop-

One of Pine's tapestry hanging designs of the Armada for the House of Lords, 1739; the tapestries were subsequently burnt

ships and carrying only a modest armament of cannon. The English commander, Charles, Lord Howard of Effingham, could muster no converted merchantman to match Sidonia's *La Ragonza*. But neither was his new galleon, *Triumph*, of 1,100 tons, matched in tonnage or power by any warship in the Spanish fleet.

Medina Sidonia's fleet for 'the enterprize of England' consisted of seventy-seven first-line ships, divided into six squadrons, or armadas, supported by forty-five storeships and smaller craft, the four galleys and the four Neapolitan galleasses. Of the main fighting force, around seven of the ships were of 1,000 tons or more, twice this number were between 800 and 1,000 tons, and the rest averaged about 400 tons. But of these only some twenty had been designed as fighting ships from the keel up; the remainder were tubby merchantmen mainly of carrack form, which had received an addition to their standard armament. Santa Cruz, the victor at Lepanto seventeen years earlier, favoured the heavy cannon, and the main artillery power of the Armada lay in cannon and demi-cannon with a short barrel and capable of firing, over a very limited range, a round shot of 60 or 30 pounds. In total weight of broadside, the English could not match the Spaniards. But the long-barrel English culverin and demi-culverin far outranged the Spanish guns. The situation was analogous to a heavyweight boxer with a short reach and a pulverizing punch challenging a flyweight with a long reach. With the English Channel as the ring, all else being

95

equal it would seem to be only a matter of time before the heavyweight triumphed. But the flyweight had a further and overwhelming advantage: he was very much quicker on his feet, and his reflexes were twice as fast.

For the only time in Britain's long maritime history, the Navy's *matériel* was the finest in the world. In Mattingley's words it was 'a fighting fleet faster and more weatherly than any that had ever been seen in the ocean before.'[9] The English galleons were 'the last word' in fighting ship development. Like the Spitfire and Hurricane fighters that prevented another attempted invasion 350 years later, their guns might be lighter, but they were nippier than the enemy at bringing them to bear. And on both occasions, the men were imbued not only with heroic patriotism but a sense of confidence in their weapons.

The English seamen of the late 1500s had made a close study of ship design and had debated the merits and demerits of a lower or higher freeboard, a larger or smaller ratio of beam to length, a greater or lesser rake forward. 'A great rake forward gives a ship good way,' wrote Sir Henry Manwayring, 'and makes her keep a good wind, but if she had not a full bow it will make her pitch mightily into a head sea.' Sir John Hawkins led the advanced West Country school of thought which preferred a lean hull with a low freeboard, and with the waist decked over: the days of boarding were past. Sir Walter Raleigh agreed; nor did he believe that size and gunpower alone made an efficient fighting ship. 'We find by experience that the greatest ships are least serviceable, go very deep to water, and of marvellous Charge and fearful Cumber, our Channels decaying every year. Besides they are less nimble, less maineable, and very seldom employed . . . a ship of 600 tons will carry as good Ordnance as a ship of 1,200 tons, and though the greater have double her number, the lesser will turn her broadsides twice before the greater can wend once.' Raleigh laid down for his ideal fighting ship these principal requirements:

'First, that she be strong. Secondly, that she be swift. Thirdly, that she be stout-sided. Fourthly, that she carry her Guns all weather. Fifthly, that she hull and try well, which we call a good ship. Sixthly, that she stay well, when bourding and turning on a wind is required.' (The *Mary Rose* disaster had not been forgotten, and Raleigh advocated 'always that your lowest Tyre of Ordnance must lie four foot cleare above water when all loading is in'.) England probably owed her salvation from Spanish rule to the theoretical and practical wisdom of great seamen like Raleigh and Hawkins, and the skill of the ship-wrights of England who met their needs with such magnificent fighting ships as the *Ark Royal* and *Triumph*.

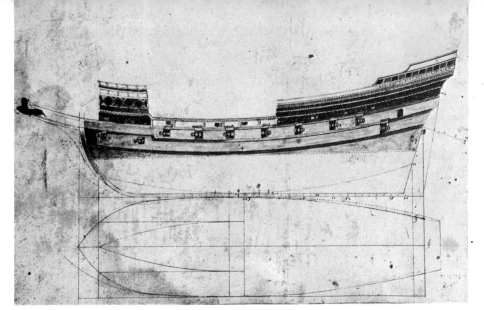

Matthew Baker's design for a ship
of the time of the Armada

The Queen's ships built under the administration of Howard as
Lord High Admiral were not in any way revolutionary. Rather, they
represented a natural and inevitable trend in fighting ship design,
impelled by the growing efficiency and ship-destroying power of
contemporary ordnance, which other nations – even the Dutch – were
slower to accept. For the first time in the history of warship design,
there is detailed documentary evidence of measurements and plans
of the vessels. Matthew Baker, the first Master Shipwright appointed
by the Crown, left a manuscript (now in the Pepysian Library at
Magalene College, Cambridge) containing elevations, plans and
sections of several ships. It is evident from these documents, and from
a list of 1600, that the English fighting ship which defeated the Armada
had a keel length at least three times its breadth; had a forecastle set
well back from the stem and a projecting beak; a strong sheer, or
upward curve of the hull towards both stern and bow; and transom,
or square, stern. The old extravagance of built up castles fore and aft
had now quite disappeared; instead, by successive stages aft of the
mainmast there arose half deck, quarter deck and poop. The rig was
four-masted in ten of Howard's ships, most of the others carrying fore,
main and mizzen only. The mizzen and bonaventure mizzen carried
single lateen sails, the main and fore masts both carried topgallant
masts and sails. Projecting galleries extended from each quarter (they
served as officers' latrines) and across the stern as a walkway. The
rudder was controlled by a whip-staff, or lever pivoted in the deck,
the lower end engaging the fore end of a tiller. The main armament
of culverins and demi-culverins was arranged on the broadside at
several different levels because it was an invariable rule that the wales,
on which the longitudinal strength of the ship depended, must not be
pierced. Because of the ship's steep sheer the gunports rose by stages
forward and aft from the waist. The lighter guns were carried in the
forecastle and the half deck, in the waist, and in the beakhead bulk-

head, which provided forward fire which was effective against men and rigging.

This was the type of English galleon which formed the most formidable attacking weight of the English fleet. The English captains were proud of them and loved them. 'I protest if before God,' wrote the Lord High Admiral to Sir Francis Walsingham, 'that were it not for Her Majesty's presence I had rather live in the company of these noble ships than in any place.' And for his flagship, his heart burst with pride (and tact) in a letter to Lord Burghley. 'I pray you tell her Majesty for me that her money was well given . . . for I think her the odd ship in the world for all conditions. . . . We can see no sail, great or small but how far soever they be off we fetch them and speak with them.'

Supported by this spirit, gifted with native skill as well as experience in seamanship, burning with zeal and a fierce hatred of the Catholic invader, with ships such as these as well as all the natural advantages enjoyed by a defending fleet close to its supplies and reinforcements, could Howard and his commanders fail?

They could have failed for several reasons. First, only a handful of the English fighting ships were of the latest swift and powerful class. While no less than 197 vessels are listed as taking part in the attacks, the vast majority of these were small merchantmen, pinnaces and fishing vessels of negligible fighting value compared with the *Ark Royal* with her 44 guns. Only fourteen of Howard's ships were of more than 500 tons, and the decisive fighting which decided the fate of England and of Medina-Sidonia's Armada was conducted by no more than some twenty ships on each side. Second, the Spanish fought with skill and tenacity, and their formation, in a loose crescent or triangle with the most powerful ships in the centre protecting the supply ships ahead, proved to be almost unbreakable. Finally, Howard's crippling handi-

Two versions of the *Ark Royal* Howard's flagship against the Armada. She was built for Sir Walter Raleigh, but then bought by Queen Elizabeth for the Navy. Lord Howard of Effingham called her 'the odd ship in the world for all conditions'. The picture (left) is a unique print of an ancient woodcut, and bears a strange resemblance to the *Great Harry* in many respects; (right) is Visscher's idea of the ship

cap was a simple logistical miscalculation of the expected expenditure of powder and shot required for the harassing attacks by the English ships all the way up the Channel.

In spite of the courage of the foe and the recurrent shortage of ammunition, the English galleons swept in time and again to a range just beyond that of the heavier Spanish guns and fired their broadsides of culverins and demi-culverins. Many of their shots damaged the Spanish rigging and plunged into the upper works to spread deadly wooden splinters among those exposed on deck. But most of them were delivered 'on the downward roll' of the ship so that the shots struck low on the stout sides of the Spanish ships: each broadside a shattering confirmation of the English determination to destroy the ship. In fact the structural damage from a culverin ball was comparatively slight; and the vast Spanish fleet sailed implacably on, and questions were asked by the Queen's Council why none of the perfidious Catholic ships had yet been boarded. This was just what Medina-Sidonia was praying for – and he could do little more under the circumstances. He had been warned that there was little likelihood of good, old-fashioned, man-to-man combat: 'The enemy will fight at long range to get the advantage of his artillery,' King Philip had told him. But it was impossible for Medina-Sidonia to follow his orders that he 'must close and grapple, taking them in your hand' when the English could beat back into the wind almost before the Spanish steersman could put over the helm. At the time it was necessary to defend Howard's tactics against ignorant criticism, while the fate of England still hung on the effective handling of a few hundred pieces of light artillery against ships containing 19,000 eager but frustrated Spanish foot soldiers. As Raleigh was to write later, 'To clap ships together without consideration belongs rather to a madman than to a man of war. . . . The Spaniards had an army aboard them, and [Howard] had none.'

Divine crisply sums up the long-drawn-out and spasmodic action that resulted in the defeat of the Spanish Armada thus:

> The English fleet sailed in a new tradition, the tradition of the gun. The tactics that had been made possible by Henry VIII and his shipwrights, that had been developed by Drake and Hawkins and half a hundred other raiders along the coast of the Spanish Main, crystallized in the conduct of the fleet from Plymouth Sound to the last rout of the Spaniards off Gravelines. Only by boarding could Medina-Sidonia hope to use his weight of numbers, the skill of his soldiers. Howard of Effingham never gave him the chance to board. The gun dominated the battle from the opening 'defiance' until the Spaniards turned to the north and found their ultimate disaster.[10]

Besides being one of the most decisive sea battles of all time, the defeat of the Spanish Armada marks the beginning of naval warfare in a form and tradition that was to endure until the aircraft took over the rôle of the cannon 350 years later. The English ships triumphed because they presaged the age of the line-of-battle and were the first battleships to take part in a major and decisive conflict. The Spanish galleons were defeated as decisively as the battleships were later defeated at Taranto and Pearl Harbor, because they remained armed troopships when the new battleship with longer-ranging artillery was manifestly the new queen of the sea; just as the steel battleship itself was defeated in the 1940s because it was vulnerable to the new longer-ranging artillery of the aircraft carrier – the bomb and the torpedo.

The Spanish defeat marked the opening of the new age of sea warfare when the *matériel* – beyond the cutlass, the pike and the sword – began to dominate sea warfare. The quality of the personnel, goodness knows, was to continue to count in the statistical results of battle and gallant combats against great odds were to touch with gold the annals of sea warfare for centuries to come. But the modern fighting ship was born, the age of dominance of the *matériel* began, when Charles Lord Howard, soon after 9 am on the morning of Sunday 31 July 1588, bore down in the *Ark Royal* on Don Alfonso de Leiva's great galleon the *Rata Coronada* and poured into her ample hull a broadside of 9-pounder and 18-pounder round shot. At 3.47 pm on the afternoon of 31 May 1916, Vice-Admiral Sir David Beatty opened fire on the German battle cruisers and began the last great combat between artillery-armed fighting ships. In the intervening years the fighting ship was to suffer many changes in its size and shape, motive power and gun power. The basic principles and conduct of maritime warfare changed not at all.

Two illustrations from Matthew Baker's 'Fragments of Ancient Shipwrightry' showing his design for a ship, and a master shipwright with a compass

Overleaf: one of a pair of oil paintings of the Spanish Armada, 1588 by Vroom, showing 'The Battle'

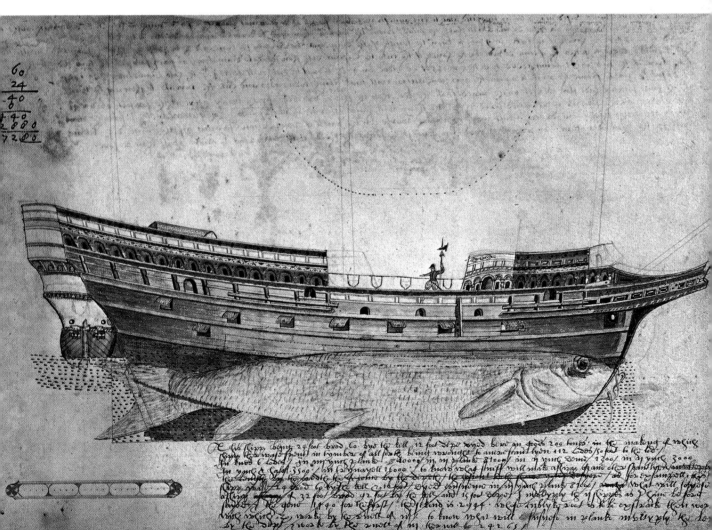

# 3. THE 1600s: DUTCH AND FRENCH PARAMOUNTCY

This century marked a period of powerful colonial rivalry and conflict, in which the chief contestants were France, Holland, England and Spain. There had been frequent and fundamental changes in the shape of the fighting ship following the introduction of the third mast and the ship-destroying gun in the 1400s and 1500s. There remained to the naval architect plenty of opportunity for radical improvement of his ships in the succeeding decades, but none that were to alter greatly the form and silhouette. This was a century of consolidation rather than evolution, when the carver and the gilder had better scope for expression than the shipwright, when sea battles occurred often enough to give the tacticians the means to develop the art of naval fighting to a high degree, when – and we must at last be grateful for this – people kept proper documents and records and preserved models of their ships. From now on there is less need for speculation and caution. In Stockholm there even exists, by a miracle of preservation, chance and enterprise, a complete fighting ship of this period.

The most dogged, sagacious and successful colonists of this century were the Dutch. Dutch colonialism and affluence were brought about by a series of historical events, one of the most important being the defeat at sea of Spain by England in 1588. But long before then the Dutch had begun to struggle free from the Hapsburg spider's web. The sea and their heroic physical struggle against it, their native acumen and acquisitiveness, had for long made the Dutch acutely maritime-conscious. In the late 1500s they were building armed galleons that could sail far beyond their native shores to bring back

The second of a pair of Armada oil paintings by Vroom, showing 'After the Battle', and (bottom) detail of a portrait of Queen Elizabeth I with two scenes of the Spanish Armada behind her

The Battle of Ter Heide, 1653, b
Beerstraten. This is a typical con
temporary version of a sea battle
In the days of wooden ships sinking
was rare, and occurred almos
solely as an artist's convention

home the riches of the East Indies – without the advantage of a call
en route at Lisbon, closed to them as a result of their own rebellion.
Good fortune assisted their courage and endeavours. The shrewd
Queen of England, who had struck such a blow at their oppressors,
died at last in 1603, and a king who misguidedly over-prized peace
ascended the throne. The English Navy decayed while Dutch sea
power soared higher and higher in unison with the wealth of the
merchants of Rotterdam and Amsterdam. In the second half of the
century the United Provinces possessed 20,000 merchantmen with a
tonnage of 900,000 – almost twice that of England's. While the Spanish
Navy recoiled from the blows of 1588 the Dutch firmly but unostenta-
tiously seized one by one the rich and distant Hapsburg monopolies.
Within a few decades, the material benefits of maritime power – in
terms of merchantmen and warships to protect them on an unprecedented scale – were demonstrated to the world. The effect on the
succeeding centuries was to be profound.

The Dutch were handicapped by the need for a small draught in
their warships, because of all their sandbanks and islands and the
shallowness of their harbours and estuaries. But while the English had
to be prepared to fight in the wild waters of the North Atlantic as well
as the more sheltered Channel and North Sea, the Dutch also benefited from the need to build ships for operating in mainly sheltered
waters – just as the Germans did 250 years later. The fighting ships
that resulted on both occasions were the finest in the world; and Admirals Maarten Harpertszoon Tromp and Michiel Adriaanszoon de
Ruyter of the Anglo-Dutch wars were the equal of Admirals Reinhard
Scheer and Franz von Hipper of 1916.

The Dutch warships of the mid-1600s were smaller and less heavily armed than the largest English ships. The need to restrict their draught limited them to two gun decks, although by judicious use of the space eighty and even ninety guns were sometimes carried. But by skilful formation of the hull and a shrewd understanding of sails and rigging and the sailing qualities of a ship, their vessels were both swifter and more manoeuvrable than their English counterparts, although these advantages were probably entirely wiped out when fighting in the open sea. The biggest vessels were three-masters, with a much reduced sheer compared with the galleons of the last century. The forecastle had almost ceased to exist, the beakhead thrust upwards more markedly, the stern – in contrast with latest English practice – was square. Dutch naval architects were the first to recognize the extreme and wasteful degree to which the tumble-home had developed, and sought by more scientific means to offset the imbalance caused by many heavy cannon above the centre of gravity. Other nations conformed to Dutch straight-sided practice, but not until much later. The Dutch gained further speed by tallowing the bottoms of their ships against barnacles, and here again they were first. Dutch skill with sails resulted in their introduction of the first modern fore and aft rig, which was widely used in their highly admired *jachts*. At the other end of the scale, the Dutch led the world, too, with their fireships – the torpedoes of the 1600s – which Dutch flagships had under their lee ready to be despatched at suitable moments in battle: one of these

The Four Days' Fight, 1666, by
torck. This was the first time,
except for isolated occasions such
as the Armada, that regular fleets
of over 100 sail a side engaged in
mortal combat – the name of the
battle is indicative. On the right is
the English ship with the royal
arms, left, is the Dutch ship with
the arms of her state and her name
in the tafferel

being at Solebay when the English flagship *Royal James* was burnt.

During the three Dutch wars against England in 1652–4, 1665–7, 1672–4 the Dutch suffered at sea, like their opponents, from indigestion caused by excess and a mixed menu. The handicap of heterogeneity in a fighting fleet had not yet been understood, so that ships with widely varying sailing qualities, speed and gunpower all sailed together. How right that one of the two rival forms of contemporary tactics was named the *mêlée*! Commanders believed in throwing in everything available that carried a gun, and the result was often rather a shambles than a *mêlée*. By brilliant seamanship and courage of high order and stubbornness quite as irresistible as the English, the Dutch got the better of many a confusing and long-drawn-out combat. (One was called the Four Days' Battle.) The English were frequently humiliated in such never-to-be-forgiven occasions as the Dutch sailing and burning up the Medway.

But in the end the Dutch came off worse, as had the Spanish nearly a century before, because – in spite of a high degree of seamanship and boundless bravery – they did not sufficiently value the ship-destroying power of the gun. Especially early on, they *still* believed that boarding and fighting hand-to-hand was the natural, decisive culmination of a sea battle; while the English – thanks to the prescience of Henry VIII and the seeds of enthusiasm for 'the big bang' he sowed a century and a half earlier – pinned their faith in the final count on the cannon and culverin. By contrast with the Armada engagements the English ships were the sturdier and less handy. But this time their solid round shot broke up the weaker hull of the enemy. The English, as a result of their experience in the Channel fights against the Spanish, formally adopted the line-of-battle. The Dutch with marvellous skill – and none was higher than the great de Ruyter's – circled about, shot at the English rigging, sent in their fireships, attempted to grapple and board; while the English cannon shot them to pieces. If the Dutch had appreciated as fully as the English that the fighting ship was a gun-platform for sailing in line with its consorts and in disciplined order battering the enemy, the outcome of those fierce combats of the mid-1600s could well have been different.

The superiority of Dutch shipbuilding before and during the Anglo-Dutch wars was widely recognized in Europe. The Swedes, the Danes and the Germans all took advantage of Dutch wisdom. Peter the Great of Russia came to Zaandam in 1667 to make a personal study of Dutch methods. The origins and inspiration of one of the other great navies in Europe can be traced back to Holland in the 1620s, long before Dutch colonial power had reached its zenith. In 1624 France possessed almost no power at sea. Richelieu, who came to office in that year, recognized this desperate weakness. With no tradition of modern fighting ship construction to draw on, he turned to the best and most experienced builders, just as the Japanese did at the beginning of the present century. Five large ships with sixty guns disposed on two decks, and with the most up-to-date sail and rigging, were ordered from the Dutch yards. They were an immediate success, and French shipwrights were ordered to study and learn. They did this with such diligence and enthusiasm that soon they in their turn were building the finest fighting ships in the world. What is more, the tradition of excellence and enterprise was maintained right through the 1700s and 1800s, so that when the French ships were captured they were imitated and when the French captured enemy ships they modified them to their own higher standards. When the 74-gun *Superbe* visited Spithead in 1672 she was so admired by the English that the King ordered her to be copied; and the resulting ship, the 70-gun *Harwich*, was so successful that nine more copies were built: a satisfactory way of keeping abreast of the competition.

The French learnt their lessons well from the Dutch. The 72-gun

Louis XIV first rate. In Louis XIV's reign Colbert, the Minister f Marine, was very interested in he growth and improvement of the Navy, and today a number of beautiful manuscripts, prepared for presentation to the King, survive, with admirable pictures of different ates of ships. This is a first rate of bout 100 guns, and such a ship, fter suitable preparation, could e put together by Colbert's well-rganized dockyards in a week

two-decker *Couronne* of 1638 was a very fine sailer and by her very dexterity (in turning to present her other broadside) could probably fire as many guns in any given period as a contemporary British 100-gun ship. Armand Jean du Plessis, Duc de Richelieu, was not only *Surintendent général de la navigation et commerce*; he was the father of the permanent French navy. He set up the first French naval bases, organized the training of shipwrights and craftsmen, ordered the provision of timber and other materials, bought cannon from the Dutch and then set in hand the expansion of domestic ordnance works and issued instructions that even the most humble shipyard must turn to naval construction. By the time the *Couronne* was launched France had thirty-eight ships, a dozen of them of over 500 tons, organized into three squadrons. France had suddenly become a major naval power as well as a military power.

France's development as a sea power was broken after Richelieu's death and there was a hiatus of some nineteen years. Ships and dock-yards rotted. The army got all the glory and all the money. Louis XIV, through the offices of his brilliant administrator, Jean-Baptiste Colbert, revived France's waning naval power. Again as a stop-gap, ships were at first purchased from Holland. Craftsmen once more found their old skills. Besides two- and three-deck ships-of-the-line, there was a revival in the building of galleys and galleasses for use in the Mediter-ranean against Barbary pirates and the ever-threatening Spaniards. By 1677 the French, with 116 fighting ships, were as powerful at sea as the English and the Dutch, and Colbert had set up arsenals, a gunnery school and the great dockyards of Toulon and Brest. The study of hydrography and charts was encouraged, and the science of ship design was now followed with as much diligence in France as in Holland. In the same year *L'Architecture Navale* by Le Sieur Dassie was published in Paris. Other treatises followed, and subjects such as the ratio of sail area to stability and speed to hull design were closely studied in technical journals.

All this intensive injection of maritime enthusiasm in his subjects resulted in Louis XIV possessing before his death the most advanced and efficient fighting fleet in Europe. (The fruits of a close scientific study were quickly gathered.) By comparison with English design, the French fighting ship in the late 1600s was faster and handier and a steadier gun-platform. In contradiction to the last great step forward in fighting ship architecture, the French went for a wider beam and shallower draft, and gained manoeuvrability and stability. Landström illustrates an 84-gun two-decker French ship from the drawings in the contemporary *Atlas de Colbert* with a scarcely discernible sheer, a very

slight tumble-home, no raised forecastle at all, and a long quarter deck beginning at the mizzen mast. She drew only $19\frac{1}{2}$ feet, and the continued threat of the more manoeuvrable galley in the Mediterranean is met by the additional heavy armament in the stern and bows, necessitating a deeply curved beakhead.

In their turn, other maritime powers made a closer and more scientific study of naval architecture during the 1600s, and benefited greatly from Dutch, French and English practice. Among these was Sweden, which built up a formidable navy in the early part of the century. Fortunately, in this case we have the unique advantage of an actual ship to study. The foundering of the Dutch-designed *Wasa* off Beckholmen on her maiden voyage in 1628 was a major catastrophe for the Swedish people; her location, and her subsequent salvaging between 1959 and 1961 was a major feat. Her presence today in her own dockyard in Stockholm represents the wonder of the material actuality of every naval historian's theorizing. The preserving quality of the brackish *teredo navalis*-free Baltic waters and Stockholm harbour's mud has yielded not just the main hull structure of this great fighting ship, but the eating utensils and clothes of the unfortunate souls who sailed in her, the carpenter's tools, the coins she carried, even the food and drink that was never to be consumed. Time has treated her so tenderly that there remains still some of the bark on the hollowed-out wooden pump. The *Wasa* measures from her figurehead (there are traces of gilding on the lion's mane) to stern 184 feet, and her beam is 38 feet. She displaces 1,400 tons and is a three-master rigged with topsail and topgallant on her fore and main and two sails only on her

mizzen. Her mainmast measures 180 feet. Her construction is of oak throughout, except for the masts, the upper and orlop decks and the deck shoring, all of which are of pine. She has four decks only, two of them gun decks. But this did not cause her designer to restrain his enthusiasm for a heavy battery of guns. It was, of course, her ordnance and her inadequate ballast that were the poor *Wasa*'s undoing, although she would have survived the slight squall she met at the harbour mouth if someone had remembered to close her gunports. She was over-armed, and therefore unstable, carrying no fewer than two 62-pounders, three 35-pounders, forty-eight 24-pounders, one 16-pounder, eight 3-pounders and two 1-pounders – all brass pieces, and all with their bar, case, chain and link shot, together with incendiary bombs. It might be said she was overbuilt: her timbers were far heavier than in later and larger ships.

'Last Sunday, just after Vespers,' ran the report with the dire news of the loss of his flagship to King Gustaf II Adolfus, 'the ship laid off with all necessary supplies and all guns well lashed. The wind was from the south south-west and the weather calm, and Erich Jönsson, Captain Söfring and Hans Jansson, on board. When the ship had come under the cliffs they set both topsails, and mizzen, and fired a salute. The ship went fast and came out in the bay of Tegelwijken where more weather came in the sails and the ship went over to larboard but came up again till it was off the island of Beckholmen where it did completely fall on its side and water came in through the gun ports until it did slowly sink with sails up and flags flying. There came out right soon many small boats but they were of no aid. . . .' The *Wasa* was not the only fighting ship to go down as a result of excessive weight of ordnance, but most of them succumbed in heavier seas than the *Wasa* experienced and at least cleared their home port.

The English navy began the new century in fine fettle. The golden glow of triumph from the victory of 1588 still lingered over the fleet

The *Wasa* in dry dock. She wa raised in 1961 after lying on the se bed for 333 years. The *Wa* museum contains the almost con plete hull of the seventeenth century warship in pristine co dition, and also guns, gear, equip ment and even the personal effec of the officers and crew and the men who had sailed out to meet Medina-Sidonia; but the sunset was near, and soon after the accession of King James I in 1603 the Navy, through neglect and absence of funds, slipped into a decline. This idealistic King even tried to stamp out free-lance English piracy, an activity which had not only filled the nation's coffers but also taught the men who fought the Armada skilful seamanship and fighting prowess. In 1607 the Venetian ambassador in London reported home that even the few serviceable fighting ships left were 'old and rotten and barely fit for service'. As a result of this misguided policy, piracy by others flourished around England's shores, trade declined, and the new colonial powers – who had drawn their own more accurate conclusions from Spain's defeat at sea – were encouraged to build up new navies.

The picture was not altogether dark. Few warships were built for the Navy, but those that were laid down were among the largest and most lavishly finished in Europe, and they were later to do sterling service against the fighting fleets of the new Continental naval powers. One or two are worth closer examination, for this reason, even if they did not greatly advance the art of naval architecture. English fighting ships of this period, and right down to the reign of William III (1689–1702), often bear the mark of the Pett family, ship designers and builders. Phineas Pett was Master of Arts at Emmanuel College, Cambridge, and it was he who designed and built the largest ship in the world, the *Prince Royal*, a 56-gun vessel of over 1,200 tons. Any tendency towards gigantism in fighting ships has always been accompanied by both bombast among promoters and predictions of disaster from those who had not built so big in the past. Pett was attacked from all sides, most of all by the aged Matthew Baker whose influence had been so powerful in the design of Elizabeth's galleons fifty years before. The *Prince Royal*'s keel was laid in October 1608, and Pett's enemies were delighted to witness her failure – through miscalculation of her size – to be launched in September 1610. She got into the water in the end, and had a long and splendid service which included two rebuilds. The cult of gigantism in England did not die with the commissioning of the *Prince Royal*, although the Navy had to await the coronation of a more vainglorious king than James I before it got anything bigger. This superb *folie de grandeur* was the *Sovereign of the Seas*. According to tradition, so heavily did the cost of this ship fall on the English taxpayer that it resulted in King Charles I losing his head. Certainly if you were going to accuse a monarch of criminal extravagance the *Sovereign* was Exhibit A in any court. There is a note on her gilding and carving, at the end of this chapter; all that need be said on this score here is that, at the time when you could get a good 40-gun fighting ship for around £6,000, the *Sovereign of the Seas* cost well over £60,000. It has also been told that on a summer day in 1634 Charles was looking over the new unfinished *Leopard* at Woolwich with Pett and, finding it wanting in dimensions, ordered him to build the biggest warship in the world. Pett met his master's wishes and went ahead with his design. On 14 May 1635, he recorded in his journal: 'I was commanded by His Majesty to hasten into the north to provide and prepare the frame timber, plank and tree-nails for the great and new ship at Woolwich. I left my son' (Peter, under whose supervision the *Sovereign* was constructed) 'to see the moulds and other necessaries shipped in a Newcastleman, hired on purpose to transport our provisions and workmen to Newcastle. The frame, as it was got ready, was shipped and sent in colliers from New-castle to Sunderland.' Later in his journal, Pett boasts of her fierce and multitudinous armament: 'She hath three flush deckes and a fore-castle, an halfe decke, a quarter-decke, and a round house. Her lower tyre hath thirty ports, which are to be furnished with demi-cannon and whole cannon . . . her middle tyre hath also thirty ports for demi-culverin and whole culverin; her third tyre hath twentie sixe ports for other ordnance; her forecastle hath twelve ports, and her halfe decke hath fourteen ports; she hath thirteane or fourteane ports within board for murdering pieces, besides a great many loope-holes

The *Prince Royal*, 1610, at Flushin The harbour could be recogniz today

out of the cabins for musket shot. Shee carrieth moreover, ten pieces of chase ordnance in her right forward, and ten right aft. . . .'

Amid outcries of extravagance and protests from Trinity House, the construction of the *Sovereign of the Seas* proceeded, and the Navy got the most magnificent as well as the biggest fighting ship in the world – a three-decker, with a displacement of over 1,600 tons, and with a grandiose rig that included a vast spritsail, topsail and royals. Her bristling ordnance together with the greatest area of gilding in the world caused her to be dubbed by the Dutch 'The Golden Devil'. Although she was later cut down to two decks, she certainly succeeded in inspiring those who sailed in her with an overwhelming sense of invincibility and those against whom she sailed with fear as no other giant warship has ever exceeded. She was never defeated in battle, served for sixty years, and was at last destroyed by someone who overturned a candle in her in 1696. If she had survived, neither in her form, size nor gunpower would she have appeared obsolete in the fighting line at the Battle of the Nile a century later.

The large ships-of-the-line like the *Prince Royal* and *Sovereign of the Seas* were followed by a number of cheaper and much less spectacular fighting ships. Over 200 ships of all sizes were added to the English navy during the period of the Commonwealth (1649–60). Unfortunately, their comparative Puritan austerity failed to attract con-

*The Sovereign of the Seas*, 1637, from a contemporary engraving by Payne. She was the great ship of Charles I's Navy, the first with three masts instead of the usual four (see the *Prince Royal*), and had royals on the main and foremast, topgallants on all three masts. She was highly decorated and became known as 'The Golden Devil', though she was only in action once. Pepys and a large crowd of his friends got inside the poop lantern, which gives an indication of her enormous size

Rigging plans of a fourth ar[
(right) a sixth rate ship from 'Do
trine of Naval Architecture', by S
Antony Deane

temporary artists as some of the ships built during Charles I's reign
had done. It was during this period, however, that the sterns of the
larger English warships took on a new shape, which was not to be
imitated by the Dutch or French for many years. At the opening of
the century all English ships had been built with a flat transom stern –
or square tuck – but it seems from the small evidence available that
during Cromwell's period as Protector, the English naval architects
decreed a change to a rounded tuck, with the planking at the stern
curved round the quarters and carried right into the rabbet of the
stern-post. Smaller warships retained the square stern.

With the restoration of the English monarchy in 1660 there begins
a period of renewed naval enthusiasm and construction. The continuing competition from Holland, the ever-growing power of France
and a wave of popular interest in all things naval – comparable with
the closing years of Victoria's reign 200 years later – which was inspired
and nourished by King Charles II, all led to a splendid renaissance.
Such was the new national maritime consciousness that, suddenly and
marvellously, our records for this period are almost complete. We can
turn to Sir Anthony Deane's *Doctrine of Naval Architecture* and *Mr
Dummer's Draughts of the Body of an English Man-of-War* (both in the
Pepysian Library); there are the magnificent paintings by the Dutch
artists, father and son, the Van de Veldes, who were employed as
marine painters to the English King. It was also decreed at this
period that scale models should be made of all important men-of-war

when they were laid down, and some of these have survived. We should be grateful enough for these priceless material records, but it is a pity that they do not begin a hundred or so years earlier when changes in design were more fundamental. However, they do record several interesting developments. While there was no inclination to follow the Dutch straight-sided practice, the hull formation had altered markedly from late Elizabethan days in order to provide better seaworthiness and a steadier platform for the much increased weight of ordnance. The strong degree of sheer which had marked Matthew Baker's galleons was also much reduced. The acute tumble-home was still there but was much less evident forward, as it was lower in order to lower the maximum beam of the ship to the waterline. Consequently, these ships were much more bluff in the bows. The forecastle was correspondingly reduced, and the ships-of-the-line at the time of the last Dutch wars gave the impression when sailing of digging deep into the water.

European naval competition in the second half of the century produced a shortage of skilled men and materials comparable with that of the years before the First World War. Timber was imported in great quantities from the Baltic, and it was not so satisfactory or long-lasting as home-grown oak. England, with her great reserves of finest standing oak, was at an advantage. But even before Charles II's Act of 1677, calling for thirty new men-of-war, unprecedented demand on the oak reserves of the Royal forests, and wilful neglect to replant in

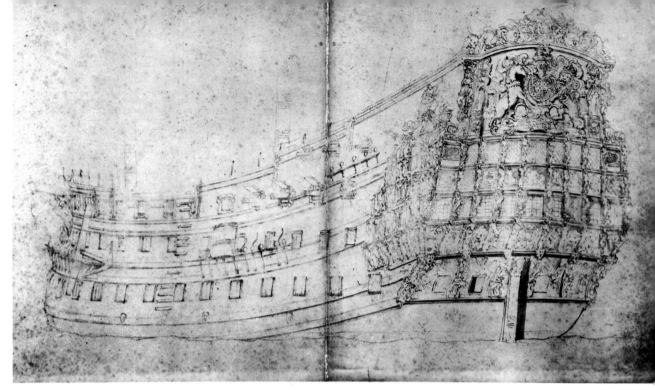

Drawing by Van de Velde of the
ornamentation on the stern of the
*Royal Charles*. The ship was carried
from Chatham to Holland by the
Dutch in 1667, and her royal arms
are now in the Rijksmuseum

the past, led to the need to import. Imported elm and beech for the
keel and lower planking of English ships proved unsatisfactory and
deteriorated rapidly. Under the stress of this shortage, iron was used
for certain internal fittings. Nails, standards and knees of iron became
more and more widely used, even in the English Navy, to the distress of
Samuel Pepys, famous diarist and secretary to the Admiralty, who
considered the departure 'most unfavourable'.

### SHIP DECORATION AND ORNAMENT

During the 1600s the embellishment of the fighting ship by carving,
gilding and painting was practised more enthusiastically and skilfully
by all the European sea powers, from the Venetians and Genoese in
the south to the Danes and Swedes in the north. The art suffered
moments of decline, as during the English Commonwealth, and also
reached such ludicrously exaggerated levels that the profusion of small
ornament defeated its own purpose, for at any distance (and ships at
sea are normally observed from a distance) the detailed skill was lost
in a confusion of gilded statuary and close-set ornamentation. The
reason for this sudden new activity among the carvers, painters and
gilders is not difficult to find, but it is very briskly told, in characteristic
style, by Van Loon:

> Why they should have provided the ship from bow to stern with beautiful
> bits of wooden sculpture is simple enough. For the ship, 'she's a lady', and
> as such she is, of course, entitled to a little extra care, to a little extra
> attention. . . . But why this entire museum of art on the stern? Why this
> . . . show of angels and mythological figures and cherubs carrying daisy
> chains, or tons and tons of anchor chains? Why these elaborate paintings

on the taffrail? . . . We should remember, however, that this was an age of ornament. The world had suddenly grown rich. . . . On land the baroque churches reared their over-elaborate façades towards heaven . . . the clocks were so densely covered with seascapes and landscapes and representations of naval engagements on the sea, with the moon and all the stars of heaven, that you never could quite see what time it was. . . .[11]

It is true that the decoration of ships usually conformed to the current practice on land, and therefore in a century of dazzling splendour everywhere, the ships of Louis XIV just outshone the strong competition. Looking at the contemporary model of the English first rate H.M.S. *Prince*, it is hard to conceive that a stern could be more elaborately carved. But the great French decorator Pierre Puget had no peer and could out-embellish the greatest carvers of his day with his pilaster work, his figure carving, his heavy balustrading for galleries, his arches and canopies over a ship's entering ports, his life-size figures on a ship's hancing pieces – the step made by the drop of a ship's rail to another level. Such was the ostentation of decoration of French men-of-war that captains were reduced to disguising them with canvas sheets in an endeavour to persuade pirate captains that they were only merchantmen. An even more graphic scene is presented by another old salt sawing off, in fury and exasperation, the great stern figures which added dangerous top weight to his vessel, and letting them fall overboard. It is fair to add, however, that the great majority of mariners accepted this burden of embellishment as no more than a further hazard to the whole dangerous business of life at sea. Thus were the fruits of the artist dealt with by the man of action. The practical Colbert protested in vain against the vulgar and expensive practice of overloading by over-carving.

The stern offered the greatest opportunity for the decorator. The introduction of windows, galleries and gunports provided the justification for further elaboration. 'The most general arrangement,' wrote Laughton, 'was that there should be a central device, a bust if the

later style of ornamentation, designed for a French eighteenth-century frigate by Ozanne. The French seventeenth- and eighteenth-century figurehead was larger and heavier than its English equivalent. This particularly ridiculous example was probably never put into practice

name of the ship suggested it, or sometimes the royal cypher crowned, with a pair of seated or reclining supporters, beyond whom to the quarters were cupids, mermaids, sea-horses and so forth. . . .'[8] Towards the end of the 1600s good sense at last prevailed among French decorators, and the stern of ships-of-the-line like the *St Philippe* revealed taste and distinction in the plainer treatment of its pillars and galleries.

The Dutch, as befitted their business-like temperament, restrained the enthusiasm of their carvers and gilders more successfully than the French or English, and early showed their good sense by exhibiting paintings by contemporary artists. The sides of their two-deckers were quite plain and business-like. The figurehead was normally a fierce but simple red-painted lion; only at the stern was there any lavishness in the treatment of carving, gilding and painting.

The English began the century in a sober frame of mind, the decorations of their men-of-war reflecting the contemporary Tudor-Gothic style of interior decoration ashore. The effects of the Renaissance took a while to cross the Channel; but soon, in the *Prince Royal*, the English had the most decorated – as well as the largest – warship in the world. The upper two of her three stern galleries were illuminated by rows of windows, and the coat-of-arms of the Prince of Wales had the plumes painted white against the surrounding gilding and background green painting (cost: £868 6s 8d). But this fighting ship was a Plain Jane alongside the *Sovereign of the Seas*, of which Phineas Pett despairingly wrote in his journals that 'she was so gorgeously ornamented with carving and gilding, that she seemed to have been designed rather for a vain display of magnificence than for the services of the state'. Her architect may have despaired of the ornamentation with which she was weighed down – buoyantly and financially; but his son Peter in his portrait stands proudly before her extravagantly-carved stern. There they all are, the cupolas and leaded windows and galleries, the monograms and mythological figures and scenes, the great royal coat-of-arms – all topped by the Goddess of Victory flanked by Jupiter and Neptune, Hercules and Jason. The bows were equally stunning to the beholder, for the royal master carver, Gerard Christmas, and his team, working to the drawings of van Dyck, had given equally special attention to the frontal aspect.

In a 'very scarce little Piece', inscribed to His Majesty King Charles I, Thomas Heywood described these bow carvings in terms of wonder, under the title *A true Description of his Majesty's royal Ship, built this Year, 1637, at Woolwich, in Kent, to the great Glory of the English Nation, and not to be Paralleled in the whole of the Christian World:*

The *Resolution*, 1669, by Van d Velde II. She was a third rate of 7 guns, and the union at the main the flag of Sir Thomas Allin, the Commander-in-Chief in the Med terranean

Overleaf: Dutch men of war an yacht, by Van de Velde II

Upon the beak head sitteth royall king Edgar on horseback, trampling upon seven kings. . . . Upon the stemine head there is a Cupid, or a child resembling him, bestriding and bridling a lyon, which importeth, that sufference may curbe insolence, and innocence restraine violence, which alludeth to the great mercy of the king, whose type is a proper embleme of the great Majesty, whose mercy is above all his workes. On the bulk head right forward stand six severall statues in sundry postures, their figures representing Consilium, that is Counsell; Cura, that is Care; Conamen, that is Industry; and unanimous endeavours in one compartement: Councell holding in her hand a closed or folded scrole, Care a sea compasse, Conamen, or Industry, a lint stock fired. Upon the other, to correspond with the former, Vis, which implyeth Force, or Strength, handling a sword; Virtus, or Virtue, a sphearicall globe; and Victoria, or Victory, a wreath of lawrell. . . . Upon the hances of the waste are foure figures, with their severall properties: Jupiter riding upon his eagle, with his trisulk, from which he darteth thunder in his hand; Mars, with his sword and target, a foxe being his embleme; Neptune, with his sea-horse, dolphin, and trident; and lastly, Aeolus upon a camelion, a beast that liveth onely by the ayre. . . .

Thomas Heywood continues his glowing tribute for several more pages, finally confessing that 'it would be too tedious to insist upon every ornament belonging to this incomparable vessel'. There were, however, those who deplored the extravagances of the *Sovereign*'s gilding and carving, including Phineas Pett himself, although he was evidently deeply proud of his ship's 'five lanthornes, the biggest of which will hold ten persons to stand upright, and with out shouldering or pressing one on the other. . . .' Lanterns were first carried in the late 1400s for the practical purpose of identification, and at first closely resembled street lanterns. Situated high on the poop, three was the standard number, but of course this was considered inadequate for the *Sovereign*.

Gunports, at first round and plain, soon proved an irresistible temptation for the carver. A wreath or foliage was a popular decoration for French, Spanish and English ships; flowers and fruit were sometimes added, and two tall carved figures were often seen flanking the protruding muzzle of a demi-culverin. The hinged lids were customarily painted on the inside, to be revealed when open, and carved on the outside. The *Sovereign* began a fashion for ornamenting the gallery turrets with ogee domes.

Commonwealth austerity – including the substitution of gold paint for gold leaf and a marked reduction in carving – was soon forgotten, and stern carving and gilding almost as elaborate as that of the *Sovereign* herself was soon again being displayed.

The *Sovereign of the Seas*, 1637, anon. Peter Pett, on the right, was a master shipwright, and his masterpiece was built for Charles I at Woolwich

## SAIL AND RIG IN THE 1600S

There was little development in sails and rigging in the first part of the century. A typical Dutch-built three-masted galleon of the 1620s already carried a topsail on the sprit topmast above the bowsprit as well as spritsail below. Fore and mainsail were furled with buntlines, clewlines and martnets; and topgallantsails were carried above the fore and mainmasts, but there were only two sails, square sail above a lateen, on the mizzen, with martnet and lift for furling. The *Sovereign of the Seas* designed a decade later sported a remarkably elaborate plan with no less than thirteen sails, although it is likely that the two royals were only for show. The main weakness of the sail arrangement in the 1600s – as it had been for centuries – was in the headsails. The sprit-sail topsail was, to the eye as well as in practice, a clumsy and inefficient makeshift, and it could not be long before the implacable conservatism of the seamen was at last overcome. As so often with 'new' inventions it was only necessary for the innovator to look backwards in time; for the canny Dutch had worked everything out in their sloops of a century earlier with their triangular-shaped headsail, or jib, stayed between the foremast and bowsprit. It was the Dutch who led the way again, adopting this same practice for their big ships, while retaining the spritsail beneath the bowsprit. The introduction of triangular headsails, which permitted dramatically more efficient sailing to windward, was the first really radical departure in sails since the introduction of the spritsail. Its long-term results were much more profound. In the early years of the next century, it led to the adoption everywhere of main and foretopmast staysails, and also to the use of studding sails which again were not new but whose qualities had not before been fully explored. The wide acceptance of the jib led to the melting away of many of the mariners' prejudices against sail innovation, so that within a few decades from the end of the 1600s the science of rigging and sails had advanced so rapidly that it was approaching the ultimately efficient degree of exploitation of wind power achieved in the 1800s.

A section of a third rate warship from Mr Dummer's 'Draughts of the Body of an English Man of War'. The officers' cabins and wardroom can be seen aft; the galley store forward

Ornamentation on models of the *Soleil Royal* and (right) the *Louis Quinze*. This magnificent flagship of Louis XV's Navy was burnt by the English at La Hogue, 1692, under the eyes of Marshal Turin and the exiled James II, who was tactless enough to cheer the English sailors on

A further notable advance in sail arrangements during the 1600s was in the method of reducing sail. For many years sail had been reduced by tying up at a line of reef points either at the top or bottom of the sail. With the introduction of the three-masted ship, bonnets were introduced. These were an additional depth of sail laced to the foot of the course, which could quickly be taken off. But the bonnet could not be used on the smaller topsails, which could only be furled when the yard was lowered. This became a more and more formidable undertaking with the increase in size of the upper sails, and reef points had therefore to be added to these sails too, their number increasing with the size of the sail so that, in the next century, as many as four lines of reef points became commonplace.

### UNDERWATER PROTECTION

The protection of a ship's bottom from corrosion and rot and the depredations of barnacles and worms and seaweed had been an occasional anxiety even on the shorter voyages in the ancient world. With the lengthening of voyages to many weeks and the tactical need to stay at sea, later perhaps for blockading purposes, it became necessary to give more serious attention to the problem, especially in ships sailing in tropical waters, where the ravages of the teredo were so

127

dangerous. In the 1500s Hawkins had thought up the idea of covering the outside of the planking with a composition of felt, hair and tar, nailing over it a sheathing of elm boards. This was a brave shot in the right direction but it did not work very well, and like a gold cap to a tooth, the decay went on beneath until the timbers at length fell apart. Lead sheathing was tried later in the 1600s, but electrolytic action caused the nails to fall out and it was very heavy. Copper sheathing was the answer, though of course it was very expensive and at first it only accelerated the corrosion of the iron bolts of the hull behind the copper. In the late 1700s copper bolts replaced these iron bolts, and all was well.

Table of all the 'principal parts and rigging' of a Dutch man of war. This was the epitome of Dutch shipping at the end of the seventeenth century; the sections show the characteristic flat bottoms. An interesting instrument, shown in the border, was the nocturnal, for finding the time at night by the Pole star

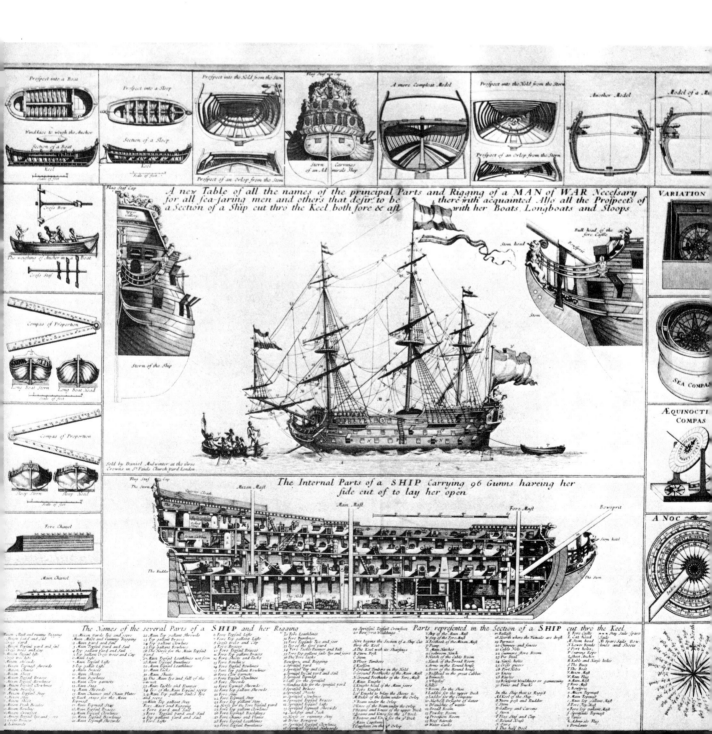

# THE 1700s: A CENTURY OF CONFLICT

This was the last full century in the life of the sailing warship. Again the one hundred years witnessed a steady and unspectacular development in all branches of naval science. In its hull formation, masting, sail plan and the disposition of its armament the sailing warship closely approached a degree of efficiency beyond which no further progress could be made. Before the century was out the first fumbling experiments were being conducted with mechanical in place of natural power for the ship, and a few far-sighted and courageous artillery enthusiasts were demonstrating the fearful effects of explosive against the structure of the wooden ship.

There was much fighting at sea during this century, mainly between the French, Spanish and English, and towards the end, the Americans too. The Anglo-French wars added lustre to the naval records of both countries. The British suffered many setbacks and defeats but proved themselves the more skilful fighters. But their ships were the worst in the three navies. 'To sum up the character of the English vessels of this period,' wrote Charnock of the early 1700s, 'in general terms, they were crank, confined, very indifferently adapted to the purposes of keeping out the sea in tempestuous weather, and in general but sorry sailers, even when it was most favourable . . . It continued the fashion of the time to attribute every superior faculty of sailing to the mere length of the vessel itself, without any or at least very trivial, regard to the form or shape of the bottom; from this circumstance, the wishes of the architect were rarely answered; and whenever they happened to be so, the success, in all probability, was more attributable to a coincidence of blunders innocently committed, so that the effect of one mistake was counteracted by another, than to any regular and established system resulting from theoretical knowledge and studious application. . . .'[3]

In spite of the stalwart endeavours of some individuals and well-intentioned official attempts to get to grips with the shortcomings of British ship design, the application of science and the experience of the men who sailed them somehow escaped the naval architects of this great maritime nation until the very end of the century. The French naval engineer possessed the priceless ability to step back and judge problems with his characteristic engineering originality, fresh and unprejudiced by tradition for its own sake. Craftsmanship by eye was a deeply ingrained English tradition. In the time of James I, Captain George Waymouth, an advanced shipbuilding theorist, complained that he 'could never see two ships builded of the like proportion by the best and most skilful shipwrights, though they have many times undertaken the same . . . because they trust rather to their judgement than their art, and to their eye than their scale and compass.'

Lewis summarizes the situation, pungently and historically, better than any other authority:

The superiority of our [British] enemies' ships was not due, however, to superior shipbuilding skill. Our shipwrights were probably, at all periods of 'wood', the best in the world. . . . Where then did the fault lie? Largely, it would seem, in over-reliance upon tradition and in a confusion of thought which failed to distinguish between ship-*building* and ship-*designing*. The former might safely be left to the long and wide experience of master shipwrights who were, as often as not, the sons and grandsons of shipwrights, and who were usually honest, industrious, and gifted craftsmen with a fine professional pride. Such people, however, are liable to preconceived ideas: they are almost certain to be hidebound conservatives. . . . The successful ship-designer unquestionably needs for success an inventive brain, a much higher standard of education than the actual builder, and a much wider outlook. And he must be countenanced, financed and encouraged. It is here that we went wrong. There was, for long, no demand for such a person: no recognition even of the fact that he was necessary. This was not so in France. From the time of Colbert in the late seventeenth century onwards, the innate logic of the French mind recognized that Science might be made to turn the scales against sheer workmanship and numbers. Naval Architecture, in fact, became a whole-time profession across the Channel long before we even dreamt of such a thing. . . .[6]

The Spanish were never able to make up for the deficiencies of their

The Battle of Gibraltar, 1782, by ... room. The explosion is probably ... e powder magazine of the Spanish ... ip igniting and blowing up – a ... ommon danger

fighting seamen. But they built some of the best fighting ships of the century by recognizing the special qualities of their friends and their enemies – by importing French engineers to design them and British master shipwrights to construct them. Such giants of the mid-1700s as the 114-gun *Real Infanta*, or the 70-gun *Isabella*, *Hercule* and *Constant*, were unsurpassed even by any French fighting ship. The British kept no more than one step behind by capturing, by superior seamanship, both French and Spanish ships and copying them. All the same, the British sailor often found himself in positions of hopeless inferiority. The French normally carried heavier guns anyway, but because the British had, in spite of the *Mary Rose* disaster, carried their lowest and heaviest guns too close to the water, the ports had to be shut up and the cannon remain silent in any sort of sea or when heeling over even at a modest angle, as when the enemy was to leeward. Time and again the canny sailing skill of the British was rendered impotent by the superior sailing qualities of French and Spanish ships – for science had been at work on the shape of their hulls and the arrangement of their sails. At

131

St Vincent in 1797 the British captured many Spanish vessels of all sizes, including the two great 2,400-ton, 112-gun ships-of-the-line *San Josef* and *Salvador del Mundo*. All, according to Bowen, were 'magnificent vessels, and even under their jury rig they outdid all the British ships beating into the River Tagus after the action. Nelson was always warm in his praise of Spanish shipbuilding and design, although he did not worry himself unduly about the odds when he was pitted against their ships in action.'[12]

A further reason for the conservatism of British fighting ship design in the 1700s was the introduction of a calculated and well-intentioned throttling process to enterprise in the shipbuilding establishments, which authorized, among other things, standard dimensions. These had been misguidedly initiated in the late 1600s and were continued in 1706, 1719 and 1745, with additional revisions in 1733 and 1741. The position improved only after Anson completed his voyage round the world, during which the shortcomings of his ships were shown up in many a stormy and distant sea. Things changed when he was appointed to the Board of Admiralty, ships were less heavily gunned, and closer attention paid to hull form and proportion. 'The ships previously composing the British Navy were so extremely long, in proportion to their breadth,' wrote Charnock, 'at the same time so

Admiral de Winter at Campe down with the *Monarch*, *Ardent* ar *Venerable*, by Serres. This battle w just after the notorious mutiny the British fleet at the Nore, 179 and it is surprising both that t dissatisfied sailors should hav fought the Dutch fleet so gallant so soon, and that the Dutch ol viously had no intelligence of t mutiny, or they would hav attacked before

deficient in bearings forward, that, in a heavy sea, they pitched, and laboured with such violence as to endanger, considering this as the slightest inconvenience they were to expect, the loss of all their masts. Reflection, at length, produced an attention to the cause. The absence of these defects, which became too discernible in the vessels of different countries, were, at last, too glaringly apparent to be neglected by Britain.'[3] Captured Spanish and French ships provided, as so often before and after, the answer. Foreign methods were studied more closely than ever. The most important result was the wonderful British 74s. Copies they may have been, but they were the best British fighting vessels of the century.

With the firm establishment in the 1600s of the distinction of the fighting ship from the merchantman, and the great increase in numbers and complexity of the fighting fleet, it had become necessary for all navies to classify their vessels in various categories. A system of 'rating' according to the number of guns had been accepted by the English Navy in the middle of that century, thus:

|             |          |
|-------------|----------|
| First-rate  | 100 guns |
| Second-rate | 52 guns  |
| Third-rate  | 46 guns  |
| Fourth-rate | 40 guns  |
| Fifth-rate  | 24 guns  |
| Sixth-rate  | 18 guns  |

With the inevitable increase in the size of ship brought about by the Dutch wars the rating requirement was raised for all but the sixth-rates. It was generally accepted that the first four rates were fit to lie in the line of battle, but there was a great deal of confusion about this, and much else too, until the administration of Anson. Anson was the Lord Fisher of the 1700s; without his clarity of vision and enterprise and energy the victories at sea against the French at the end of the century would never have happened. Besides introducing some measure of standardization into ship construction (not much perhaps, but it was a start), he laid down that nothing under 64-gun ships should stand in the line of battle. Later in the century and during the Napoleonic wars the British line-of-battle was even more neatly made up from two-gun-decked 74s and flagships of 100 guns or more. Although the sailing quality of the individual ships in these two categories varied widely, for strict uniformity in ship construction was still a hundred years away, this near-homogeneity added immeasurably to the power and control of the line-of-battle.

The shape of the ship-of-the-line changed, but not very markedly, during the century. The most noticeable difference between, say, the *Prince* of 1670 and the *Victory* built just 105 years later was the absence of rake, which had been steadily diminishing over the years since the acute almost hoop-like form of the carracks of the 1400s.

The forward castle had quite disappeared by the mid-1700s, and survived in name alone, as the forecastle deck, raised from the waist of the ship, and growing longer decade by decade. The aftercastle, too, had gone, even to its name. Its vestigial remnants were the quarter deck, raised above the main deck just abaft of midships, and above it again the poop, under the break of which the ship was still steered – no longer by the whipstaff but by a wheel, except in smaller ships, from the early years of the century. A glance at the bows helped to confirm the distinction between a large fighting ship, whether Spanish, French or British, of the late 1700s from the late 1600s. The head became progressively deeper and shorter and, starting with the smaller vessels, then began to disappear altogether so that the bow reverted to a shape more closely resembling the old rounded form. This had the twin advantages of keeping the ship much drier in a head sea and allowing for an increase in the number of guns that could be brought to bear on either bow. The reshaping of the stern became evident, too, during the 1700s. Although the stern-walk had made its first appearance in English ships in the late 1600s, some years passed before it began to project beyond the stern. The single stern-walk of the two-deckers was doubled up in three-deckers normally, but there was no hard-and-fast rule about this.

By the end of the 1700s the fighting ship was almost fully matured in its sails and rigging. Every stay had its own staysail, and there was a jib set on the jib-boom, although the spritsail and spritsail topsail were sometimes retained as well, for no apparent good purpose except to please the traditionalists and provide the men with yet more exercise. These two redundant sails slowly disappeared after 1750, although they were still to be seen more than half a century later. With the exception of the royals, every sail on fore and main masts had its own pair of studding sails. There were important changes on the mizzen mast, too. The lower sail, or course, was greatly reduced in size until the whole sail lay abaft the mast, and the lateen yard developed, through a gaff, to a driver which projected over the stern and was set by a long boom.

French ship design retained its ascendancy throughout the century, from the vast and magnificent three-decker 120s like the *Commerce de Versailles* to small sloops. They rarely built a bad sailer, and never

e Battle of the Nile, 1798, by
cock. This was painted to be
graved as an illustration to
arke and McArthur's standard
ife of Nelson', produced in two
lumes in 1816. The French fleet
at anchor; it is dusk; the English
et is sailing towards the head of
e French line, which Foley in
e *Goliath* is rounding (left of apex
two lines); the English then
ubled on the head of the French
ne, and worked down in a pincer
ovement. *L'Orient*, which blew
, is seventh from the right of the
ench line

anything as bad as the British 80s which were poorly balanced and
poor sailers and generally despised by friend and foe. By contrast the
French contemporary 80 (actually a 92) like the *Franklin* of 1797,
was built to two decks, carrying thirty-two 36-pounders on the lower
deck, thirty-four 24-pounders on the main deck, fourteen 12-pounders
on the quarterdeck, six 12-pounders on the forecastle and six 36-
pounder carronades (*cf. below*) on the poop. The length of her gun-
deck was 194 feet, her keel 160 feet, while her beam was just short of
52 feet. Her displacement was 2,257 tons. It was heartbreaking for the
French to witness the rapid transfer to the enemy of fine ships like the
*Franklin*. She was captured, a few months after commissioning, at the
Nile, where she flew the flag of Rear-Admiral Armand Blanquet and
was nearly consumed by the fires following the blowing up of the
*Orient*. Renamed *Canopus*, she later took part in the pursuit of Villeneuve in 1805, and like other French captures, had difficulty in
holding herself back to the snail's pace of Nelson's British-built vessels.

After a period of decay and neglect, French fighting strength at sea
enjoyed a revival in the second half of the century, until it achieved
unprecedented power and status at the reopening of hostilities in 1778.
The superb quality of the *matériel* and personnel was largely due to the
endeavours of the Duc de Choiseul, who did as much for the French
navy in the 1760s as Colbert had accomplished in the time of Louis
XIV. The naval bases and dockyards at Rochefort, Toulon and Brest
were cleaned up and strengthened and a new base was created at the
port of Marseilles. Choiseul, like Anson and later Fisher in the British
navy, brought about a revolution in the training and education of
officers and men. In 1767 a special corps of seamen gunners was formed.

135

Besides gunnery, special attention was paid to improving navigation and signalling. A new shipbuilding programme was put in hand. Science played its full part, and the ships that resulted were far ahead in almost every aspect to those of France's old foe across the Channel. 'The most ingenious mathematicians were consulted,' wrote Charnock, 'and experiments repeatedly made in ascertainment or decision of all points which were considered in the smallest degree doubtful.'[3] La Roncière and Clerc-Rampal emphasize the great advances made in French shipbuilding between the reigns of Louis XIV and XV: 'the difference which separates the work of a simple labourer from the work in collaboration of mathematicians, scholars and skilled engineers;'[13] while Destrem in the catalogue of the Musée de la Marine cites the work not only of such brilliant architects as Ollivier, Coulomb and Groignard, but traces back the scientific tradition in French shipbuilding to the first half of the century and the designs of Daniel Bernoulli.

Choiseul had been deposed before 1778, but when the fighting began in that year France's fleet of some 105 ships-of-the-line owed almost all their qualities to him. The six first-rates of 104 or 110 guns – the *Bretagne*, *Invincible*, *Majestueux*, *Royal Louis*, *Terrible* and *Ville de Paris* – were magnificently designed and built and were formidable vessels indeed. Of them, the *Bretagne*, 'which was by no means the most superior among them, far exceeded not only all the English first-rates which were contemporary with it, but even surpassed those which, in augmentation of the former establishment, were ordered to be constructed some years later.'[3] On the French 74s, Charnock is especially interesting as he was writing before the destruction of French naval power in 1805. This class in the fleet of 1778 'not only considerably outnumbered every other, but exceeded all of them combined. . . . From the agility, capacity, velocity, stability, and ease, with which the French ships, mounting 74 guns, were able to bring the whole of their force into action, or, in plainer terms, to open their lower deck ports, even in stormy weather, they were, independent of their numbers, justly considered as the strength of the French navy.'[3]

Judged on her overwhelming advantage in *matériel*, France should soon have dominated the war at sea. There are many reasons why she did not do so. On the whole, French ordnance and gunnery were inferior to the British, and so was French seamanship. Excepting only Suffren, France possessed no admirals of the genius of Rodney and Collingwood, St Vincent and Nelson. Below that rank the disparity was even more evident. The French officer class, for all the efforts of the Duc de Choiseul, remained more deeply concerned with the distinctions of rank based on the aristocratic hierarchy on land than the professional qualities of its officers at sea. Hannay, in his life of Rodney, underlines the distinction between the British and French officers. The French were 'so conscious that they were nobles as to somewhat forget the fact that they were officers. They thought little of their rank compared with their common nobility. They all messed together, they thee'd and thou'd one another in the friendly second person singular. This easy good-fellowship must have been socially more pleasant than the stern subordination of an English ship, on which the captain lived apart in solitary grandeur, and the midshipman looked up with awe to the lieutenants. But of the two, ours was the better system of discipline.'[14] This discipline and the battle fibre it germinated filtered down the ranks and was as strongly evident on the lower decks of British ships as in the wardrooms.

In essence, then, for the following thirty years when maritime power once again foiled Continental expansionist ambitions, the handicaps of inferior British *matériel* were more than offset by superior personnel. The French were wholly professional in the manner of their naval architecture; in the tradition of Hawkins and Anson, the British better understood how to train and work the men who manned and fought their inferior fighting ships. The finest fighting unit in the world was a captured French ship manned by British seamen.

This combination was equally formidable when the ship was Spanish. The Spanish Navy, too, had undergone something of a revival and revolution, and many formidable warships were built at Cartagena and Ferrol during the second half of the century. Spain entered the conflict with nearly a hundred first, second and third rates. Of these the *Santisima Trinidad*, the greatest fighting ship in the world, was the subject of awe and wonder throughout her life. This monster four-decker (she was said to have carried up to 140 guns on occasion) provided a target that the most unpractised gunner could hardly fail to hit, and had a chequered career. At St Vincent (14 February 1797) she formed the central mass of the Spanish fleet with the *San Josef* 112, *Mexicano* 112, *Salvador del Mundo* 112, *San Nicholas* 80 and *San Ysidro* 74, and was one of the targets of Nelson's shrewd and courageous single-handed attack with the two-decker *Captain*. He was soon joined by Troubridge and Collingwood and others, and in the succeeding fierce *mêlée* all the Spanish first-rates were taken except the giant four-decker. At one time the *Excellent* (Collingwood), *Blenheim*, *Orion* and *Irresistible* were all pouring their fire into the *Santisima Trinidad*. 'The four-decker is said not only to have struck,' wrote Clowes, 'but to have actually hoisted British colours; yet, be this as it may, she became no prize, for, relieved by two of her van ships, which wore to her support, by the two vessels which all day had been coming up from the west-south-west, and by the approaching junction of the Spanish lee division, she at length got clear of her foes.'[15]

The military and moral value of the ship as a prize would have been very high. She was towed away from the scene of action by a frigate, was sighted and pursued six days later, and on 28 February was visited again by the little *Terpsichore* 32 at dusk. The next morning Captain Richard Bowen had the temerity to attack her unaided. 'He was naturally unable to effect much against his huge antagonist, but he nevertheless kept company with her until, off Cape Spartel, she fell in with the Spanish fleet.'[15] The monster *Santisima Trinidad* survived a further eight years, suitably meeting her end at Trafalgar. Here, as the flagship of Rear-Admiral B. H. de Cisneros, she was one of Nelson's first targets. Towering above her consorts, she fought gallantly and for long before at last, late in the afternoon, she was boarded from the *Prince* and then taken in tow. But the British were to gain nothing from her. In the rough weather on 24 October she became a danger to her crew and was scuttled at Collingwood's orders.

Much had happened between the outbreak of war in 1778 and the moment when the greatest enemy ship-of-the-line went down in 1805. The British Navy started the war in a state of appalling neglect, thanks to the ministry of Lord North who had declared a few years earlier, 'I do not recollect to have seen a more pacific appearance of affairs than there is at this moment. This is the time, if ever there was a time, for a reasonable and judicious economy.' Ships, stores, dockyards were all neglected, and morale was at a low level. 'When Kempenfelt went down with twice four hundred men,' Cowper would have us believe that

> A land-breeze shook the shrouds
> And she was overset. . . .
> She sprange no fatal leak,
>     She ran upon no rock. . . .

when in fact the bottom fell out of the *Royal George* because no one had bothered to clean it and replace her rotten timbers. By prodigies of reorganization and effort from a new generation of administrators, like Sir Charles Middleton (later Lord Barham); by the skilful seaman-ship and fighting prowess of a new breed of commanders, like Colling-wood and Nelson; by the swift construction of new men-of-war of a vastly improved kind, Britain withstood the onslaught at sea during the wars from 1778 to 1805, and while the American colonies were lost, Bourbon and Napoleonic threats were frustrated by 'those far distant, storm-beaten ships, upon which the Grand Army never looked [which] stood between it and the dominion of the world'.[16]

### SAIL AND RIGGING IN THE 1700S

Attempts had been made in the past to standardize the spars and sails in a large fleet of ships so that these could be interchangeable if damaged in storm or battle. As the line-of-battle ship increased in size, further efforts were made in all navies to extend this standardization to individual ships. The consumption of spars by a large fleet at sea during a long cruise was very heavy, and there never seemed to be enough. To help the situation further, the long mizzen lateen yard was retained in larger ships as a reserve, although it was no longer needed and had disappeared from smaller ships. In the British Navy the attempts to bring about rigging uniformity were frustrated by independently-minded captains. Very often official sail plans were altered and rigging warrants ignored so that they could make their own choice: a ship's rigging reflected the personality of the man commanding it, and non-conformity was practised, too, as a deliberate affront by the active sailor to the sedentary administrator, who, it was believed, did not know what it was really like to beat against a half-gale.

By the end of the century the full-rigged fighting ship had reached

quare sails and driver of a 20-gun ip, 1794, by Steel

the ultimate stage of development in its sails and rigging. Nothing remained to be done. Clowes summarized the situation: 'Every stay had its appropriate staysail, while a large jib was set on the jib boom. Earlier in the century the mizzen mast had been lengthened by the addition of a topgallant mast, in order to set a topgallant sail, and 1788 saw the general introduction, even in small ships, of royals set flying, in light winds, above the topgallant sails on all three masts. . . . The flying jib boom, as an additional spar projecting beyond the jib boom, and spreading the flying jib, was an innovation of 1794, and it would seem that the final extinction of the spritsail topsail was not long delayed. Both mainmast and foremast were provided with a pair of studding sails to each sail, except the royals. . . .'[5]

## GUNNERY IMPROVEMENTS

At the beginning of the century there was small evidence of any substantial improvement in the accuracy and destructive power of a fighting ship's artillery since the Armada had been fought 120 years earlier. The ship-of-the-line still carried everything from heavy ship-destroying cannon to man-destroying sakers, and the seaman with the musket high in the fighting tops was to continue to play an important rôle (including the killing of Lord Nelson) for another hundred years and more. Cannon became heavier, their recoil more powerful and violent, requiring ever bigger and heavier ships. When firing heavy shot, the cannon had a more or less accurate range of some 400 yards; but the hole it made in the enemy's timbers could, given resolution and speed, be plugged. Even a 42-pounder cannon firing at point-blank range might not pierce the two-feet-thick timber at the water line of some of the heaviest ships. It took a lot of firing to sink a big ship as a direct result of cannon fire. The most likely way of destroying the enemy was by the chance ignition of his powder, which was all over the gun decks and mainly unprotected. In spite of this very high explosion and fire risk, ships were still much more often captured than sunk.

The French, Spanish and British all attempted to apply science to improve guns and increase their range and destructive power. The British were lucky enough to capture in the *Mars* the documents relating to the latest French experiments, which helped to keep the two countries level in their spasmodic progress towards improvement in ordnance. Both navies benefited from the re-introduction of the iron cannon in place of the brass piece. As the size of the brass cannon increased, its weight had become impossible to sustain. Better casting methods brought about an iron gun that was both lighter and more

The captured *Santa Brigida*, wi the *Naiad*, the *Alcmene* and t *Ethalion*, 1800, by Whitcombe, a (bottom) the Battle of La Hog after Admiral Rook's attack, 169 by Van Diest

Overleaf: 'The *Royal George* Deptford', by Clevely the Eld Deptford, Chatham, Plymout Portsmouth and Woolwich we Britain's 5 arsenals at that time

durable, although brass continued to be used for smaller guns.

The carronade was the most notable new weapon of the late 1700s. Its invention is attributed to General Robert Melville, and it was named after the River Carron near Falkirk in Scotland. Ironworks had been set up here because of the area's coal and iron deposits, and one of the largest was the Carron Company. The 'smasher' as the carronade came to be called was really an improved version of the old perrier – a stumpy-looking gun with a wide bore and a thin barrel designed to fire a hollow shot with great penetrating power over a short range. Its lightness was its great merit. The fighting sailor's demand for more and more big and heavy cannon in a vessel that was still swift and handy had set the naval architect an impossible task. The carronade helped greatly to solve the problem of compromise. The barrel itself was light, and this meant a light truck carriage, to which it was secured by lugs to a piece of timber which slid into the carriage. There were, therefore, no trunnions. The hollow shot called for a lighter charge, and thus less recoil. It was elevated by a screw fixed to the slide. The carronade was not only a most effective ship-destroyer; it was so light that it could be mounted high up in the ship, even on the poop or quarterdeck. Its one great drawback was its short range – a mere 100 yards. So a ship carrying only 'smashers' (and some did) could be smashed at long range by a well-handled ship carrying only cannon.

There were other drawbacks. 'Several captains complained of the carronade,' wrote William James in his *Naval History* of 1888. 'Some, of its upsetting after being heated by successive discharges; others, that, owing to its shortness, its fire scarcely passed clear of the ship's side. . . . The captains of some of the 32-gun frigates, in particular, represented that one pair of the quarterdeck carronades was so much in the way of the rigging as to endanger the lanyards of the shrouds, and begged to have their established number reduced from six to four.'

But there was no denying their smashing power, as well as their power to intimidate the enemy. It was some time before the French caught on to them, and meanwhile they were often greatly embarrassed and discomfited. In 1781 the British fitted out the old *Rainbow* 44 with an all-carronade armament, thus increasing her weight of broadside from 318 to 1,238 pounds. In April of the following year she sailed in search of prey. As James recounts, 'All the well-known skill and enterprise of her captain (Henry Trollope) failed, however, to bring him within gunshot of a foe worth contending with until the 4th of the succeeding September, when, being off Isle de Bas, he came suddenly upon a large French frigate. Owing to the latter's peculiar bearing, one of the *Rainbow*'s forecastle 32-pounders was first discharged

Detail of the Battle of 1 June 1794, by de Loutherbourg

145

at her. Several of the shot fell on board, and discovering their size, the French captain, rationally concluding that, if such large shot came from the forecastle of the enemy's ship, much larger ones would follow from her lower batteries, fired his broadside "pour l'honneur du pavillion", and surrendered. . . .'

The British carronade really came into its own and justified itself at the Battle of the Saints Passage in 1782. On this occasion the French were also surprised and savagely damaged by another British innovation. This was oblique fire, introduced into the service by a clever officer named Sir Charles Douglas. Douglas was the most inventive gunnery expert of the 1700s. He diminished the violence of recoil by combining ingenuity with simplicity: he put an inclined plane behind the rear wheels of the gun carriage and placed springs in the breeching. He also made things much safer for the gunners (though their job continued to be extremely hazardous for many years yet) by suggesting that the charge could be safely ignited by a lanyard-pulled flintlock instead of a lighted match. The introduction of oblique fire was another of those seemingly obvious improvements in gunnery which make us, with the advantage of hindsight, wonder at the slow-wittedness of our ancestors. Until almost the end of the 1700s a ship's broadside could be fired to hit the enemy only when it bore close to 90 and 270 degrees – or at right-angles to the vessel's course. The act of traversing, thought up by Sir Charles Douglas, allowed each gun

The Leeward Islands convoy being delivered by the *Portland* to the *Thames*, 1776, by Luny. From early times, and particularly during the mid-seventeenth-century wars with the Dutch, it was customary to gather merchant ships into fleets to be convoyed through enemy-controlled waters

to be swung and fired 45 degrees before or abaft the beam. It astonished the French and revolutionized tactics by signalling the end of the formal set-piece battle with the opposing fleet sailing in strict line-ahead on parallel courses blasting off at once another as fast as the guns could be re-loaded. The oblique-firing gun helped to instil a new sense of freedom of operation in the conduct of sea battles.

SHIP DECORATION AND ORNAMENT

The carver, painter and gilder had a mixed century, their opportunities increasing with the expectations of peace and falling with the actuality of war. In Britain the demands of the War of the Spanish Succession (1702–13) called for the reduction of the most extreme embellishment of the fighting ship, and after an enquiry into 'how the great charge of carvers' and joiners' and other ornamental works may be lessened on board her Majesty's ships for the future', it was decided 'that the carved works be reduced to only a lion and trail board for the head, with mouldings instead of brackets placed against the timbers: that the stern have only a tafferel and two quarter pieces, and in lieu of brackets between the lights of the stern, galleries and bulkheads, to have mouldings fixed against the timbers: that the joiners' works on the sides of the great cabin, coach, wardroom, and round-house of each ship be fixed only with slit deals without any sort of moulding or cornice, and the painting be only plain colour. . . .' Similar restric-

he Dutch bringing in the cap-
red *Royal Charles*, 1667, by van
est. This was after De Ruyter's
id on the Medway; the English
sign at the stern is debased; in
e left corner is a Latin inscription
d the name of the victorious
utch admiral 'D. D. Cornelio de
itt'

tions were made by the other belligerents, and had as brief an influence as the British order. From a variety of motives – perhaps vanity or a concern for his ship's *esprit de corps* or a deep-grained tradition that rich ornamentation raised the will to fight of his own company and depressed that of the enemy – carving, gilding and painting were soon once again much in fashion. In Britain this was acknowledged officially by a relaxation in 1727 of the order of 1703. Long before this the gilders and varnishers, the painters and carvers, had been in full employment, working on their angels and dragons, their oxen and their unicorns, their greyhounds and lions. St George fought the Dragon time and again, cupids and draped female figures supported patiently the royal coat of arms, all gazed down upon by bevies of massed angels.

Eastern influence spread by way of the Dutch and British East Indiamen, whose decoration had for long been designed to impress the locals, and had in some cases adopted the eastern style for this purpose.

A model of a 60-gun ship of 17 showing the influence of Chinc serie in its decoration. The men lavatories can also be seen; t officers' are inside the bows. T chaplain was classed with the me for this purpose, and there is a sa poem, 'The Chaplain's Lamen about how he wanted a key to t indoor lavatories

The Dutch, who had never aspired to the extravagance of the French and British even in the 1600s at the height of their naval power, were especially susceptible to the Oriental influence, retaining as a figurehead their favourite red lion with the golden mane. The British for a short time early in the century made a fine display of Chinoiserie. Chinese figures appeared on the counters, on the undersides of the gunport lids and on the beakhead bulkhead. Even the figurehead lion became orientalized.

In the later 1700s the Dutch and the British turned over from the lion to individual figureheads, even down to sixth rates and sloops. This extended further the opportunities of the artists. For example, an extract from the original specification of the *Victory*'s figurehead (1765) tells us that 'the principal figure is a large drapery figure representing Britannia, properly crowned, sitting on a rich triumphal arch, and in one hand holding a spear enriched and the Union Flag hanging down from it, and with the other hand supporting the bust of His Majesty, with one foot trampling down Envy, Discord and Faction, represented by a fiend or hag: at the same side above and behind Britannia is a large flying figure representing Peace crowning the figure Britannia with laurels and holding a branch of palms denoting peace and the happy consequences resulting from victory. At the back of the arch is the British lion, trampling on very rich trophies of war, cut clear and open, and the arch on this side supported by two large figures, representing Europe and America properly dressed agreeable to the countries; and at the lower part of this side the head piece is cut a young Genius, holding in one hand a bunch of flowers, belonging to a rich cornucopia denoting abundance or plenty. . . .'

The quarter galleries offered greater decorative opportunities during the first half of the century. Towards the end of the 1700s they had everywhere become more standardized, with small pilasters framing windows set three in a tier.

The French showed the best sense of style and taste in their decoration. There was rarely any flamboyance. Classical figures were popular and busts came in at the end of the century. Some of the prettiest figureheads of all originated in France. Laughton reminds us of the *St Louis* (1721) with its simple angel and with the main rail curved over as a canopy. The figure of Fame was especially popular with French carvers. Of French painting in the second half of the century La Roncière and Clerc-Rampal write that 'it is blue between the batteries and the forecastle and quarterdeck, with gold border, the port lids are red, the lines of the batteries maroon, the whole aspect is sober and elegant.'[13]

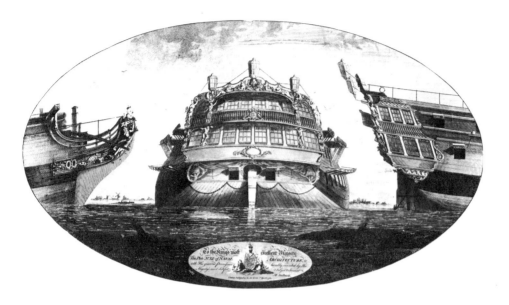

## THE AMERICAN WAR OF INDEPENDENCE

The genesis of the naval power of America in the present century can be found in the maritime enthusiasm and skill of the early settlers as merchants, shipbuilders and mariners. Marcus has admirably set the scene:

Bow, stern and quarter of a battl ship, from Stalkartt's 'Naval Arch tecture' of 1781

> The tough Yankee stock bred some of the very finest seamen and shrewdest merchants of their day. The trading and fishing fleets of these northern colonies were manned by successive generations of hardy, adventurous youngsters attracted to the sea by the lure of high wages. The keener spirits among them made voyage after voyage; acquired skill and experience; studied, qualified, and became masters and mates in their turn. Navigation schools arose in almost every port of consequence on the New England coast. Resource and initiative were the leading character-istics of the able merchant interest who directed the manifold business activities of the northern colonies.[17]

The boldness and the expertise of the American fighting sailor in the War of Independence, and later in 1812, were derived from the generations of rugged experience of these northern seamen among the cod fishing banks off Newfoundland, farther north in search of whales to bring back to Nantucket Island, and from the long trans-Atlantic voyages from New England to the ports of the Old World. At the start of the Revolution in 1775 the colonists could draw on a vast merchant marine of several thousand vessels, mainly of a very modest tonnage. Not one had been built with combat in mind. Orders were given to fit out a number of these with guns to serve as privateers and to harass British communications. In December 1775 the Continental Congress decided to build thirteen men-of-war. Although several fighting ships had been constructed in Massachusetts in the past, including a ship-of-the-line in 1690 and a frigate, the *America*, in the 1740s, for the Royal Navy, these frigates of 24 to 32 guns – the *Boston, Delaware, Montgomery, Trumbull, Congress, Providence, Effingham, Virginia, Warren, Randolph, Raleigh, Hancock* and *Washington* – formed the foundations of a navy which 170 years later was to be the most powerful in the world. By 1778 all but four of these ships had been lost, but the new Continental Navy had added greatly to its strength through purchases, captures and new construction.

There was never any question of a fleet action between the Revolutionary Navy and the British. The British battle fleet, later to become the business of the Colonists' French allies, was never in hazard. But the depredations of the frigates and the smaller privateers among British merchantmen on both sides of the Atlantic became very serious. 'They were of the very greatest service in preying on the enemy's commerce.' Morison has written, 'intercepting his communications with America, carrying terror and destruction into the very chops of the Channel, and supplying the patriot army with munitions, stores and clothing at Johnny Bull's expense.'[18] When British ships bombarded and raided the coastal towns of New England, the most famed privateer of all time proved the truth of his own claim that 'not all their boasted navy can protect their own coasts' by sailing on 10 April 1778 from Brest in the *Ranger* up the Irish Sea, attacking shipping on the way, and raiding and burning the shipping at Whitehaven in Cumberland. In little more than an hour of spirited action John Paul Jones also overcame and captured the British sloop *Drake*. He returned the next year with an old East Indiaman, the *Bonhomme Richard*, equipped with six 18-pounders, twenty-eight 12-pounders and eight 9-pounders. With four other ships, ranging from a frigate to a cutter (a motley, insubordinate lot) he set off the following summer for a cruise that was to have devastating results, and has since become identified with the very roots of American historical lore. No nation in the world is more sensitive than Britain to raids, even at the modest level, on her coastline – as the Germans were to discover with the trivial bombardments of East Coast towns in 1914 and 1915. No damage was done to British property, and British shipping losses were negligible, but the appearances of the squadron off the east coast of Scotland and England spread alarm through the land, while the inhabitants of Scarborough and Bridlington were able to witness at first hand from the cliffs of Flamborough Head Jones's fighting skill and tenacity in an action with the powerful British frigate *Serapis*. 'The heavy shot of the *Serapis* quickly began to tell,' wrote Wilson in Clowes's History. 'The *Bonhomme Richard* received several hits between wind and water; and she had her fourteen 12-pounders disabled and dismounted, and seven of her deck guns put out of action, so that she was left with a battery of only three 9-pounders, one of which had to be shifted over from the starboard side. In these circumstances Jones determined, as his only hope of safety, to close with the enemy; and Captain Pearson of the *Serapis* was foolish enough to allow his half-beaten opponent to lay himself alongside. The *Serapis* evaded the *Bonhomme Richard*'s first attempt to grapple. At the second the *Bonhomme Richard*'s mizzen-shrouds caught the *Serapis*'s jib-boom, which was promptly lashed fast by the American captain himself. . . . Meantime the *Bonhomme Richard*'s men, driven from the 18- and 12-pounders below, had swarmed to the deck and the tops, whence they swept the *Serapis* with a steady musketry fire, and from time to time pitched hand-grenades on board her. Below, the port lids of the *Serapis*'s 18-pounder battery had been closed when the two ships swung alongside, for fear of boarders. The guns were fired through them, and speedily reduced to splinters the hull of the American.'[15] These thunderous broadsides at a range of a few feet were eventually to sink the American ship, but they killed no one as the men were all up on deck, and the *Serapis* herself caught fire and was blazing fiercely. 'Yet, in spite of this, victory was decidedly inclining to her when a terrible mischance befell her. An American seaman climbed out on the *Bonhomme Richard*'s main-yard, which overhung the *Serapis*'s deck, and dropped a hand grenade down the main hatchway into the *Serapis*'s gun-room, where a number of 12-pounder cartridges had been placed. The grenade fired the cartridges, and the explosion ran aft between the rows of guns, scorching or killing officers and men, and disabling five of the guns. Thirty-eight were killed or wounded at this one blow.'[11] The tide of battle was finally turned by the American marksmen up in the rigging, who prevented the British from boarding, and finally caused the British captain to haul down the flag in his ship – which by this time was almost keeping afloat the shattered American privateer.'[11]

Attacks by American privateers – and there were many almost as evasive as John Paul Jones – on both sides of the Atlantic sent marine insurance rates rocketing, diverted naval effort to the provision of convoys, and gravely injured British morale at sea. Nor was the British Navy able to interfere seriously in the vital military and commercial trade between France and the American colonists before the French intervened in the war.

Frigate action, and (bottom) bri fighting

# 10. THE FRIGATE AND SMALLER FIGHTING SHIPS

From almost its earliest days the fighting ship has been supported by its minions, its messengers, its protectors, its scouts. The Mediterranean galley had its *fregata*, a close replica of itself in miniature, to act as a swift tender. In northern waters the term frigate was first used in the 1500s to describe a small, sail-driven vessel, very like the galleons it served but narrower in proportion to its length. As naval fighting became more sophisticated, as it became increasingly possible for fleets to travel great distances and to remain at sea for long periods, the need arose for small craft for scouting and communications. Hawkins had his scouts – his 'eyes' – to watch what was going on in Spain in 1587 and 1588. He had eighteen ocean-going pinnaces, and they did not miss a thing. When the Armada sailed, its daily progress, its distance from British shores, were both known. Thus it was quite possible for Drake, while awaiting its appearance, to play bowls calmly on Plymouth Hoe – although he did no such thing.

The classic frigate, the three-masted swift, single-gun-decked fighting ship – the type which Nelson would have had engraved on his heart for want of them, had he died in 1798 – did not make its appearance until the mid-1700s. The frigate did not find its real shape and form before this time although many different types were built, and some of them – especially the Dutch ones – excellently fulfilled their rôle. In the 1600s the French and Spanish navies used a number of small, swift craft armed with a single tier of perhaps six or twelve guns. There is a drawing by Willem van de Velde the Younger of a Dutch frigate of 1665 with a complete gun deck. She has a high quarter-

Two frigates before the wind, b[...] Brooking

deck and poop, but no forecastle at all. Britain's first contribution is popularly supposed to be the 30-gun *Constant Warwick* of 1646. She was called a frigate at the time, and often since, but, as Clowes pointed out, 'she was not a frigate in the modern sense, and several vessels very similar to her were added to the Navy while she was still a privateer, cruising for the profit of the Earl of Warwick, Peter Pett, and others. But she and other craft of 1646 marked the beginning of a progressive tendency in naval architecture. It lay in the direction of making ships of medium size less high out of the water, of finer lines, and of longer proportionate keel than before, and thus obtaining faster vessels and steadier gun platforms. The developments in this direction continued under the Commonwealth; but they did not go very far. . . .'[5]

In the early 1700s most of the northern nations continued their search for the ideal frigate-type of vessel which could keep to the seas for long periods. A wide range of two-deckers carrying a few light guns, and perhaps a tier of oars beneath them, was built. These grew bigger and lost their oars and gained more guns as the century advanced. The British built under the Establishments of 1733, 1741 and 1745 a number of two-deck 44-gun frigates of between 678 and 914 tons. They had nothing to recommend them and were referred to in the fleet as 'the forty thieves'. The short quarterdeck of these vessels was abandoned in 1753, and instead the quarterdeck was carried right forward to the mainmast, which made the ships both more habitable and more efficient. In 1780 the British built several scouting craft, like the *Diana*, *Juno*, *Southampton* and *Vestal*, carrying first twenty-eight

n English brigantine of 1750, by
levely and (right) a man of war
rigantine, by Brooking. Pictures
naval brigantines under sail are
re – the jack and pennant indicate
is one

9-pounders and then thirty-two 12-pounders.

The needs of war suddenly brought about the right blend of qualities for which the architects had been striving for so long. The Seven Years' War began in 1756. In the following year the British built, to the designs of Sir Thomas Slade, two single-gun-decked three-masted frigates, the *Pallas* and *Brilliant*. These frigates, and the French *Aurore* built at the same time, set the pattern for the genuine 36-gun frigates, which were to be built by the score for the French, Spanish, Dutch, British and American navies over the following fifty years, and were to serve so successfully in their multitudinous duties all over the world, convoying, scouting, patrolling, attacking and protecting commerce. The French and British built the most, and the French frigates were notably superior. Once again size and science counted. Look at these comparative figures for the *Aurore* and *Brilliant*:

|  | Tons | Keel | Beam | Guns |
|---|---|---|---|---|
| *Brilliant* | 718 | 106′2½″ | 35′8″ | 36 |
| *Aurore* | 946 | 118′9″ | 38′8½″ | 36 |

A year later the British captured the *Aurore*, renamed her *Aurora*, admired her, took her measurements and learned many lessons from her.

Many different classes of frigate – from 40 to 20 guns – were built by the British during the second half of the century. Typical of her type was the *Minerva*, launched in 1780, the first of a new 38-gun class. When she joined the fleet she carried twenty-eight 18-pounders on her main deck, and on her forecastle and quarterdeck ten 9-pounders and eight 18-pounder carronades, together with 14 swivel guns. At this time, over a period of some eight years, thirty 28-gun frigates were built. Representative of this class was the *Ariel*, of which there is a beautiful model in the Science Museum in London. Under the command of Captain Thomas Mackenzie she was pursued by the French frigate *Amazone* on 10 September 1779 and after an action lasting ninety minutes, during which she lost one of her masts and suffered twenty-four casualties, struck her colours.

The trim, elegant frigate of the late 1700s, like their counterparts and namesakes of the Second World War, were the workhorses of the French and British fleets and were in frequent action. Neither the French, Spanish, Dutch, Americans nor British ever had enough of them. The British navy possessed thirty-five in 1760. In 1798, when Nelson so deeply felt his lack of them, there were around a hundred in commission.

The Americans built the best frigates in the world – see next chapter.

## THE CORVETTE, OR SLOOP

The nomenclature of the various classes of fighting ship at different dates is almost impossible to sort out – even by authorities as eminent as Lewis, who finds it 'indeed a puzzling subject',[6] while Landström

An English snow-rigged sloop 1720

considers it 'at times a hopeless job trying to straighten out the terminology especially as regards small vessels'.[19] Even the origin of some of the terms – let alone the ships they describe – is obscure. Does the word 'sloop' come from shallop, the rowed pinnace of the 1500s? Very likely it does. By the 1700s the British sloop – called a corvette in France – had grown up into a junior frigate, with perhaps eighteen guns on the upper deck. She would be fully rigged, the sloop with three masts, the brig with two masts, but for a while oars might still be used as a last resort. By the end of the century a French corvette might be as formidable an antagonist as a British frigate, with three masts and guns on a gun deck – 12-pounders at that, instead of 6- or 9-pounders. The functions of the sloop or corvette were like those of the frigate – escorting, patrolling, attacking and protecting commerce.

### THE BRIGANTINE AND SNOW

The meaning of this classification is as subject to overlapping and confusion as the sloop. It began life at the end of the 1600s as a square-sailed two-master mainly for carrying dispatches. It might have carried half a dozen or a dozen light pieces on its main deck. It could also be called a snow when the boom mainsail was hooped to a trysail mast abaft the mainmast. Inevitably, its size increased and its sail plan became more elaborate during the 1700s.

A late eighteenth-century French corvette, by Baugean

snow and (below) a cutter close
~~~uled~~ , by Brooking

### THE CUTTER

The cutter shared the patrol and dispatch duties also performed by the brigantine, but carried a single mast and a yard with a single square sail, over which was set a square topsail. In its developed and enlarged form in the later 1700s, an English cutter of 150 tons carried around twelve guns, a pair of carronades and one or two swivel guns.

### THE SCHOONER

This was pure Dutch-American in its origin – a fast, two-masted vessel, fore-and-aft rigged, with the mainmast somewhat taller than the fore mast, but sometimes carrying square topsails on both masts. When the British seized New Amsterdam from the Dutch in 1664 (and changed its name to New York after King Charles II's brother), most of the Dutch settlers decided to stay on. Among them were many who had inherited the instinctive Dutch ability for ship design and ship-building. The building of fine sloops was a Dutch speciality, and from these was derived the first schooner. The story goes that the first genuine schooner with a triangular headsail was built at Gloucester, Massachusetts, in 1713. As she was leaving the stocks and entering the water, so it is said, someone exclaimed, 'Oh, how she scoons!' Overhearing this, her builder replied : 'Very well, then, a scooner let her be.'

late eighteenth-century Maltese
~~tter~~

## THE BOMB KETCH

By contrast with these fast and handsome small fighting ships, the bomb ketch was a crude and cumbersome but extremely efficient weapon carrier. It was pure French in its origins. Well-defended forts had always been a problem for cannon-armed men-of-war. When Admiral Abraham Du Quesne departed from Toulon on 12 July 1682 with a powerful squadron of galleons and galleys to deal with the pirate town of Algiers, he brought with him a number of *galiotes à bombes*, the invention of one Bernard Renau d'Eliçagaray, a young Basque, of whom it was said he was '*particulièrement savant dans toutes les parties de la construction et de la navigation, doux, simple, modeste et vertueux, fort brave et fort honnête homme*'.

A bomb ketch by de Passebon. This was really a square rigged three master without the foremast – in its place was a short-muzzled cannon that hurled shells into enemy fortifications

The Battle of the Saints, 1782, was Rodney's great victory in the West Indies over the French fleet. The French flagship, the *Ville de Paris*, surrendered after very heavy casualties and the rest of the French fleet escaped by flight. Rodney was blamed for not pursuing closely enough, but he had won a notable victory. When they took possession the English were shocked to find the blood on the deck of the French flagship came over the tops of their shoes

Mortars firing primitive but large bombs had been used effectively in land warfare, especially for siege work, for many years. Their application to sea warfare was to have devastating consequences, in the narrow rôle to which they were necessarily restricted, 'The vessel built for this purpose,' wrote Charnock, 'was in burthen about 200 tons, constructed with every possible attention to strength, and was of much greater breadth in proportion to its length than was ever thought necessary. Its masts were two in number, the tallest being in the centre, the shorter in the stern, occupying the place of that which in ships is called the mizzen; on the fore part, which was purposely left open, were placed the mortars; and, in order to take off or lessen that dangerous effect which it was imagined the sudden explosion of so great a quantity of powder fired in the necessary direction, and surmounted by a bomb, weighing nearly two hundredweight, would have on the vessel, the whole, or at least the greater part of the hold between the mortars and the keel, was closely packed and laid with old cables, cut into lengths for the purpose. The elasticity and yielding quality of the support obviated the apprehended inconvenience, and a trivial practice raised the art to a species of perfection almost unprecedented, so that a bomb vessel soon became one of the most dreadful engines of naval war.'[3]

Certainly Mediterranean naval warfare had seen nothing like the firing of a bomb ketch's mortar since the old days of Greek fire. With a projectile more than four times heavier – and explosive at that – than

163

the largest cannon ball, the effect on Algiers was appalling. Besides destroying the forts, the town was set on fire and some 700 of its inhabitants were killed in the bombardment, and 'the destruction of Algiers struck the whole piratical fraternity with immediate awe'.[3]

Inspired by the instant destruction wrought by his new weapons, Louis XIV sent Du Quesne off to wreak vengeance on Genoa for helping the Spanish. 'The orders,' continues Charnock, 'were executed with the utmost promptitude and exactness. An incessant shower of bombs, which continued, till the whole number, amounting to fourteen thousand, with which the fleet was furnished, had been expended, laid the greater part of the city, and the whole of the many superb buildings which it contained, completely in ashes.'[3]

The bomb ketch was largely instrumental in giving the French complete control of the Mediterranean, and in keeping it until supremacy was challenged by the British Navy. But the bomb ketch was too slow and unhandy, its accuracy too speculative, for its shattering power to be used in ship-to-ship combat. The high-explosive shell was still a long way away.

The *Ramillies* bearing away, 1782, by Dodd. Most of the French prizes after the Saints, including the *Ramillies*, were lost in a hurricane

# 1. AMERICAN FRIGATES

No nation in the world has created a navy with greater success and greater reluctance than the Americans. Three times in their history – at the end of the 1700s, in the early 1900s and in the 1940s – the Americans have deemed it necessary, against their national inclination, to create a fighting fleet to protect their shores and their trade. On the second and third of these occasions they rapidly modernized and added to the strength of an existing fleet. In 1794 they had no nucleus on which to build, and the decision to do so was reached by a new, still loosely-knit nation whose mores and constitutional spirit were strongly opposed to military expenditure of any kind. It remains a wonder that this new fighting force, built with anxiety and parsimony by a people with a negligible fighting tradition at sea, turned out to be the most advanced and successful in the world, a tiny *corps d'élite* of super-frigates which had no peer during their life-time.

In 1793 the maritime condition of the Union was precarious. Following the conclusion of the War of Independence, American finances and trade were highly vulnerable. Even if America had wanted a navy, she could have scarcely afforded the construction of a single sloop. The surviving units of the old Revolutionary Navy had been sold off. Nothing remained. In 1793 France and Britain were at war again, taking liberties with American merchant shipping. The Barbary pirates were, as always, disrupting trade in the Mediter-ranean and demanding outrageous yearly tribute in default of which American ships were captured and their crews sold into slavery. In order to secure the release of these captives the government at one time had been obliged to build a warship, the *Crescent*, 'one of the finest specimens of elegant naval architecture which was ever borne on the Pascataqua's waters', load with her many valuable presents – including twenty-six barrels of silver dollars – for the Dey of Algiers, and hand over ship and cargo complete to this dictator.

'But out of the national humiliation,' wrote Spears, 'sprang a new navy. The people who had called every legislator that spoke for the honour of the flag a blatant demagogue; the people who had feared naval tyrants, who had feared taxation, and who had argued that a small navy was worse than none – the peace-at-any-price men had been in a great majority.'[20] But even the most ardent peace-man rebelled at the idea of building warships for foreign robber barons in order to obtain free passage for Yankee merchantmen. On 27 March 1794 the United States Congress reluctantly and by a narrow majority passed an act authorizing the acquisition or construction of six men-of-war for the protection of American trade. This is the real date of birth of the United States navy, although there were to be many hold-ups before even this token force could be completed. And what use could

The Battle of Lake Champlai 1776. In this war on the Nor American lakes, Britain defend Canada against the newly inc pendent America

it be, many people quite reasonably asked, when these six fighting ships were ready for their first commission? American trade spread over tens of thousands of miles of ocean, and these were hazardous times. Privateers, besides Barbary pirates, were still rife, the vast fighting fleets of Britain and France and Spain were loose – and in combative mood – on the seas of the western world.

The man who was to be responsible for the overall conception of these six ships believed that if they were properly designed for their task they could be of immense value. He was Joshua Humphreys, a Quaker of Philadelphia, who had been laying down keels for thirty years and was recognized as the ablest shipbuilder in the New World. President Washington approached Humphreys for his views, and these were delivered, in one of the most notable summaries of requirement in naval history, to the Secretary of War, General Knox.

'As our navy for a considerable time will be inferior in numbers,' wrote Humphreys, 'we are to consider what size ships will be most formidable and be an overmatch for those of an enemy; such frigates as in blowing weather would be an overmatch for double-deck ships

*The Serapis and the Bonhomme Richard.* John Paul Jones, a Scottish gardener's son, was the original hero of the U.S. Navy. With French help he fitted out two ships in which he proceeded to conduct operations against his old friends around Whitehaven, Cumberland, which he had known as a boy. He attacked an English convoy in the North Sea and after a fierce engagement captured the English frigate *Serapis.* However, she successfully defended the escape of the convoy

and in light winds to evade coming to action. Frigates will be the first object, and none ought to be built less than 150 feet keel, to carry thirty 24-pounders on the gun-deck. Ships of this construction have everything in their favour; their great height gives them the advantage of sailing, which is an object of the first magnitude. They are superior to any European frigate, and if others be in company, our frigates can always lead ahead and never be obliged to go into action but on their own terms, except in a calm; in blowing weather, our ships are capable of engaging to advantage double-deck ships.'

Design in all things utilitarian is a judgement of degree of compromise. Naval architects for generations had been assessing the merits and demerits of the features which together made up a good fighting ship – speed, manoeuvrability, stability, area of sail and weight of armament to be carried. No class of vessel demanded a higher degree of finesse in the calculation of compromise than the frigate, which had to be swift yet a good sea boat, remain at sea for long periods yet be capable of fighting a pitched battle with a foe that might even be a two- or three-decker.

The frigate class of fighting ship had been exercising the skills of the naval architects of Spain, Holland, France and Britain all through the 1700s. The French tended to build big and fast, the British medium, blunt and robust. Everyone had to face up to the major dilemma of balance, explicit in the definition of the frigate as a single-gun-decked fighting ship. In order to be able to fight in rough seas the frigate's single tier of guns must be high up in the ship – where, if judgement of balance was not very fine, they would raise the centre of gravity so high that there would be a risk of capsizing. In a two- or three-decker the port-sills of the largest guns were only about four feet above the water, where they usefully offset the weight of the guns in the upper gun decks. For this reason the 18-pounder was considered to be the heaviest piece of ordnance which a frigate could reasonably and safely be expected to carry: anything larger would demand a wide beam, and a wide beam – if speed was to be a consideration – would demand an exceptionally long keel. But this was not the solution either. For a frigate capable of carrying 24-pounders together with the vital chase guns at bow and stern would have to be so long that she would strain – if not break – her back in heavy weather.

How could a Quaker shipbuilder, citizen of a nation but a few years old, hope to succeed beyond the considerable achievements of French naval architects like Ollivier and Coulomb? Fletcher Pratt opens the door a fraction and casts a narrow beam of light onto the dark mystery of how Joshua Humphreys acquired stability, speed and unprecedented armament in his first great frigates: 'Many a time had he seen the slim Baltimore clippers ghosting through Delaware Bay; long ships, slim ships, cadaverous in the cheeks, fish-shaped along the run, raked sharp at bow and stern. They had a turn of speed like nothing on earth, yet did not tip or bounce when high gales blew; product of generations of ingenious builders who had added an inch here, taken one off there, till in the ideal test tank of their landlocked bay they had found just the point at which speed, stability and capacity were united in a *mariage à trois*. Then why not build the new frigates to these same lines, gigantic Baltimore clippers?'[21]

And yet it was not quite as simple as this. These were to be fighting ships and had to carry a great weight of armament. Humphreys drew further inspiration from the French masters themselves. The French marine had cleverly cut down a number of their three-deckers – 'razoring-off' their two upper decks. These *razées* made immensely strong and steady, if mighty slow, frigates. Humphreys later wrote: 'As soon as Congress had agreed to build the frigates, it was contemplated to make them the most powerful, and at the same time the most useful ships. After the most extensive researches and mature deliberations their dimensions were fixed and I was directed to prepare the draughts; which was accordingly done and approved. Those plans appear to be similar with those adopted by France in their great

*The Independence*, by Schmidt

experience in naval architecture; they having cut down several of their 74s to make heavy frigates. . . . From the construction of [our] ships it is expected the commanders of them will have it in their power to engage or not any ship as they may think proper; and no ship under 64 now afloat but what must submit to them. These reasons are paramount to all objections, and annihilate opposition.'

These recommendations were accepted by the President and by the War Department – the Navy Department was not formed until 30 April 1798 – and the six frigates, the finest to be built anywhere at any time, were ordered to be laid down. They were:

*Constitution*: builders, Hartt's Shipyard, Boston, Massachusetts
*President*: builders, Forman Cheesman and Christian Bergh, New York
*United States*: builders, Humphreys, Philadelphia
*Chesapeake*: builders, Gosport Navy Yard, Norfolk, Virginia
*Constellation*: builders, Samuel and Joseph Sterrett, Baltimore, Maryland
*Congress*: builders, Lancaster Burling, Poughkeepsie, New York

The first three were rated 44s, the second three rated 36s. All were delayed during construction, for political or financial reasons (construction of the *President*, *Chesapeake* and *Congress* was held up after peaceful agreement had been reached with Algiers), and because, as the Secretary of War emphasized, when stating the unpreparedness of the nation for the construction of fighting ships, 'the wood for the frames is standing in the forest, the iron for the cannon lies in its natural bed, and the flax and hemp are perhaps in their seed'.

It is convenient to single out one of these frigates for closer examination; and none is more suitable than the *Constitution*. In brief, these are the specifications of this famous fighting ship:

  Overall length: 204′
  Beam: 43′6″
  Displacement tonnage: 2,200
  Waterline length: 175′
  Depth of hold: 14′3″
  Highest logged speed: 13½ knots

Her armament varied considerably through her long life, but in her famous battle with the *Guerrière* she carried:

  Thirty long 24-pounder cannon on the gun deck
  Sixteen 32-pounder carronades on the quarter deck
  Six 32-pounder carronades on the forecastle
  Two 12-pounder bow chasers

The *Albemarle*, by Robertson. Sh was a 28-gun frigate captured fro the French, and one of the fir ships Nelson commanded as ca tain. He took her to America ar joined Hood at New York in th 1781–3 war

## MASTS AND SPARS

Her masts were of solid white pine, cut at Unity, Maine, and dragged to Sheepscot River, whence they were towed to Boston. The following dimensions of her masts and spars are extracted from the 1932 pamphlet on the frigate published by the United States Navy's Bureau of Construction and Repair:

| Name | Whole length | | Diameter | | Mast head lengths | | Yard arm lengths | |
|---|---|---|---|---|---|---|---|---|
| | Feet | Inches | Feet | Inches | Feet | Inches | Feet | Inches |
| Foremast | 93 | 8 | 2 | $5\frac{1}{2}$ | 16 | 10 | | |
| Fore topmast | 57 | 2 | 1 | $6\frac{3}{8}$ | 8 | 5 | | |
| Fore-topgallant mast } 1 mast | 30 | 0 | 0 | 11 | | | | |
| Fore-royal mast } | 28 | 0 | 0 | 7 | | | | |
| Mainmast | 104 | $3\frac{1}{2}$ | 2 | 8 | 19 | $6\frac{1}{2}$ | | |
| Main topmast | 64 | 10 | 1 | $8\frac{1}{8}$ | 10 | 0 | | |
| Main-topgallant mast } 1 mast | 33 | 0 | 1 | $\frac{1}{8}$ | | | | |
| Main-royal mast } | 32 | 0 | 0 | $8\frac{3}{4}$ | | | | |
| Mizzenmast | 86 | 4 | 1 | $11\frac{1}{2}$ | 13 | 6 | | |
| Mizzen topmast | 48 | 0 | 1 | $3\frac{5}{8}$ | 7 | 0 | | |
| Mizzen-topgallant mast } 1 mast | 24 | 6 | 0 | $9\frac{5}{8}$ | | | | |
| Mizzen-royal mast } | 24 | 0 | 0 | $6\frac{3}{4}$ | | | | |
| Fore yard | 82 | 0 | 1 | $7\frac{1}{2}$ | | | 4 | 0 |
| Fore-topsail yard | 62 | 0 | 1 | 2 | | | 6 | 0 |
| Fore-topgallant yard | 42 | 0 | 0 | 9 | | | 2 | 3 |
| Fore-royal yard | 27 | 0 | 0 | 6 | | | 1 | 2 |
| Main yard | 94 | 0 | 1 | $10\frac{1}{2}$ | | | 4 | 6 |
| Main-topsail yard | 71 | 0 | 1 | 5 | | | 6 | 6 |
| Main-topgallant yard | 46 | 0 | 0 | 10 | | | 2 | 6 |
| Main-royal yard | 30 | 0 | 0 | $6\frac{1}{2}$ | | | 1 | 6 |
| Mizzen yard | 70 | 0 | 1 | 2 | | | 6 | 0 |
| Mizzen-topsail yard | 46 | 0 | 0 | 10 | | | 4 | 0 |
| Mizzen-topgallant yard | 31 | 0 | 0 | 3 | | | 1 | 9 |
| Mizzen-royal yard | 19 | 0 | 0 | $4\frac{1}{2}$ | | | 1 | 0 |
| Bowsprit | 64 | $8\frac{3}{8}$ | 2 | 8 | | | | |
| Spritsail yard | 60 | 0 | 1 | $1\frac{1}{2}$ | | | 4 | 0 |
| Spanker boom | 56 | 0 | 0 | $11\frac{1}{8}$ | | | | |
| Spanker gaff | 40 | 0 | 0 | $11\frac{1}{8}$ | | | | |
| Jib boom | 47 | 6 | 1 | $2\frac{3}{8}$ | | | 1 | 9 |
| Flying jib boom | 59 | 0 | 0 | 9 | | | 2 | 0 |
| Lower studding sail boom | 50 | 10 | 0 | $10\frac{1}{2}$ | | | | |
| Fore-topmast studding sail boom | 44 | 0 | 0 | 9 | | | | |
| Main-topmast studding sail boom | 48 | 0 | 0 | $9\frac{3}{4}$ | | | | |
| Fore-topgallant studding sail boom | 31 | 0 | 0 | $6\frac{1}{2}$ | | | | |
| Main-topgallant studding sail boom | 35 | 0 | 0 | 7 | | | | |
| Fore-royal studding sail boom | 21 | 0 | 0 | $4\frac{1}{4}$ | | | | |
| Main-royal studding sail boom | 23 | 0 | 0 | $4\frac{3}{4}$ | | | | |
| Fore-topmast studding sail yard | 22 | 0 | 0 | $4\frac{1}{4}$ | | | | |
| Main-topmast studding sail yard | 25 | 0 | 0 | 5 | | | | |
| Fore-topgallant studding sail yard | 17 | 0 | 0 | $3\frac{1}{2}$ | | | | |
| Main-topgallant studding sail yard | 19 | 0 | 0 | $3\frac{3}{4}$ | | | | |
| Fore-royal studding sail yard | 11 | 0 | 0 | $2\frac{1}{2}$ | | | | |
| Main-royal studding sail yard | 13 | 0 | 0 | $2\frac{3}{4}$ | | | | |
| Lower studding sail yard | 18 | 0 | 0 | $3\frac{3}{4}$ | | | | |

The *Constitution*'s sails, with their total area of more than 42,000 sq. ft, were manufactured of flax at the Old Granary Building in Boston in 1797-8. For the ship's restoration in 1927-31

he *Erie*, 1824, by Camilierre, and
ottom) the *Constellation*, by de
mone

the following table of sail areas was adhered to:

| Foresail | Square feet | 2,300 | Main-topgallant staysail | Square feet | 970 |
|---|---|---|---|---|---|
| Fore-topsail | | 2,640 | Main-royal staysail | | 760 |
| Fore-topgallant sail | | 1,050 | Mizzen-topmast staysail | | 630 |
| Fore royal | | 560 | Mizzen-topgallant staysail | | 570 |
| Mainsail | | 3,340 | Spanker | | 1,690 |
| Main topsail | | 3,400 | Gaff topsail | | 930 |
| Main-topgallant sail | | 1,260 | Lower studding sails (per pair) | | 3,600 |
| Main royal | | 680 | Fore-topmast studding sails (per pair) | | 2,400 |
| Mizzen topsail | | 1,620 | Fore-topgallant studding sails (per pair) | | 1,100 |
| Mizzen-topgallant sail | | 650 | Fore-royal studding sails (per pair) | | 530 |
| Mizzen royal | | 330 | Main-topmast studding sails (per pair) | | 3,000 |
| Flying jib | | 1,180 | Main-topgallant studding sails (per pair) | | 1,260 |
| Fore-topgallant staysail | | 640 | Main-royal studding sails (per pair) | | 650 |
| Jib | | 1,720 | | | |
| Fore-topmast staysail | | 660 | | | |
| Main-topmast staysail | | 2,600 | Total | | 42,720 |

42,720 square feet = 4,746 square yards.

The *Constitution* matched the expectations of her name. Not only was she built in one of the most famous shipyards in the land. The materials for her construction came from as far north as Maine, as far south as Georgia. Her timber included live oak, white oak, red cedar, pitch pine and locust. Live oak had never been used in Europe for warship construction, and she was the object of a good deal of derision from British sailors (and some Americans, too) who saw her being built: she was too crank by half, and moreover was nothing but an old 'pine box'. Many years later, after the frigate called at Portsmouth, England, she created more mirth and newspaper comment. 'The opinions they expressed were, of course, a repetition of those expressed by British naval officers, who had visited her at various times. . . . They spoke of her as " a bunch of pine boards", and as "a fir-built ship with a bit of striped bunting at her mast-head", and "their opinions gave rise to various excellent jokes that were uttered in and out of the British Parliament at the commencement of the war"'.[20] Her copper bolts and spikes were supplied by Paul Revere himself after he had written to the Secretary of War that he could furnish them 'as cheap as anyone'. The *Constitution*'s total cost was $302,718.

The frigate was laid down at Boston and was built under the supervision of Colonel Charles Claghorn and with Captain Samuel Nicholson as inspector. Her launching on 21 October 1797 was not a happy occasion. Like the monster *Great Eastern* sixty years later she got stuck on her ways which were not steep enough, and she had to be got into the water with the assistance of jack screws, ten feet at a time. She put to sea for the first time nine months later, on 22 July 1798, her first commander being her inspector. Nor was her early career very distinguished. Privateers of the Union's old allies, the French, were at

The *Constitution*, engraved Bowen. American frigates of th type were heavily armed and ga a good account of themselves in t 1812–15 war. The *Constitution* w popularly known as 'Old Iro sides' and her remains are pr served at Annapolis. (Below) th *Guerrière* being captured by t *Constitution*, engraved by Birc One account of this famous actic describes the surprise of the Engli sailors when 42-pounder cannc balls came crashing *through* th ship's sides instead of lodging in th woodwork. Their cannon shot 1 pound balls

this time creating havoc with commerce off the east coast and among the islands of the West Indies, and the *Constitution* was ordered out on patrol with orders to run down these pirates. She met with no success until, twelve months later, as flagship of the Santo Domingo Station, she seized three privateers, including the 24-gun *Niger*.

All the effort, expense and heart-searching which had gone into the construction of America's pocket-size Navy, were justified in the early years of the new century. In 1803 once again the Barbary pirates were proving troublesome to American trade in the Mediterranean, and on 14 August the *Constitution* sailed for the shores of Tripoli under the command of Captain Edward Preble, where she acted as flagship of the Mediterranean Squadron. The daring plans for the destruction of the captured *Philadelphia* were made on the *Constitution*'s decks, and her successful blockading and bombarding activities in this theatre played a large part in bringing the war to a successful conclusion.

The tales of the *Constitution*'s combats during the War of 1812 have added a wonderful touch of colour to the fabric of early American history. It is worth recalling two of the most famous of the battles because they reveal not just the superior calibre of the American fighting sailor at this time (the spirit and morale of the British Navy decayed seriously after the triumph of Trafalgar) but the splendid fighting capacity of Humphreys' frigates. During this war at sea the British, who had been so disparaging of America's first real fighting ships, gained increasing respect for the *Constitution* and her consorts, and were

The capture of the *President*, 181 by Walters. From left to right t ships are the *Endymion*, *Majest Tenedos*, *President* and *Pomone*. S was overpowered after a long chas and her name has been carried in the British Navy. HMS *Presid* on the Victoria Embankmer London, commemorates the ca ture of a ship named after t President of the United States

more inclined to call them 'disguised 74s', from their part-*razée* origins.

In July 1812 the *Constitution* went to war again, this time under the command of Captain Isaac Hull. Five days later the war was nearly over for her. She sighted five sail and believing them to belong to the squadron she was meeting, she attempted to join up, only to find, too late, that it was a British force, which included the powerful frigates *Guerrière* and *Shannon*. Under ordinary circumstances the swift *Constitution* could have shown her heels without trouble. But the wind failed at this moment, and in one of the greatest pursuits in naval history, lasting two days, the *Constitution* got clear only by the extreme measure of kedging – that is, by dropping anchors in turn half a mile ahead from boats and drawing in on the line, literally walking the frigate away from the enemy.

A month later, the American frigate again sighted the *Guerrière*, and this time the British ship was alone. Captain Hull began to shorten sail. 'The breeze was steady and fresh, and the water fairly smooth. It was just the kind of weather he would have chosen for such a battle.' Spears has written of this epochal moment in American naval history, when a British and United States frigate confronted one another for the first time:

Perry's victory on Lake Erie, 1813, by Birch

All the light sails, including the topgallant sails, were furled, the courses were hauled up to the yards, and the royal yards were sent down. Then the topsails were double-reefed, and as the men came down from the topsail yards the drums beat to quarters. [Captain Hull held his fire while the *Guerrière* fired at the American's rigging at long range, doing little damage.] The *Guerrière* had meantime steered away before the wind; the clipper stem of the Yankee was overreaching the Englishman's quarter only a few yards away from it; our guns were brought to bear, and then stooping till 'he split his knee-breeches from waistband to buckle', Captain Hull straightened up again to his full height and shouted in a voice heard all over the ship:

'Now, boys; pour it into them!'

With a yell they obeyed. The broadside was as a single explosion. The crash of the balls through the splintering timbers of the *Guerrière* came back as an echo, and as she rolled with the swell the blood of the dead and wounded gushed from her scuppers. . . . For fifteen minutes the roar of the cannon and the rattle of musketry, and the crash of solid shot that struck home was incessant. The ships were literally yardarm to yardarm, rising and sinking over the long swells as they drove away before the wind.[20]

The masts of the British frigate began to topple. At 6.20 am a round shot carried away her mizzen. 'Hurrah, my boys! We've made a brig of her!' Captain Hull is supposed to have shouted. The two frigates became locked together, and preparations for boarding were made on both sides. Instead, an exchange of musket fire was followed by the *Constitution* breaking clear. The two other masts of the *Guerrière* toppled down, and she was no more than a hulk, with thirty round-shot holes below her waterline.

The *Guerrière* was a smaller and less heavily armed ship than her victor, but the action had proved the superiority of American fighting prowess as well as the effectiveness of Humphreys' basic frigate design. The story has often been told of the British seaman's distraught cry, when his vessel's broadsides appeared to make no impression on the *Constitution*'s hull, 'Huzza! her sides are made of iron!' And how the Boston-built frigate was forever after called 'Old Ironsides'. This victory early on in the war with Britain added strength and spirit to the American will to resist and, with John Paul Jones' successful capture of the *Serapis* years earlier, helped to instil a sense of maritime consciousness and responsibility in this new nation.

Late in the same year of 1812, the USS *Constitution* took part in the second great combat of her long career. Now under the command of Commodore William Bainbridge, the frigate ran out of Boston on 26 October, and on 29 December fell in with the British frigate *Java*, which had been the French *Renommée* before her capture off Madagascar the previous year. Again it was a demonstration of how superior

ne *Shannon* and the *Chesapeake*,
13. Captain Broke of the *Shannon*
ockaded the *Chesapeake* in Boston
arbour and sent in a personal
allenge under a flag of truce be-
use he was running out of pro-
sions. Captain Lawrence came
t, followed by pleasure craft of
e Boston inhabitants, who had
ranged a victory banquet ashore
r that night. In twelve minutes
e was mortally wounded and the
*hesapeake* captured. This greatly
eartened the British, who had not
en victorious for some time

seamanship, fighting spirit and gunnery – above all of gunnery –
could rapidly bring about the surrender of the foe: just as the British
had proved time and again in combat with the French and Spanish.
In addition, the American frigate was again markedly superior in
size and weight of fire, though not speed, for here the Toulon-built
ship had the edge on the frigate from Boston. After an exchange of
broadsides, the two ships closed to musket range, where much damage
was done to both sides and many were wounded, including Commodore Bainbridge himself. But the American gunnery soon showed
its deadly accuracy. The *Java* missed stays, and as she hung in irons,
with 'no movement in any direction', Pratt describes this moment:

*Constitution* wore round like a yacht, reached the new tack first and raked her opponent frightfully. *Java*'s lieutenants were screaming, pounding men about the head with speaking trumpets and the flat of their swords; they got the ship round somehow and down she came with her bowsprit over *Constitution*'s quarter and her bugles singing 'Boarders!' as brave Captain Lambert ran forward to lead a hand-to-hand charge. There was a rattle of musketry, a thud from *Constitution*'s carronades and the boarders were down, Lambert in their midst with a bullet in his spine. A swell swung the American frigate's head; she raked with every gun of her battery, then jerked clear as *Java*'s foremast came crashing down.

For a moment more the ships hung side by side, firing all they could, but *Java* much weaker now with so many men killed and the wreck of the foremast masking some guns. Then *Constitution* gained, turned under *Java*'s bows and raked her savagely before they once again ran parallel. Everything was going on the British frigate, her men still cheering indeed, but in desperation, the shouts mingled with swearing and sobs, their guns firing ragged or not at all, the sails of the broken foremast catching fire at every discharge. Down came her mizzenmast in the final exchange; *Constitution* shot away ahead and, sure of her victim, stood off a little distance to repair her cut ropes. . . .[21]

But it was all over. The *Java*, with sixty dead and over a hundred wounded, struck her colours. 'The Public will learn, with sentiments which we shall not presume to anticipate,' commented one British newspaper, 'that a third British frigate has struck her flag to an American. This is an occurrence that calls for serious reflection – this and the fact that Lloyd's list contains notices of upwards of five hundred British vessels captured in seven months by the Americans. Five hundred merchantmen and three frigates! Can these statements be true? Anyone who had predicted such a result of an American war this time last year would have been treated as a madman or a traitor. . . .'

Not all actions in the War of 1812 were concluded so satisfactorily for the Americans; nor did all Humphreys' frigates match the record of the *Constitution*, the *President* for one being captured and taken to Britain as a prize. The big American frigates, like the battle fleets of later years, inspired the Navy with self-confidence and valour, and caused dismay to the enemy; but the material damage to the foe – the loss of the vast majority of those five hundred British merchantmen – was brought about by the small privateers (the submarines of 1917 and 1941) working often in pairs and armed with perhaps a single carronade.

This is not to denigrate the achievements of these magnificent American fighting ships. A précis of the record of the other five of Humphreys' original six super-frigates speaks for itself:

The *Constitution* blowing up the *Java*, 1812, by Pocock, and (bottom) the *United States* and the *Macedonian*, 1811, by Coates

Overleaf: the *Serapis* and the *Bonhomme Richard*, 1779, by Paton

USS *President*: launched 10 April 1800. Blockaded Tripoli 1804. 30 June 1816 captured French privateer. 16 May 1811 badly damaged British frigate *Little Belt*. In War of 1812 fought running battle with British frigate *Belvidera*, which escaped; captured five British merchantmen and recaptured American vessel; captured fifteen more British ships the following year. Ran British blockade into New York 14 February 1814. 15 January 1815 fought running battle with British ships *Endymion*, *Tenedos* and *Majestic* before forced to surrender. Broken up 1817–8.

USS *United States*: launched 10 May 1797. 1798–9 cruised the West Indies, capturing four French merchantmen. 25 October 1812 fought and captured British frigate *Macedonian* off Madeira. Broken up 1865.

USS *Chesapeake*: launched 2 December 1799. Patrolled West Indies in search of French privateers, capturing *Le Jeune Creole* 1 January 1801. 1802 Commodore Richard Morris's flagship in Mediterranean, blockading Tripoli. June 1807 fired on and damaged by HMS *Leopard*. In War of 1812 captured five merchantmen. June 1813 with fresh untrained crew met crack British frigate *Shannon* and was captured after furious battle. Taken into the British Navy, broken up 1820.

USS *Constellation*: launched 7 September 1797. 9 February 1799 fought and captured 40-gun frigate *L'Insurgente*. Captured two French privateers. 1 February 1800 fought 52-gun frigate *Vengeance* which struck but subsequently escaped in darkness. May 1800 recaptured three American merchantmen. 1802–5 operated actively in Mediterranean, blockading, bombarding and protecting American interests. Spent much of War of 1812 blockaded in Hampton Roads, but prevented destruction of Craney Island fort. Again fought in Mediterranean 1815–7, capturing Algerian frigate *Mashuda*. Until 1865 employed at various times in supporting American interests, protecting American shipping, putting down slave traffic, serving in Mediterranean during Civil War in defence of Union shipping. Recommissioned 1840, later serving as relief flagship of C-in-C Atlantic Fleet. At present public memorial at Baltimore.

USS *Congress*: launched 15 August 1799. 1800 served in West Indies to protect American shipping against depredations of French privateers. Recaptured merchantman *Experiment*. Patrolling and blockading in Mediterranean 1804–5. 1812 captured thirteen British merchantmen in opening months of war. Operated against West Indies pirates 1822–3. Broken up 1834.

The *Constitution* and the *Guerrière*, 1812, by Birch

# 2. TRAFALGAR
# AND THE LAST YEARS OF SAIL

The business of an English commander-in-chief being first to bring an enemy's fleet to battle on the most advantageous terms to himself (I mean that of laying his ships close on board those of an enemy as expeditiously as possible), and secondly, to continue them there without separating until the business is decided. . . .

From the battle plan of Vice-Admiral Lord Nelson, 1805

I do not propose to go in search of the enemy; I even wish to avoid him in order to arrive at my destination; but, if we should meet him, let there be no shameful manoeuvring; it would discourage our ships' companies, and bring about our defeat. . . . Every captain who is not under fire will not be in his proper station; and a signal to recall him thither will be a dishonouring blot upon him.

From the battle plan of Vice-Admiral Villeneuve, 1805

The contrasting nature of these two directives accounts in some measure for the overwhelming defeat of the combined Franco-Spanish fleet off Cape Trafalgar on 21 October by a British fleet inferior in numbers and *matériel*. Several captains on the allied side suffered these 'dishonouring blots', just as others like Captain Lucas of the *Redoutable* and Commodore Charucca of the *San Juan Nepomuceno* fought with unsurpassed heroism. This great and decisive fleet action was won by the superior spirit, self-confidence and fighting prowess of the British seamen, whose trust lay in their officers and in the righteousness of their cause. Except for ships captured from the French (like the *Tonnant* taken at the Nile), the British ships of the line at Trafalgar were markedly inferior to the French and Spanish ships. There was no ship-of-the-line on the British side to match the mighty Spanish *Santisima Trinidad*, with its four tiers of ordnance, or the 80-gun *Bucentaure*; but a fatally high proportion of the French and Spanish officers were lacking in zeal, and many of the men who served under them were recently recruited and disaffected peasants without sea-going or fighting experience. They did not stand a chance against the seasoned and ruthless English fighting men.

The Battle of Trafalgar was not only one of the most decisive battles – by sea or by land – of the Napoleonic wars and one of the greatest naval battles of all time. Strategically, it represented the culminating triumph of the British Admiralty in its mature experience and its comprehension of the meaning of sea power to an island nation. It justified all the resolution of men like Rodney and Howe, the administrative

Detail of the Battle of San Domingo, 1806, by Pocock. The French three-decker, left, is losing her main topmast

brilliance of Sir Charles Middleton and the intellectual prescience of men like the Vicomte Bigot de Morogues and Vicomte de Grenier, and the Scotsman, Clerk of Eldin.* These were the men who were instrumental in breaking up the set piece battle, in which two fleets in parallel lines exchanged broadsides and endeavoured to batter each other to pieces. In the last battles of the 1700s, it had become clearly evident that long-established tactical principles were being dropped overboard; at Trafalgar Horatio Nelson relaxed formality to a degree which permitted extraordinarily wide individual freedom and enterprise among his commanders. The way everyone seemed to do just what they liked looked to be simple effrontery at the time, and astonished the enemy. But Nelson knew his foe and did not regard him very highly. Trafalgar, then, marked the full return of individual initiative to combat at sea; with the difference that now there was organization and communication behind the apparent confusion.

The position on the morning of 21 October 1805 was this: Admiral Villeneuve with his allied fleet of thirty-three ships-of-the-line (2,626 guns) had recognized that he could no longer hope to avoid battle, and drew up his ships as well as he was able into a single line (actually a crescent, and a confused one at that) headed north off the coast, with

*Tactique Navale, ou traité des évolution et des Signaux by Vicomte Bigot de Morogues (1763); L'Art de la Guerre s Mer by Vicomte de Grenier (1787 Essay on Naval Tactics by Clerk of Eld (1782).

The Battle of Trafalgar, 1805, b Pocock. This is another illustratio to the 'Life of Nelson' (cf. the Batt of the Nile, page 135). As battle joined Collingwood in the Roy Sovereign leads the English and first to break the Franco-Spanis line (travelling diagonally forward from left to right). The back (hor zontal) line of English is led b Nelson's Victory

Nelson fatally wounded at Trafal-
ar, by Dighton

Cadiz some twenty miles distant in the north-north-east. A light wind
was blowing from the west-north-west. The commander-in-chief,
flying his flag in the *Bucentaure*, had ten ships ahead of him, and the rest
of the fleet, including Admiral Gravina's 'reserve squadron' astern.
Decks were cleared for action. French and Spanish ships were
arbitrarily mixed together as a precaution against the dangers of
jealousy and recrimination.

During the night the allied fleet had been scrupulously observed by
the British *Euryalus*, a new frigate commanded by Henry Blackwood.
'All through the long, dark, and unsettled night preceding the battle
the frigate kept vigil, and dogged the enemy's movements. At each
tack of the enemy she fired a signal gun; at every hour, to show the
Admiral that she was still watching, a blue light was burned.'[22] Then
'as the day dawned,' wrote one of the British officers, 'the horizon
appeared covered with ships. The whole force of the enemy was discovered standing to the southward, distant about nine miles, between
us and the coast of Trafalgar. I was awakened by the cheers of the
crew and by their rushing up the hatchways to get a glimpse of the
hostile fleet. The delight they manifested exceeded anything I ever
witnessed.'[2]

Nelson at once formed his fleet of twenty-seven ships-of-the-line (2,148 guns) into two divisions, each in single column. His flagship *Victory* led in the northerly column, while Vice-Admiral Cuthbert Collingwood, flying his flag in the *Royal Sovereign*, led the lee column, with the assignment of destroying the rear of the enemy. Before the battle, Villeneuve had told his captains, 'The enemy will not be content himself with forming a line of battle parallel with ours, and with engaging us with his guns – a business wherein not necessarily the most skilful, but rather the most lucky is commonly successful. He will seek to surround our rear and to pierce our line; and he will endeavour to concentrate upon, and overpower with groups of his own vessels, such of our ships as he may manage to cut off.' In the event, when the two British columns began their advance, slowly in the light breeze, Nelson's tactics appeared suicidal. 'It was contrary to ordinary prudence,' wrote a French officer of the *Intrépide*, 'for the British ships, reaching us one by one, and at a very slow speed, seemed bound to be overpowered in detail by our superior forces.' This same officer also added: 'But Nelson knew his own fleet – and ours.'

Collingwood's *Royal Sovereign* (100 guns), built at Plymouth in 1787, renowned for her dull sailing qualities, had recently been refitted and copper-sheathed. In contradiction to her nickname, the 'West Country Waggon', she surged ahead. These silent anxious minutes of approach over a grey-green swell that was soon to be stained red and soiled with the sad squalid litter of battle, and the moment of confrontation and blasting first broadside, have been many times described by French and British writers. Instead, let America's greatest naval historian briefly take up the narrative:

> Immediately ahead [of Villeneuve] was the huge Spanish four-decker, the *Santisima Trinidad*, a Goliath among ships, which had now come forth to her last battle. Sixth behind the *Bucentaure*, and therefore eighteenth in the order, came a Spanish three-decker, the *Santa Ana*, flying the flag of Vice-Admiral Alava. These two admirals marked the right and left of the allied centre, and upon them, therefore, the British leaders respectively directed their course. . . . Collingwood came within range, his ship, outstripping the others by three-quarters of a mile, entered alone, and for twenty minutes endured, unsupported, the fire of all the hostile ships that could reach her. A proud deed, surely, but surely also not a deed to be commended as a pattern. The first shot of the battle was fired at her by the *Fougueux*, the next astern of the *Santa Ana*. This was just at noon, and with the opening guns the ships of both fleets hoisted their ensigns; the Spaniards also hanging large wooden crosses from their spanker booms.
>
> The *Royal Sovereign* advanced in silence until, ten minutes later, she passed close under the stern of the *Santa Ana*. Then she fired a double-

shotted broadside which struck down four hundred of the enemy's crew,
and, luffing rapidly, took her position close alongside, the muzzles of the
hostile guns nearly touching. Here the *Royal Sovereign* underwent the fire
not only of her chief antagonist, but of four other ships; three of which
belonged to the division of five that ought closely to have knit the *Santa
Ana* to the *Bucentaure*, and so fixed an impassable barrier to the enemy
seeking to pierce the centre.[16]

At last Collingwood was relieved by the slower consorts of his
division, which penetrated the Franco-Spanish line and set about the
*Fougueux, Monarca, Algésiras,* the *Swiftsure* and *Argonaute* and the others.
'See how that noble fellow, Collingwood, takes his ship into action!'
exclaimed Nelson from afar, where he could just see the *Royal
Sovereign*'s mastheads above the billowing smoke of battle. And
Collingwood, at about this time, is reported to have called out to his
flag-captain, 'What would not Nelson give to be here!'

Nearly an hour passed after Collingwood received his first broadside before the *Victory* reached the French flagship. 'The latter was
raked with the same dire results that befell the *Santa Ana*; but a ship
close to leeward blocked the way, and Nelson was not able to grapple
with the enemy's commander-in-chief. The *Victory*, prevented from
going through the line, fell on board the *Redoutable* . . . between which
and herself a furious action followed.' This was the close action for

which Nelson had planned for so long, and which, within half an hour, was to result in his own death. This was the moment when not only the quality of the weapons and the skill and experience in handling them was to decide the fate of Britain and of Europe; here, at this time, amid the bloody turmoil and cacophonous noise of battle (many gunners were never to hear again), it was nerve and fighting will that would prevail. A savage and fearsome gallantry marked the conduct of many of the Spanish and French officers and men. But the weight of disciplined skill and determination was too great, and further imbalanced by unworthy admirals. Far away to the north Admiral Dumanoir Le Pelley felt disinclined to become involved at all, and in spite of frantic signals from Villeneuve, remained out of gunshot range and slipped away safely with four ships-of-the-line, and Admiral Gravina escaped with eleven more ships, a number of which saw scarcely any serious combat. The speed and accuracy of British broadsides, the British marines' skill at boarding the enemy and countering their attempts at boarding, and the faultless British seamanship, were all too much for those of the allies who chose to stay and fight to a finish. Nelson died with the certain knowledge that victory was his. By 3 o'clock the tide of battle was already turning, by 5 o'clock it was almost all over. Nelson had called for the capture or destruction of twenty of the enemy. By 4 November, when the errant Dumanoir and his four ships were at last caught up and captured, the total of French and Spanish losses was raised to twenty-two.

The victory at Trafalgar in October 1805 spelt the end of Spanish

The *Victory* at close quarters with the *Redoutable*. Between firing at the enemy the sailors threw water onto her to stop a blaze that might spread back to them

sea power for all time, and it took the French navy a quarter century to recover from the calamities of that autumn. But above all, the destruction of Villeneuve's fleet finally terminated any hopes Napoleon still nursed of invading England. Instead, 'Napoleon henceforth set his hopes on exhausting England's resources, by compelling every state on the Continent to exclude her commerce,' wrote Fyffe in his *History of Modern Europe*. 'Trafalgar forced him to impose his yoke upon *all* Europe, or to abandon the hope of conquering Great Britain. . . . No victory, and no series of victories, of Napoleon produced the same effect upon Europe.'

Trafalgar was the last decisive fleet action fought with sailing fighting ships, and these were not to be radically reshaped or radically improved in their fighting quality before the introduction of steam, shell and armour plate fifty years later. Although ships were shattered and dismasted by the fearful power of a full broadside of perhaps fifty cannon, 350 years after the introduction of gunpowder to sea fighting it was the destruction of men rather than ships (none was sunk during the battle) that decided the outcome. Many, including the British C-in-C, fell to the grenade and musket fired at point-blank range. 2,000 years after the great galley battles of the Mediterranean, when ships had been sunk by the score, and 150 years after the development of the formal and disciplined battle in line, naval fighting at Trafalgar – after the tactically brilliant opening moves and approach – had reverted to the close medieval *mêlée*. The revolution in *matériel* which was to bring about the final shape of the fighting ship, and to conclude once and for all the age of fighting when man was the target and you could see him, was still a half century away.

Many of the ships on both sides at Trafalgar had been designed and built ten, twenty or more than thirty years earlier. The most modern Spanish, French and British ships-of-the-line and frigates showed evidence of the structural and rigging changes which were being introduced at the turn of the century (see above pp. 139-40) and were to bring the sailing fighting ship to its culminating point of development. The lessons learned from Trafalgar were far-reaching. The devastating damage and murderous slaughter caused during this battle by the raking fire from the broadside of a three-decker at point-blank range further hastened the modification of bow and stern. The beakhead bulkhead had always been a clumsy and dangerous way of closing off the two uppermost decks. By building up the bow – a process which had begun in smaller ships in the late 1700s – and by completing it above the middle deck to give the fighting ship a 'round bow', the architect at once greatly reduced the ship's vulnerability from raking fire, permitted the siting of guns to defend the bows of the ship, and made the ship drier in a head sea. Today it seems remarkable that the advantages of this improved formation of the bow took so long to be appreciated.

The sterns of the English and allied ships at Trafalgar had suffered as much as the bows from the effects of raking fire. There was obviously further room for improvement here. The old, flat, windowed stern, with its galleries rising like the ornate gilded boxes of some great opera house, made a stunning target for even the worst shot with the crudest means of sighting. The stern and its quarters were only lightly defended by guns. In the British Navy, the 84-gun *Ganges* of 1819 was one of the first battleships to carry a circular stern, and a means of defending it with heavy armament firing from the quarters. In the 1820s the circular stern was again modified into an elliptical shape, which allowed – to the relief of the ship's officers – the revival of quarter galleries and stern windows: shipboard life without these pleasant conveniences was somehow not quite the same as it had been. For a brief period in the early years of the new century, British practice reverted to the square tuck for the stern, but the round tuck soon regained favour, which it held until the end.

For many years after Trafalgar the British Navy was so omnipotent that, with the important exception of American frigate construction, the advance of naval architecture can be judged by British standards alone. Nevertheless, foreign influence still dominated British design. Any seaman who had come up against the mighty Spanish *Santisima Trinidad* or the French *Bucentaure* during the Napoleonic wars was confirmed in his belief that he was fighting at a serious *matériel* disadvantage; even one of the excellent 74s like the *Colossus* was itself a copy of the best French practice. So the experiences off Cape Trafalgar in 1805 influenced not only the shape of bow and stern, completing the 'rounding-off' process, but also, once again, the size of the fighting ship. Although laid down before Trafalgar, the British *Caledonia* was not completed until 1808, and in many features – but above all in her size – her design was based on the French monster, *Commerce de Versailles*. The *Caledonia* carried 120 guns on her three decks, was 205 feet long, and her tonnage exceeded 2,600. No more smaller three-deckers were built, and the fine 74s of 1,700 tons were replaced by two-decker 78s, 84s, and 92s of between 2,000 and 2,600 tons. The British two-decker achieved its full flowering in the *Albion* class of 1842: 3,100 tons, ninety 32-pounders and 8-inch guns. French influence was also seen in the gradual acceptance of the sturdy bulwarks, built up solid

on the poop, quarterdeck and forecastle, which had been introduced into the French Navy from about 1790. The advantages were so clear that, once belatedly recognized by the British Admiralty, they were incorporated into the design of most ships from three-deckers to frigates, and a number of older ships were modified to carry them.

A further important development of the early years of the new century was the final closing in of the waist of the fighting ship. Until the mid-1700s the upper deck, linking forecastle and quarterdeck, had not really been a deck at all. This open space had been used for the storage of spare spars and the ship's boats, with the further advantage that the smoke and fumes from the discharge of the guns on the upper gun deck were soon dispersed. The advantage of directly linking the forecastle and quarterdeck with gangways set above the guns was recognized and became increasingly common in the second half of the century. These gangways, at first only temporary, were enlarged and became permanent structures. The upperdeck became an actuality, and from the 1830s the waist of the ship finally closed, ventilation being provided by more large grills.

Two men were especially influential in bringing the British fully-rigged, sailing man-of-war to its ultimate condition. They were Sir Robert Seppings, Surveyor of the Navy from 1813 to 1832, and his successor Captain William Symonds. Between them these two men were instrumental in applying science in the French manner to naval architecture, and bringing the standards of design of British fighting ships at last up to the level of the French. Both men were especially concerned with hull configuration and construction. Seppings introduced to the construction of a ship's hull a method of diagonal strutting, the need for which was brought about by the ever increasing size of the biggest ships. These diagonal timbers added greatly to the strength of the structure and diminished the hogging strains, which for so many centuries had created anxiety and exercised the ingenuity of shipbuilders. But these added timbers also greatly increased the weight

195

of the ship and so reduced its speed – for which Seppings was harshly criticized. When Captain Symonds took over office his first need was to increase the speed of British warships. He went for a finer under-water section to achieve this, but necessarily had to increase the breadth on the waterline. 'Just as before, and many times after,' wrote Chatterton of this period, 'England had shown herself to possess a genius not so much for inventiveness as for improving on the ideas of others, so now she began to design and build vessels that could not be surpassed by the French themselves. During Symonds' regime the golden age of the wooden walls of England was reached. It was he who was responsible for the design of such ships as the *Vernon*, the *Queen*, and about 180 others. Seaworthiness combined with speed were their out-standing virtues, and these he obtained by improving their under-water lines and making them less heavy and clumsy. Internally the ships were constructed so as to provide more room and more air.'[1] Symonds' ships were highly regarded and satisfied the service's need for greater speed, but they heeled acutely and made indifferent gun-platforms.

The French Navy continued its decline after Waterloo, and during the reign of Louis XVIII (1815–25) suffered '*diminution des armaments, licenciement du personnel, réduction extrême de tous les crédits.* . . .'[13] Not until the 1830s was there evidence of a serious renaissance. When it came the French, as always, built well. But their superiority was no longer evident – and this time they were not above learning from others. The influence of Humphreys' American frigates was profound. The size,

The *Caledonia*, 1808, engraved b Dutton

Right: the *Prince*, 1828, jury rigge at Portsmouth, etched by Cook She was the guardship at Por mouth and seldom put to sea. was said she was 'grounding on h beef bones'

Overleaf: the *Nelson*, 120 gun 1809, a construction drawing b Pringle. As a result of lesso learned at Trafalgar she was d signed to be more powerful tha her predecessors

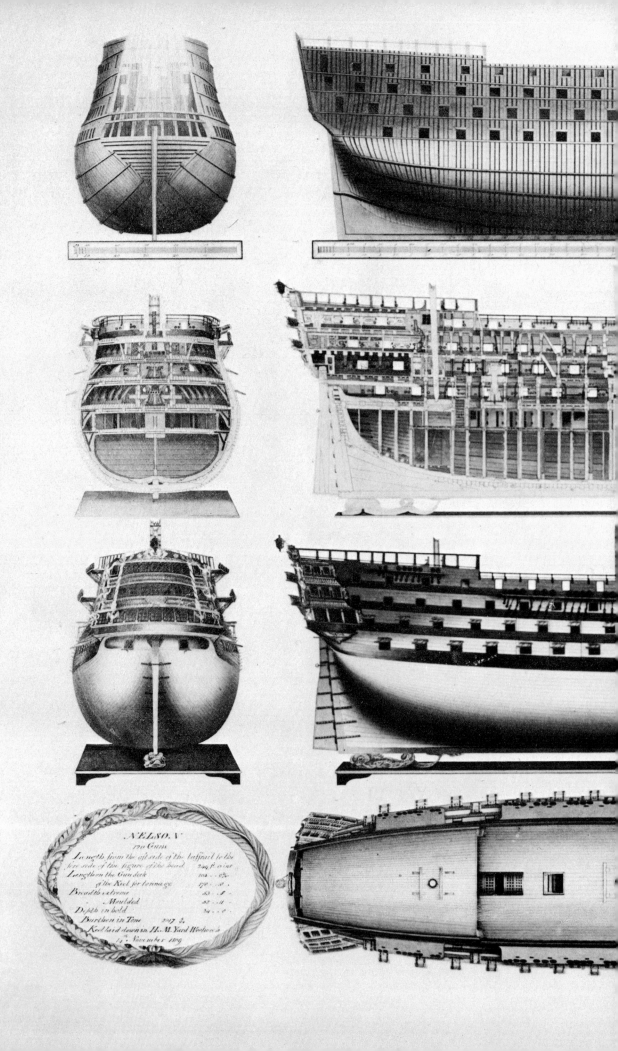

NELSON
170 Guns

Length from the aft side of the taffrail to the
fore side of the figure of the head    244 ft. 0 in.
Length on the Gun deck                  205 .. 0½
of the Keel for tonnage                 170 .. 0
Breadth extreme                         53 .. 4
Moulded                                 52 .. 4
Depth in hold                           24 .. 0
Burthen in Tons        2617 ¾
Keel laid down in H. M. Yard Woolwich
14ᵗʰ November 1809

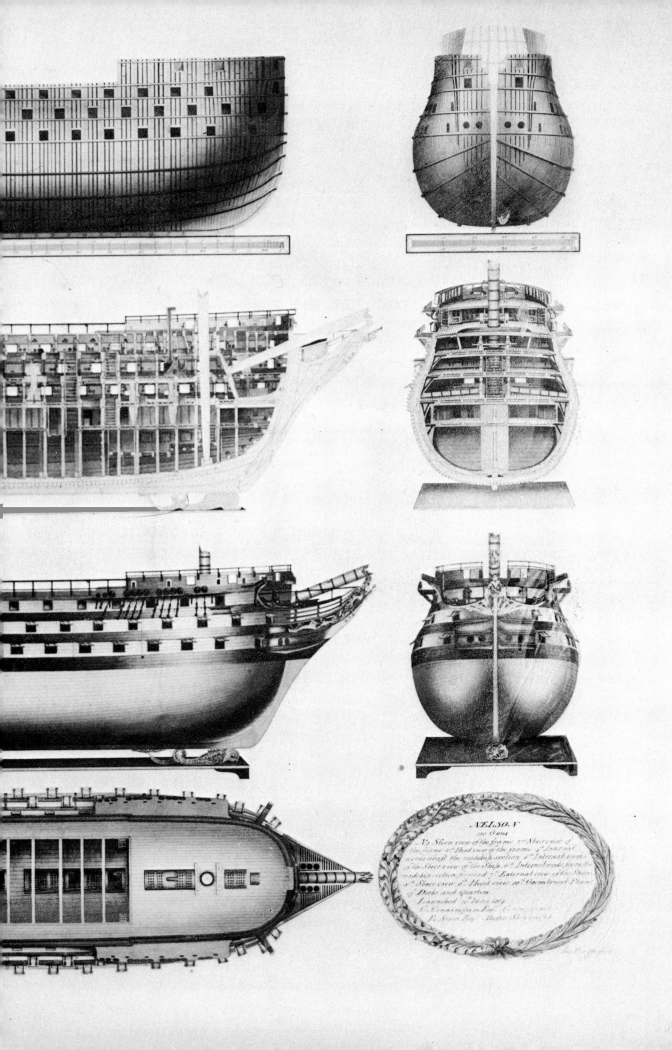

NELSON
120 Guns

N.º 1 Stern view of the frame, 2.º Sheer view of
the frame, 3.º Head view of the frame, 4.º Internal
works abaft the midship section, 5.º Internal works
of the Sheer view of the Ship, 6.º Internal works forward the
midship section, 7.º External view of the Stern,
8.º Sheer view, 9.º Head view, 10.º Quarterdeck Plan
of Decks and Quarters.

Launched 4.º June 1814

C. Cunningham Esq.r Commissioner
R. Seppings Esq.r Master Shipwright

power, speed and excellent sailing qualities of ships like the *Constitution* had been noted among all shipbuilding nations. The British had built two formidable double-decked frigates, the *Leander* and *Newcastle*, in an attempt to match the American ships; and when France began building seriously again, like the British and Americans, she built big. Landström has drawn one of these – *La Belle Poule*, built at Cherbourg in 1834, the ship which six years later brought back from St Helena the remains of Napoleon I. Like the *Leander* she actually mounted her guns on two decks, and the size and number of her guns – thirty-two 30-pounders, two 80-pounders and twenty-six 30-pounder carronades – made her as formidable a foe as any 74 ship-of-the-line in Napoleon's day. She measured 209 feet overall.

There was little room for further improvement in a ship's rigging during the 1800s. After about 1815 trysails, set on small masts below the main and fore-tops, began to replace the staysails. Of other small refinements in the rigging of the last sail-driven fighting ships, Clowes comments: 'The greater importance of head sails also had the effect of rendering the spritsail yard a fixture and of gradually relegating it to the position of a spreader for the shrouds of the jib-boom and flying jib-boom. By 1830, although the yard was still retained, the spritsail had entirely disappeared . . . while twenty years later the yard itself was only represented by two light spreaders, fitted with jaws, for the shrouds of the jib-boom and the flying jib-boom. An improved method of securing the futtock shrouds, by bringing them to the mast, instead of to the lower shrouds, was introduced into East Indiamen in 1811, and spread to the Navy within the next ten years. The year 1811 also saw the introduction of jackstays on the yards, to which all the square-sails were secured, instead of being lashed round the yards themselves. . . .'[5]

A new system of rating was introduced into the British Navy in 1817 which belatedly included carronades in the calculation of a fighting ship's power:

First Rates: three deckers, 104 to 120 guns
Second Rates: two deckers, 80 to 84 guns
Third Rates: two deckers, 74 to 78 guns
Fourth Rates: two deckers, 58 to 60 guns, including *razéed* 74s and 50-gun
    frigates
Fifth Rates: 42 to 48 guns
Sixth Rates: 24 to 32 guns

This rating method was modified again in 1811, when a ship's rate was based more closely on the size of the ship's company.

The *Victory*, by Swaine

Overleaf: the Battle of Trafalgar 1805, by Wilson. Both Wilson and Stanfield painted the *Victory* with her stern gallery, although it had in fact been removed in the 1800-repair

# 3. TRANSITION AND COMPROMISE

Mister McAndrew, don't you
think steam spoils romance at sea?
    Rudyard Kipling, *McAndrew's Hymn*

The three-decker *Sovereign of the Seas* of 1637 could have fought usefully and creditably at Trafalgar. And she would not have looked very strange or antiquated going to sea with the British fleet 200 years after she was launched. The pace of development of the fighting ship had scarcely increased over the centuries. This may partly be explained by the slow and hesitant progress of science, which still offered nothing better than canvas to catch the wind and a primitive muzzle-loading cannon firing various kinds of shot; and partly by the condition of unthreatened omnipotence of the ship-of-the-line. The battleship of the 1830s really was mistress of the seas. She could meet any foe of inferior size, under any circumstances, with complete confidence. She could leave port and sail safely anywhere in the most unfavourable weather. She could remain at sea for as long, and travel as far, as any nuclear submarine of the 1970s. Much of the wonder and splendour of the great three-decker 'wooden walls' of the last days of sail lies in their arrogant consciousness of unchallengeable power. Look at Admiral Roussin off to force the entrance to the Tagus in 1831 with the *Suffren*, *Trident*, the *Ville-de-Marseille* and the *Marengo* and the other great ships of his squadron; or look at Captain Charles Napier leading into Beyrout the *Ganges*, *Thunderer* and *Edinburgh* in 1840 to put the fear of Britain into the hearts of some rebellious Egyptians. Such occasions brought a special glory to the last years of supremacy for the ultimate fighting ship. At that time there was no other deterrent to a fleet of battleships than a greater fleet of battleships. 'I hate your pen-and-ink men,' wrote Nelson to Lady Hamilton. 'A fleet of British ships of war

Queen Victoria being received at Cherbourg by Napoleon III, and (bottom) Napoleon's ashes being transferred to the *Belle Poule*, by Isabey

205

are the best negotiators in Europe; they always speak to be understood and generally gain their point: their arguments carry conviction to the breasts of our enemies.'

It was a golden autumn all right, but a brief one. After its centuries of power, only a few decades were left to it. In less than half a century, the ultimate weapon at sea would be a graceless, noisy, low-lying slug of steel belching black smoke from a pair of dark funnels, nosing its way through the seas in fear that a single projectile or a new and sinister underwater form of high explosive might blow it sky high. The new weapons of science were to shape the heavy fighting ship during its last century of power and the results were at first unpleasing to the eye. The steel battleship was to rediscover a new grandeur and a new and satisfactory balance of rig before she went down in a maelstrom of bombs and torpedoes; but the fighting ship's final touch of peerless beauty began to diminish when the first engine was installed on board and a vertical iron cylinder to carry away its effluence pierced its wooden deck. No wonder the sailor fought the onslaught of science against his beloved man-of-war, for he was a lover of beauty and a deep believer in 'what looks right is right', as well as a conservative.

The unlovely fighting ship of the mid-1800s came about as a result of momentous strides forward in three fields of science, all inter-related and concurrent. First, there was the revolution in ordnance; then in the fighting ship's motive power; and lastly in the material from which it was constructed. In less than two decades the shape and the power and the speed of the fighting ship were all transformed. And with this revolution, there arrived the need to reappraise everything concerned with maritime power – from strategy through *matériel* to the quality of the sailor himself. Ashore, more men had to be sent burrowing for more coal and more iron ore, while others applied themselves to the complex new skills of gun-making and shell-making. New skills in shipbuilding practice were suddenly demanded. A steam-driven fighting ship could be sighted from afar by its plume of black smoke. And now that motive power was no longer the free wind, it had to be paid for; while the navy of every nation had to provide itself with accessible coaling bases, or colliers, wherever it was required to operate. Tactical flexibility on the one hand was greatly increased at the cost of strategic flexibility. The denuded forests of Europe were at last given some peace. The list of consequences is legion. Oil and coal dust appeared in the unlikeliest places on board, and affronted the older generation of seamen with its grime.

There was stout resistance to these sudden developments, and as a result, much delay in their whole-hearted acceptance. Conservative elements were supported by many early failures. Every time an iron vessel went down, a shell gun blew up or a thundering engine broke down it was a discouraging event, and those who had said 'I told you so' scored another point. And changes would have happened quicker if there had been a few big wars to spur them on. Even that miserable affair in the Crimea in 1854–6 acted as a stimulus. These technical revolutions were not instant in their effect, nor were they unpredictable. People had been thinking about and experimenting with steam engines, explosive projectiles and iron hulls (and even armour plate) for many years before bold and persuasive experimenters got their way at last.

The progress and acceptance of the scientific inventions which transformed the fighting ship from the 1840s to the 1870s were marked by a number of notable events and the endeavours of a number of clever men. There can never, now, be a just share-out of credit. Most great scientific advances have been brought about by the simultaneous and parallel work of a number of people persuaded by the

Leonardo da Vinci's fifteenth-century designs for a paddle boat and (right) Robert Fulton's first sketch for a steam boat in the eighteenth century

needs of the time, by the circumstances of their life, by the materials available, and by their ability to promote their work and claim their share (more or less) of the credit. But penicillin has its Alexander Fleming, the aircraft its Wilbur Wright and the motor car its Gottlieb Daimler, and the names of certain men whose accomplishments sealed the fate of the fully-rigged wooden fighting ship have come down to us over the years.

To propel a ship through the water by mechanical means requires first a source of contrived power and second a means of transmitting it. Both were available long before anyone put them together and made them work. The idea of paddling a boat through the water by rotating a number of paddles instead of working a single paddle horizontally goes back (like so much else) to the Romans, to the Chinese, and to the drawings of Leonardo da Vinci. If Chinese drawings are to be believed, they had a man-powered paddle ship (slaves in a treadmill) back in the 1500s. Towards the end of the next century a French doctor called Denis Papin did better by suggesting in a memorandum that power to paddle wheels could be supplied by a piston drawn down a cylinder by air pressure when steam was condensed beneath it. For the next hundred years or so the spasmodic progress was shared about equally between Britons and Frenchmen – men like Jonathan Hull and Newcomen, Jouffroy and Savery, Worcester and Watt.

Of these perhaps the Marquis de Jouffroy d'Abbans and James Watt performed the most enduring work. Jouffroy had a 46-metre-long paddle steamer working effectively on the Saône in 1783. The Scotsman, Patrick Miller, collaborated with the steam engine manufacturer William Symington, and soon had a paddle boat doing five knots.

The American, Robert Fulton, arrived on the scene at the right time with the right blend of ingenuity, business sense, determination and recognition of objective. Fulton, more than anyone else, brought steam power to the fighting ship in the 1800s. Fulton was born in Pennsylvania in 1765, and later studied in England and France, and learned well from the failures of others in the field of marine power. He ran a tiny steamboat on the Seine in 1803, and returned to America to make his fortune. His next steamboat travelled from New York to Albany in 32 hours. Six years later, in 1813, he built the first steam-driven fighting ship. At this time the American Navy was buoyed up by the successes of its fine frigates against the British, and those who commanded them. These and others were the men who encouraged Fulton, in this hour of need, to build a steam-powered ship to defend New York. The war was over before it was completed, so the British never had the opportunity to test steam against sail in combat. But they did not like whatever they heard about it, and determined to give her crew no quarter if they did come up against such a diabolical man-of-war. For not only was the *Demologos* (the voice of the people) powered by a steam engine working a paddle between two catamaran hulls, but she was to be armed with thirty 32-pounders firing shot heated in a furnace. On her trials she managed 6 knots, but whether she would have remained afloat in any sort of a sea was problematical. She had no opportunity to prove herself and was blown up in an accident at the Brooklyn Naval Yard in 1829.

There was every justification for prejudice against the use of steam power and its transmission through paddle wheels. The engines were heavy, unreliable, inefficient and even dangerous. They did not only make a mess and a noise. They – and their nasty black fuel – took up cargo space in a merchantman and gun space in a warship. The fire risk was increased many times over. A paddle box made a large and vulnerable target. And one round of solid shot in the engine, or worse still the boiler – well, it was best not to contemplate such a catastrophe. But steam tugs were useful for towing big three-deckers into or out of harbour, and in the 1820s and 1830s the French were especially progressive in applying paddle-transmitted steam power to larger warships – even to corvettes and frigates. These vessels made a new sight at sea, a sight that was fearsome or ridiculous, depending on the sailor's age and prejudices: a trim 1500-ton frigate like the French *Gomer*, fully rigged, sails taut in the wind, but amidships a single tall funnel belching black smoke and red hot sparks (a hazard if you like!) while, attached seemingly as an afterthought to both sides, was a huge semi-circular box, with the froth and foam from the rotating paddle wheel beneath it. This would not do, of course. The 450 horsepower of the *Gomer* was usable and even useful from time to time, but when it was not the paddle wheels upset the sailing qualities of the vessel. While the steam engine provided only secondary or auxiliary power, a form of transmission less clumsy and inefficient than the paddle wheel would have to be found.

It was, of course, found and perfected very quickly. In spite of all the prejudices against mechanical power, the advantages of a form of propulsion that did not depend on the vagaries of the wind or the endurance and muscle power of the oarsmen were so obvious that only a handful of reactionaries could seriously oppose further development. The history of the screw propeller, like that of the steam engine, is marked by numerous tentative and experimental projects, many of which got no farther than the drawing board. Among the claimants for bringing the screw form of transmission to a workable condition are the Swede John Ericsson, the English farmer Francis Pettit Smith, and the French engineer Frédéric Sauvage. It is Ericsson's name which has popularly endured, partly because he was a good business-man, and partly because he initiated other great advances in naval architecture. Ericsson, working in England, took out a patent for a submerged steamship screw in July 1836. Under the patronage of the American consul in Liverpool, Francis B. Ogden, he built a screw steamer (of this name) which was launched in April 1837. The British Admiralty expressed no interest in it, so Ericsson took himself off to the USA, to the enormous profit of himself and that country. Francis Smith was working on similar lines at the same time, but in London. His patent was dated May 1836, and his little 6-ton screw steamer was showing its paces on the Paddington Canal later in the same year. Sauvage's patent was dated four years earlier, but his practical development seems to have been slower than that of the two men working in England. In America, Ericsson busied himself through the 1840s, experiencing great advances and one or two nasty setbacks. He succeeded in having two steam frigates, the *Princeton* and *Mississippi*, built with screw propulsion, telescopic funnels and fans for forced draught fire. There was novelty in their armament, too, and while the screw of the *Princeton* was being successfully demonstrated up the Potomac one of the 950-ton frigate's monster 12-inch guns was fired. It blew up, killing the Secretary of State as well as the Secretary of the Navy. This event, by a rather tortuous political process, was unjustly made to reflect on Ericsson himself, and even the reputation of his propeller was indirectly tarnished.

In spite of this mishap, the development of screw propulsion went ahead fast in America. In Europe, too, some modest official encourage-ment was given to a form of transmission that patently possessed great advantages over the clumsy paddle wheel. Where Ericsson had failed

The *Basilisk* against the *Niger* 1849, and (right) the *Rattler* against the *Alecto*, 1845, in paddle versus screw contests

to persuade the British Admiralty, Francis Smith had a modest success. The 880-ton sloop *Ardent* was converted while under construction to carry a 200 horsepower steam engine which was married to a Smith-designed two-bladed screw. It was launched in April 1843 as the *Rattler*. Two years later, she was lashed on a calm sea stern-to-stern with another steam sloop of equal size and power, but paddle-driven. With seeming effortless ease, the *Rattler* towed her fellow away at 2.8 knots. There could no longer be any serious question of the screw's superior efficiency.

For once, the British Admiralty were rather precipitate in their acceptance of the screw, and much money was wasted on the unconsidered conversion to screw propulsion of ships already built or on the stocks. 'The French took a longer time to consider the screw principle before applying it to their ships of war, and thus they derived the full benefit of matured experience without the necessity of making ruinous experiments,' wrote one contemporary German writer. 'Their "constructors" – more scientific than those in England – pondered well over the invention before accepting it, and it was not till the success of the new propeller had been thoroughly proved that it was adopted by them. But its powers having been once ascertained, there was no delay.'[1]

By the late 1850s, the screw fighting ship, though still of course fully rigged, formed the backbone of the fleets of the major powers, and the paddle was left to the tug and smaller craft, which it nobly served for another hundred years. Reliance on the vagaries of the wind alone was now finished. By 1859 an authority commenting on the state of the British Navy was writing: 'Of the long array of sailing line-of-battle ships, frigates, and corvettes, that now figure in the Navy List, only a very limited number can . . . be considered as seaworthy. They have an imposing appearance, it is true, as they "repose in perfect stillness

on their shadows" at Sheerness, Chatham, or at Devonport; but never more "will they, at the call of patriotism or of necessity, ruffle their swelling plumage, nor, putting forth their beauty and their bravery, collect their scattered elements of strength, nor awaken again their dormant thunder".'[2]

It was the mariner's deep and traditional fear of fire at sea which had provided one of the strongest obstacles to the acceptance of a furnace and boiling water and steam, in addition to large quantities of gun-powder, on board a man-of-war. The same perfectly reasonable anxiety delayed the introduction of the explosive shell. Carrying hand grenades to lob on to enemy decks from the rigging was hazardous enough, and those who had seen the *Orient* blow up at the Battle of the Nile remembered the horror of that event for years afterwards. Besides the traditional conservatism of the sailor, there was another very different and seemingly very curious reason for opposing the explosive shell in naval warfare, long after the shell gun had become a practical proposition. Among fighting seamen who lived like pigs and were treated like savages, and were sometimes known to despatch their prisoners without a thought, there was a very surprising prejudice against the explosive shell for humane reasons. Finally, as far as the omnipotent British were concerned, there was the more practical prejudice against the explosive shell because it might be effective enough to offset the sheer weight of numbers enjoyed by the Royal Navy. The French, for this same reason, zealously encouraged experimental work on shell guns and gained a temporary advantage. The

The paddle frigate *Terrible*, 1845 engraved by Papprill. There is a significant contrast between her funnels and black smoke, and the white canvas and beautiful lines of the three-decker. Steam frigates saw service in the Crimean War the introduction of shell fire in this war was the death knell of wooden warships

man most responsible for this was Henri-Joseph Paixhans; but there were many others before him who recognized that the ship-destroying power of the smooth-bore cannon firing solid shot was absurdly limited, and that the Greeks, Phoenicians and Romans had been better – 2,000 and more years earlier – at *sinking* ships.

The object of all this work was to combine the destructive advantages of the bomb-throwing mortar with the longer-ranging, horizontal-firing cannon. A few early experiments in combat had shown how devastating could be the effect. Shells with short fuses, fired from 24-pounder cannon, had proved themselves at the Siege of Gibraltar. A British shipwright and artillerist, Sir Samuel Bentham, showed his employers, the Russian government, what could be accomplished by shell fire in the Sea of Azov in 1788. The Russian 'fleet', consisting mainly of longboats, but armed with shell-firing guns to Bentham's designs, annihilated a much larger Turkish force. The French began to take explosive shells seriously before the end of the 1700s, although the results were not seen in the naval war with Britain. In 1794 a French artillery officer, Lieutenant-General Count Andréossy, presented to Napoleon a *Mémoire sur le tir des corps creux, qu'on propose de substituter au tir à boulets rouge dans les combats de mer*. In the following June experiments against mocked-up ships with shell-firing cannon from 18- to 24-pounders were conducted at Toulon. The results were reported as satisfactory. There were further experiments in the following years, their success being prejudiced by some damaging premature explosions of shells which had been issued to units of the French fleet. Another drawback of the explosive shell which had to be overcome was that, being 'hollow' and therefore incapable of withstanding a heavy charge, its range and penetrating power were restricted. Both were soon improved by the metallurgists.

Then there were more experiments in America, where British bombardments of the New England coastal towns in the War of Independence, and later experiences in the War of 1812, pointed to the need for better shore defence. A book published in Philadelphia in 1809, called the *American Artillerist's Companion*, drew attention to General Andréossy's work in France and emphasized the advantages of horizontal-firing shell artillery for coast defence. This was followed by the introduction of the Columbiad (after Joel Barlow's poem) gun, 'a long chambered piece, combining some of the qualities of the gun, howitzer and mortar, and capable of firing both solid shot and shells',[3] and the mainstay of American defence artillery for several decades.

A certain amount of unsponsored shell gun experiment went on in England and among the minor naval powers during these early years of the century. But it was in France, a nation still smarting from the military and naval setbacks of the first fifteen years of the century, that the final catalyst occurred. Here was a country that had nothing to lose and everything to gain by disturbing the *status quo* in the fighting ship in its endeavours to regain its lost prestige and greatness. Paixhans initiated the renaissance of the French fighting ship with the publication in 1822 of his *Nouvelle Force Maritime et Artillerie* and three years later of *Expérience faites sur une arme nouvelle.*

Henri-Joseph Paixhans was born at Metz in 1783, attended the Ecole Polytechnique and served in the army during the Napoleonic campaigns as an artillery officer. This dynamic, irascible, brilliant scientist-artillerist, the apotheosis of all genius inventors, was a battalion commander with vast experience to draw on when he published his first work. He extended his theories far beyond the advocacy of shell artillery. He was after a real revolution that must change the whole nature of sea warfare. Paixhans wanted also to abolish all sailing ships-of-the-line and frigates, replacing them with swift steamships armed with shell guns of uniform calibre. With smaller, more efficient fighting ships, armed with fewer but vastly more destructive artillery and manned by smaller crews he saw a fighting force that must dominate the seas by its speed, hitting power and flexibility, while being more economical to maintain in peacetime. This was heady talk. But it would have been wiser if Paixhans had stopped short at his shell gun; for at that time his super-frigates and super-battleships would have been paddle-propelled, and he was opposed to the introduction of armour plate to defend his vessels from the explosive shells of an enemy. As an innovator, Paixhans was a little ahead of himself and his time. The French Ministry of Marine recognized this, but also saw good sense in his theories on the effects of shell fire against a wooden man-of-war. They were even prepared to try them out. In 1824 a commission was appointed to study the results of shellfire against an unarmoured wooden hull. The 80-gun *Pacificateur* was selected as a target, and Paixhans's shells tore the old ship to pieces.

Surely, here was enough evidence to convince the most extreme sceptic. Yet several years passed before all the other objections to shell artillery in the fighting ship were overcome. Not until the late 1830s was the shell gun generally introduced throughout the French Navy. Filled with a confused disquiet about the consequences on the one hand of following French practice and on the other of failing to do so, the British Admiralty hesitantly permitted the gun complements of some, but only a few, British ships to be converted to shell firing. The results of the Battle of Sinope, in which a Turkish force was annihilated

by Russian shellfire, and the Crimean business a year later, settled the
fate of round shot. By the 1850s the big naval shell gun had arrived,
and this long cylinder of steel with its fearful promise of distant
destruction was to dominate naval architecture and tactics for almost
a century, culminating in the monster British and Japanese 18-inch
weapons of the two World Wars.

Once the technical difficulties and the human scruples had been overcome, means had to be found to prevent or at least diminish the
devastating results of a shell exploding within a wooden ship. Like all
the technical innovations of the fighting ship of the mid-1800s, there
was nothing novel about protecting the hull of a ship from shot and
fire. Leather had often been tried in Mediterranean galleys, and in
Jerome Osorio's *History of Portugal*, published in the mid-1500s, there
is an account of a naval engagement, which took place between the
inhabitants of Diu and the Portuguese in the earlier years of the
century, during which 'when the fight had nearly ended, there
remained one ship, which was the largest and best equipped of any in
the whole fleet: it was covered completely with leather, or to speak
nearer the truth, perhaps, with raw hides. . . .'

At about this same period the Koreans, of all people, are reputed to
have used against the Japanese a turtle-decked vessel armoured not
only with plates of iron but also *studded with spikes* – better against ball

215

*and* boarders. The Genoese admiral, Andrea Doria, was supposed to have had one of his ships encased in lead. Less dramatic forms of protection were sometimes resorted to when there was to be a bombardment against shore batteries, such as securing another layer of timber to the sides, with another layer of cork to soften the cannon blow. But the fact was that the ship-destroying gun did not often actually destroy the hulls of big wooden two- and three-deckers. They cut up the rigging and shot away the masts, they killed the men inside, and they made a lot of holes in the hull. These were sometimes bad enough to sink the ship, especially if the weather was bad. But mostly naval combat was still a matter of killing men and capturing ships.

The advent and acceptance of armour plate and the iron ship roughly coincided in time. There was strong resistance, both practical and emotional, to the use of iron for building ships. In spite of the success of Isambard Kingdom Brunel's iron transatlantic steamer *Great Britain* in 1838, and the successful bombardment by shellfire of the Kinburn forts in 1855 by a trio of French armoured steamships ($4\frac{1}{2}$ inches of iron over 17 inches of wood), Britain still placed her reliance on the wooden three-decker, even though they carried shell guns and auxiliary steam power, for the real fighting strength of her fighting fleet. No British iron warships took part in the Crimean War, and it was with misgivings and the utmost reluctance that the Admiralty ordered small armoured iron-built bombardment vessels after the successful French pattern. Experiments using solid shot conducted by the Admiralty in the late 1840s had proved that hits on the hull left iron plates with holes that were 'open and sometimes very jagged', whereas damaged oak planking could speedily be plugged, and was moreover partly self-sealing. The results of these experiments were still influencing British ship-of-the-line policy when the enormous

The *Marlborough*, 1854, by Pickering. There is a lady in the Admiral's cabin (left); cows and sheep are stabled in the waist; sick are in the fo'c'sle sickbay; and below are engines, amidships, and a long shaft leading to a large propeller which could be hoisted up a tunnel into the stem to facilitate sailing

(7,000-ton) three-decker *Victoria* was launched in 1859 – an uneasy compromise, a mass of contradictions and the last of her kind in the world. She was one of a class of four, all fully rigged yet with 4,300 horsepower engines, built of good solid oak yet carrying shell-firing guns. Except for the single funnel amidships they were little different in silhouette from Nelson's flagship at Trafalgar.

During this transitional period the French and Americans were ahead of the British. There were a number of reasons for this. The Americans still had to build exceptionally well if their naval power was to count at all, for in numbers it could not hope to influence events. But America possessed two great advantages – unlimited materials and clever designers: the genius of Humphreys still lived through his successors. America had not only vast quantities of timber, but also unmeasured riches in iron. It was in the economic interest of this nation to be forward-looking in its fighting ship design. As early as January 1842 the Secretary of the Navy, Abel P. Ipshur, said that 'it seems no longer doubtful, that iron ships will answer all the purposes of coast and harbour defence, and probably also of ocean cruising. It is the wish of this Department to construct as many vessels as possible of this material. This is desirable, not only on account of its superior durability and cheapness, but because by extending the use of it, the Government would afford a well-deserved encouragement to the industry of a large class of people, and aid in developing and bringing into action, a most important part of our country's resources'. These were challenging words, and were acted upon with the construction of the 582-ton all-iron *Michigan*, which served on the Great Lakes from 1844 right up to 1923. Next came the *Alleghany* of nearly twice her size, and it looked as if the New World would be the first to have an iron fighting fleet. Instead, everything went wrong with this ship. She was not fast enough and not strong enough; and the Bureau of Construction reported that it was 'of opinion that the material of which she is constructed prevents her being suited for the purpose for which she was designed'. So when Congress authorized the construction of six steam frigates in 1854, they were formidably armed with shell guns (the 4,600-ton *Niagara* had fourteen 11-inch guns) and could steam at about 10 or 12 knots, but they were of wooden construction and were unarmoured.

The French naval revival of the 1850s, like the earlier revivals in France and Britain, was the result of royal enthusiasm financing and encouraging the architects. After the uneasy alliance during the Crimean War, France and Britain quickly reverted to their customary condition of jealousy and hostility. The ambitions of Napoleon III were boundless, and after the Orsini conspiracy crisis they included the invasion of Britain. Unlike Bonaparte, Napoleon III recognized the need to neutralize the British fleet as a *first* priority. And while he possessed armies five times more powerful than the British, he was at heart a navalist. He was also in the happy position of possessing a splendid ministry and the greatest naval designer in the world. In the Emperor Napoleon III and the designer Stanislas-Charles-Henri-Laurent Dupuy de Lôme, France enjoyed the greatest source of naval architectural inspiration in the world.

Dupuy de Lôme was born 16 October 1816 at Ploemeur, Morbihan. He showed early promise in his technical training, and in 1842 was sent to Laird's shipbuilding yard in Britain, one of the most advanced in Europe. Shortly after his return he published his report entitled a *Mémoire sur la construction des bâtiments en fer*, which advocated the use of iron in ship construction and later became an accepted classic in its highly specialized field. In 1845 he put forward plans for an iron fighting ship of 2,400 tons, in which the sails would be auxiliary, armed with a few heavy guns behind armoured bulwarks, and with side armour plates reinforced by the coal bunkers. This was too *avant garde* for the ministry at that time. Nonetheless, Dupuy de Lôme was not discouraged and his career as an architect was watched with interest. His first classic design came three years later. In 1848 the keel was laid of a 5,000-ton battleship, the *Napoleon*, which might, from a quick glance, be mistaken for a 90-gun two-decker. She was built of wood, and she was fully-rigged. But she was armed with shell guns, her sails were only a secondary source of power, and her 900 horsepower engines gave her a speed of 11 knots. When she was completed in 1852 she was the most formidable fighting ship in the world. Of Dupuy de Lôme's appointment as *Directeur du Matériel* in 1857, the great British designer Nathaniel Barnaby commented: 'In boldness of conception and in executive skill he takes first place among the naval constructors of our time.'

At once Dupuy de Lôme set about his greatest masterpiece, the fighting ship for which he will always be remembered. At this time the balance of naval power between Britain and France was very fine. Both forces possessed great numbers of wooden three- and two-deckers, frigates and sloops and other smaller vessels, a number of which had been converted by the installation of auxiliary engines, besides a small number of frigates and others originally designed to steam as well as sail. (Unlike the British, the French had given up building wooden three-deckers.) The Emperor and Dupuy de Lôme – and all the young forward-looking elements in the French Navy –

believed that the future ship-of-the-line, the final arbiter in naval combat, must be an armoured, iron, fast, steam-powered vessel armed with shell guns. Everything else was useless. If France could build enough of these quickly, it was claimed, she could gain command of the seas in any future war: *l'Albion perfide* would be annihilated. In March 1858 four of these first sea-going ironclads were ordered. Unfortunately (and this rather spoils the neatness of the pattern) France, unlike America, did not have the resources to smelt all the iron needed for these ships, and only one of them was iron-hulled.

This does not affect the historical importance of the project, nor did it diminish the acuteness of the anxiety it caused across the Channel. There followed the first of the major Victorian naval crises in Britain, with the setting up of the inevitable Parliamentary committee and feverish articles in the popular and specialist press. 'Such is the opinion of French naval officers,' wrote one British authority, 'respecting the tremendous power of these ships, that they fully anticipate the complete abolition within ten or a dozen years, of all line-of-battle ships.'[2] The prophecy was more rapidly fulfilled than this. Frigates these new ships might be in name, because their guns were carried on a single deck. But they were as big as any wooden three-decker, and they could send one to the bottom with a few well-aimed broadsides.

The first of Dupuy de Lôme's ironclads to be completed was the *Gloire*, an ugly stubby vessel of 5,675 tons armed originally with thirty-four 5-ton 16-centimetre guns and armoured with plates more than 4 inches thick backed by 26 inches of wood. She could steam at 13 knots, but was also fully-rigged, originally as a barquentine.

It was British naval shipbuilding policy at this time to avoid any radical innovation that might result in jeopardizing the quantitive superiority of the fleet and wasting the vast expenditure incurred in creating it. It was wiser and more convenient to await developments abroad and copy them and even improve on them. This could be a fairly leisurely business if the innovation was a minor one. The laying down of the *Gloire* and her sisters was so alarming, however, that instant action was publicly demanded, and for once was swiftly taken. The situation in Britain was favourable to rapid decision and production. Experiments with armour plate had been going on between 1856 and 1858, and the design for a 5,600-ton ironclad had been considered and rejected only three months before news of the *Gloire* reached Britain. The *Warrior* was laid down in May 1859 as an armoured all-iron steam frigate, and because of her speedy construction was ready before France's *Couronne*, Dupuy de Lôme's own 'pure' ironclad. The *Warrior* was therefore, by a nice distinction, the world's first ironclad fighting ship. She was, moreover, superior in her speed and offensive power to her French rival, and with her sister ship *Black Prince* was successful in recovering for Britain the status and statistical superiority she had briefly surrendered.

By the 1860s the ironclad age had arrived, and the first stage in the revolution in all branches of naval architecture was complete. It is true that vast developments lay ahead in the field of ordnance, that suspicion of iron and shortage of iron caused the two great sea powers to continue building armoured wood-hulled fighting ships for several more years, that the marine engine had scarcely completed its first stage of maturity, that the science of armour plate design and manufacture was still in its infancy, that masts and sails were to add unnecessary weight, obstruct the decks and guns and contribute only a sad reminder of the days of grace. In spite of all this, the ironclad, in all its hideous, fascinating wonder, was the new monarch of the seas. The minor powers soon followed. Spain built the 6,200-ton ironclad *Tetuan*, Russia the 3,300-ton *Pervenetz*, and Italy asked France to build two 2,700-ton armoured ships for her navy.

In America, a minor episode in the Civil War registered in laughable inconclusiveness that a new age of naval fighting had arrived. The need to protect fighting ships against shellfire was well appreciated by both North and South; the desperate needs of war accelerated the pace of development in the early 1860s. The first ironclad battle in history occurred in Hampton Roads in March 1862; the fact that both combatants were freaks and incapable of serious ocean sailing does not deprive the *Monitor* and *Virginia* (ex-*Merrimack*) of their privileged place in history. The *Merrimack* was one of the formidable 1854 group of American wooden frigates, a 3,200-ton vessel armed originally with forty guns varying in calibre from 8 to 10 inches. During the war she was burnt out to the lower deck and sunk in Norfolk Navy Yard. Ingenuity and desperation raised her, her engines were somehow restored, and on to her was slapped an iron citadel with sloping sides. Her freeboard was so minimal that nothing else really showed, except a squat funnel and the ports for her 7-inch rifles and 9-inch and 6-inch smooth-bore guns. Her designers claimed her to be invulnerable, and so she proved herself.

There was nothing in the world like the *Monitor*. She was the brainchild of that fiery genius John Ericsson, and was based on plans for an invulnerable fighting ship he had presented unsuccessfully to Napoleon III after the Battle of Sinope had shown what shells could do. She consisted of an armour-plated hull 124 feet long, absolutely flat and

(Left) the Battle of Hampton Roads, lithograph by Currier and Ives. The *Monitor*, with two guns in a rotating tower, fought the *Virginia*, with ten guns, in the first fight between ironclad warships, 1862. The fight lasted into the next day, but was inconclusive. (Right) the Russian coastal defence ship, *Novgorod*, 1873; she had two 11-inch guns

with a freeboard of less than 3 feet. Her flush deck was broken amidships by an armoured rotating gun tower housing two 11-inch guns, a tiny steering house forward, two ventilators and two squat funnels. All except the gun tower were removed when cleared for action. She, too, was utterly invulnerable.

The *Monitor* nearly sank on her way from New York to Hampton Roads to put a stop to the depredations of the *Virginia*. Pratt describes her journey thus: 'They hit a storm; the turret base leaked, waves washed through the hawsepipes, the blowers almost drowned in ingested sea water, and noxious gases filled the hull, while horrible shrieks and groans came from the anchor well. . . .'[4] When at last these two bizarre vessels, both of them archetypal prototypes of the ugly age of the ironclad they heralded, finally confronted one another, what could they do but harmlessly throw shot and shell, until the *Monitor*'s ammunition was exhausted and the *Virginia*'s gunnery officer, asked why he was no longer firing, could only reply, 'I can do as much damage by snapping my fingers every three minutes.'

What this comic combat seemed to indicate was that the gun as a ship-destroyer had again utterly failed, after all – after some three centuries, and after the discovery at last of a new form of explosive projectile which had been hailed as the scourge of the fighting ship. This ironclad escapade proved nothing of the kind. All that it did was to mark the opening of one of the most prolonged and certainly the most expensive theoretical combats in the history of warfare, the battle between the ship-destroying gun and the ship-protecting plate of armour. It was to be a campaign of chemistry, metallurgy and ballistics fought out mainly in the laboratories of the scientists and only rarely and magnificently and tragically in real battle. The *Monitor* and *Virginia* affair aptly prefaced its folly and futility.

# 4. THE AGE OF THE IRONCLAD

The *Warrior*, 1861. With the *Warrior*
frigates became superior to the
huge, old-fashioned two-deckers.
She is still afloat in Pembroke Dock,
Wales, as an oiler

This was an unsightly period in the life of the fighting ship. The naval architect had been presented in the mid-1800s with such a sudden glut of innovations – new guns and shells, new machinery, new constructional materials, new means of defence – that he did not quite know what to do with them. Nor did it help that there were such few opportunities for trying them out. Because there was almost no practical fighting experience to draw on, for almost fifty years these architects were working in the darkness of theory. The results of the theorizing which emerged from the shipyards in Europe and America were therefore speculative, and in appearance often strange, sometimes downright bizarre, and by contrast with the ships of the age of sail, always inelegant. Great designers like Edward Reed and Nathaniel Barnaby in Britain, Benedetto Brin in Italy, Dupuy de Lôme and Emile Bertin in France, worked and died without seeing the qualities of one of their ships tested in battle. The results of the few engagements were seized upon and minutely examined, but they were often misleading and the knowledge derived was misread. At the Battle of Lissa in 1866, for example, the Austrian flagship *Ferdinand Max* rammed full amidships the Italian *Re d'Italia* at $11\frac{1}{2}$ knots, sinking her instantly. In this new age of technology, with its mighty breech-loading shell guns and armour plate, the ram had apparently proved itself as effective a ship-destroyer as it had been 2,000 years earlier. Overnight the ram became again highly fashionable. The construction of 'ironclad rams', the most weird form of fighting ship of all time, which had been actively used during the American Civil War, was everywhere stimulated. The

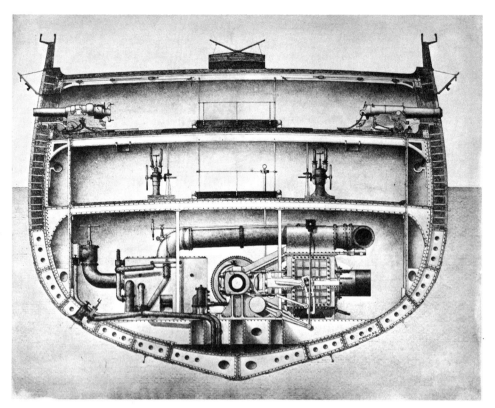

ram bow was retained in the design of ironclads for many decades and
for long after the effectiveness of long-range artillery had been proved
in practice – and even after it had sunk a Russian fleet at Tsushima in
1905.

A transverse section of the *Warrio*

Clowes has written of the naval designers' dilemma during this
period of rapid development: 'Very heavy guns were called for by
some; very thick armour was considered indispensable by others; and
while one party asked for a complete waterline belt, another party
urged the naval architects to devote even more attention to the protection of the armament than to the protection of the life of the ship.
Yet other conflicting and almost irreconcilable claims were put
forward on behalf of high speed, of great coal-capacity, of large sail-
power, of lofty freeboard, of seaworthiness and steadiness of gun-
platform, and of small size, shallow draught, and comparative invisi-
bility to an enemy's gunners. For nearly twenty years these and other
problems troubled the minds of naval architects all the world over.'[5]
The ironclad battleship was increased in size, reduced, and increased
again. The size of the gun followed the same pattern, emerged from its
turret into an open armoured barbette, and with the revival of breech-
loading, partly disappeared inside again; while the variations in its
numbers and disposition were almost infinite. Sails were reduced in
size and number, were dispensed with, had a brief revival, and finally

disappeared altogether in the battleships of the 1880s, to the undying distress and regret of those who had been brought up with them. The advent of the torpedo coincided approximately in time with the departure of sail, and was equally influential in shaping the appearance and development of the fighting ship. The coincidence was an especially convenient one because it was a puzzle and an anxiety to know what to do with sailors who could no longer be sent aloft for exercise and to pass the time. But the torpedo brought with it the need to protect big ships at anchor with enormous steel nets like a crinoline, weighing hundreds of tons, and which required to be swung out and in again. This was as strenuous and complicated a business as reefing a topsail in a gale.

The birth of the ironclad was a sudden affair, its evolution to its culminating point of maturity in the 1940s mainly leisurely and spasmodic. Two periods of acute naval rivalry, between France and

*he Minotaur, completed in 1868, as single screw with exceptionally eavy armour and armament and speed of 14 knots*

Britain in the 1860s, and Germany and Britain in the early 1900s, provided the two great impulses forward with the *Gloire* and *Warrior*, and then the *Dreadnought* and *Nassau* of 1906 and 1909. Napoleon III, like Kaiser Wilhelm II forty years later, thought that Britain had no business to be distressed about foreign naval rearmament, which was purely a domestic affair: France had as much right as Britain to protect her interests. On both occasions, Britain's view was that for a great Continental land power to attempt to rival the sea power of Britain – itself possessing a tiny army and wholly dependent for its security on its navy – was a provocative act demanding counter measures. Thus, when the French programme of 1860 called for thirty ironclads, the British replied by doubling their own programme. For The next ten years development in big ship design did not advance much beyond the standards set by the *Gloire* and *Warrior*, and both programmes fell far short of expectation because of a shortage of either iron or money or both. A number of the battleships delivered to both navies were wooden hulled or were cut-down two-deckers partly iron-sheathed and armed with shell guns. Development of the gun, however, went on apace. Since the *Monitor-Virginia* abortive contest, the gunsmiths everywhere had been needled into finding a formula for a gun that could again sink ships. The dominance of armour plate was short-lived. With the acceptance of rifling in all heavy ordnance, with the discovery of new means of building up the structure of guns, the advent of new and more powerful charges, and new forms of much more efficient shells, above all by the increase in its sheer size and weight, the gun began again to take command of the situation. In America the giant Dahlgrens were enormously destructive at short range. In Britain, the competition between the Royal Gun Factory at Woolwich and those two monarchs of ordnance, Whitworth and Armstrong, resulted in giant strides forward during the decade. Armstrong's breech-loaders appeared for a short time to be a real breakthrough, but they blew up too often and were very quickly discarded. The weight of the projectile rose from 50 to 100 pounds and more. Armstrong produced an experimental gun that threw a 600-pound projectile; and the calibre rose to 10 and 12 inches. For the first time since the 1500s effective gun range began to increase, to 2,000 yards and then much farther.

Obviously no battleship could carry as many 68- and 100-pounder shell guns, whether smooth bore or rifled, as Nelson's ships-of-the-line had mounted smaller cannon. The day of the hundred-gun ship was finished, until its revival in the 1930s and 1940s with the need for multitudinous quick-firing small-calibre weapons to fight off the aircraft.

The *Warrior*, 1861, lithograph by
[Du]tton. She was the first English
[iro]n warship

The *Gloire*, 1859, by Le Breton. She
[wa]s the first French iron ship, but
[in] fact her armour was hung over
[th]e wooden hull

The *Conqueror*, 1883, the new steel,
[ar]mour-plated turret ship

The *Glatton*, 1872, the first British
[sin]gle-turret ship. Her low free-
[bo]ard made her a curiosity

What the new big guns of the 1860s demanded was a new approach to their siting and their protection. It certainly appeared to be wasteful to place these guns on each broadside, when their numbers could be halved without reducing the offensive power of the ship by siting them on the centre line in order to be able to fire on either broadside. Ericsson's turret had worked admirably – no one could dispute that. But the *Monitor* had been a monitor – a vessel for fighting in river estuaries or close inshore, not a sea-going battleship. The origins of the idea of placing a gun in a revolving cupola to fire on either broadside, like all the inventions of the 1800s, is obscure and controversial. But the two men chiefly responsible for its acceptance were Ericsson himself in America, and Captain Cowper Coles of the British Navy. Three years before the *Monitor* fought the *Virginia*, Coles had proposed a 9,200-ton cupola ship carrying twenty heavy guns in ten rotating turrets. All sorts of objections were put forward against this design, the most powerful and the most reasonable being that the masts and shrouds (for there was no question of doing without sails) must severely restrict the arc of fire of the guns. Coles persisted in his crusade and acquired the support of the press and many people of influence. One of these was Prince Albert, the Prince Consort, who lent his name to the first British sea-going iron turret ship which the Board of the Admiralty were finally persuaded to authorize in 1862 – a coast defence ship of a mere 3,800 tons armed with four 9-inch guns and with simple gaff sails that hardly interfered with the arc of fire of the guns. Like the work of many pioneers, the *Prince Albert* was so far ahead of her time that her precursory qualities were not fully appreciated, even by her builders. It was, as Parkes has written, 'the perfect battleship in miniature', and the basic layout of her design – four centre-line turrets, two masts, raised superstructure forward of the funnel and full armour protection – could be discerned in the final phase of the battleship's life some eighty years later.

Numerous fighting ships armed with broadside guns in ports continued to be built by all the naval powers throughout the 1860s, but the turret gained increasing favour for the battleship. It was not only a new sense of enlightenment that caused this. These were good years for the innovator. Fear, and the pressure of competition between Britain and France, accelerated the acceptance of *matériel* novelties. The new big guns of the mid-1860s with their great high explosive shells meant not only that they had perforce to be fewer in number, but that they must be disposed so that they could be used to the maximum effect, and that they must be better protected.

Two battleships, one French and one British, serve to exemplify two

phases of transitional development of the ironclad battleship in the 1860s, which had been shadowed by the little *Prince Albert*, laid down in 1862. The 7,000-ton *L'Océan* of 1868 mounted its main armament of four 10½-inch guns in a central armoured redoubt in open armoured barbettes. By this disposition, it was no longer necessary to spread the thickest armour plate now demanded by the big new shell guns over the whole length of the ship; instead *L'Océan* was effectively protected over her vitals – her biggest guns, her engines, her magazine and shellrooms – and with a reduced thickness of plate along the water-line: concentrate the armament, concentrate the armour. The British replied in 1869 by laying down an ironclad which marked almost as important a stage of development of the modern fighting ship as the *Gloire* and the later *Dreadnought*. The *Devastation* represented the final justification of the work of Cowper Coles, whose turret ship *Captain*, fully rigged and highly unstable as a result, capsized in a gale, drowning nearly all on board including the brilliant Coles. The 9,300-ton *Devastation* cut free from the heavy, encumbering and now wholly superfluous masts and yards. The sail, it seemed, was at last finished, the 'mastless' battleship arrived. In appearance she was like a giant monitor with a very low freeboard for the full 285 feet of her length. Her central battery consisted of four enormous 35-ton guns in two turrets – and nothing else – divided by the upperworks and bridges and two funnels. She was protected from end to end with armour plate never less than 8 inches thick, backed by 17 inches of teak, and increasing to a foot over her vitals and 14 inches on her turret faces. Her armour weighed more than 2,500 tons, her full capacity of coal weighed 1,600 tons. Parkes quotes a contemporary writer's summary of this most formidable vessel – the exemplar of the Victorian iron-clad – as 'an impregnable piece of Vauban fortification with bastions mounted upon a fighting coal mine'.

The cult of gigantism was seized upon by all nations aspiring to a first line battle fleet, and lasted for some twenty years. During this period there was no fleet engagement anywhere from which useful experience could be drawn, while at the same time still bigger and more devastating guns demanded thicker and more efficient protec-tive plate. The result at first was inevitable. The battleship became a crude floating steel citadel, in which everything was sacrificed to functionalism and ferocity of demeanour. The Italians took things forward a further stage with the 10,000-ton, *Duilio* and *Dandolo*, the brain children of the architect Benedetto Brin, whose temperament was well matched to the age of the massive ironclad. These two freaks contrived to combine a speed of 15 knots (the Italians have always

*he Royal Albert*, screw steamer, *ing* launched at Woolwich in *54*. She was one of the last three-ckers

231

liked fast ships) with four 15-inch 100-ton guns in two turrets arranged *en echelon* amidships between the two funnels and separated only by a single pole mast. Steel armour was used for the first time, and it varied in thickness from 17 to 21½ inches, making the vitals of the ships absolutely invulnerable to the largest shells then in use. But because of its armour weight, which was some 25 per cent of total displacement, the rest of the ship had to rely for survival on watertight bulkheads and a thinly-protected deck. These were the first modern battleships to conform to the 'all-or-nothing' principle of protection, revived by the Americans in 1912 (see below, page 273), and based on the contention that a well-built properly buoyant ship could survive to fight another day, however grievously damaged it might be, if its machinery and magazines are properly protected. E. J. Reed's condition for the acceptance of the 'all-or-nothing' armoured citadel ironclad type was that 'the proportion which the armoured citadel bears to the unarmoured ends must always be such as to enable the ship to keep afloat all the time that the armour itself holds out against the attacks of the enemy: so that injuries to the unarmoured ends, however great or multiplied, shall not alone suffice to destroy the ship'.[6]

The British Chief Constructor believed that the Italian monsters did not conform to this condition, and this spurred the eager Brin on to further excesses. His *Italia* and *Lepanto* of 1877–8 were the ultimate manifestation of his big-gun-in-an-invulnerable-citadel theory. This time he placed his four 103-ton guns on turntables in open barbettes, disposed *en echelon* as in the *Dandolo*, covering the barbettes and ammunition hoists with compound (steel-faced iron) armour more than a foot and a half thick. Except for a 3-inch curved protective deck, and armour gratings over the boiler hatches, the ships relied entirely on an ingenious system of indirect protection in the form of multiple watertight bulkheads, cork-filled cells backed by coal, and a highly elaborate system to pump out water in the event of a hit below the waterline. With their six funnels adding the final touch of the bizarre, and their 16,000 horsepower giving them a speed of almost 18 knots, and their fearsome armament of big guns supported by eighteen 6-inch weapons behind shields, the *Italia* and *Lepanto* were the most provocative and discussed ships of their day.

In this race of the giants the French entered *L'Amiral Duperré* protected by 17½-inch armour, *L'Amiral Baudin* and the *Formidable*, Britain the *Inflexible* completed in 1881 and carrying four 16-inch 80-ton guns, disposed in imitation of the Italians *en echelon* amidships, and protected by the thickest armour plate of all time – but as a last sop to the old brigade, with auxiliary sails again: she was brig-rigged. The

The *Devastation*, 1873, was the first
sea-going 'mastless' turret ship. She
had hydraulic loading gear. Here
she is seen passing the old three-
decker training ship, the *Duke of
Wellington*

The *Inflexible*, 1881, had anti-roll-
ing tanks, electric light, two 60-foot
torpedo boats and new torpedo
equipment, very thick armour, the
heaviest guns in the service, and a
minimal brig-rig to exercise the
sailors. She was under the command of Captain 'Jacky' Fisher in
the attack on the Alexandrian forts
in 1882

The *Royal Sovereign*, 1890, was the
first class to exceed 12,000 tons

The *Majestic*, 1895, was the most
numerous class ever built

maximum thickness of armour on the British *Inflexible* was 24 inches. This folly had reached the limit. Science stepped in to correct the imbalance it had initiated with the invulnerable *Monitor* twenty years earlier, and the giant gun it had brought into being. The metallurgists redoubled their efforts, and over the succeeding two decades Harvey in America, Krupp in Germany, Armstrong in Britain, Creusot in France, busied themselves with nickel and carbon and manganese in their steel, producing ever more effective rolled plates which offered much greater resistance to penetration with much reduced thickness and weight.

The gunsmiths struggled against these new steels, and here too progress led to refinement and reduction in sheer size. The 12-inch muzzle-loaders in the British *Monarch* of 1869 could fire a 600-pound shell 7,000 yards twice a minute, while the French 27-cm. (10½-inch) breech-loader of the same date had a range for its 475-pound projectile only slightly less. The 16-inch muzzle-loaders of the *Inflexible* threw a 1,680-pound projectile which could pierce 23 inches of iron armour at 1,000 yards. Fifteen years later the same shell would have made little impression on American Harveyized steel half this thickness. In the 1880s the search was for higher muzzle velocity which gave better penetration at the same range. A slow-burning propellant was the answer, and because this demanded a much longer barrel, with all its attendant inconveniences when reloading, the British at last came back to the breech-loader, which had been such an expensive *débâcle* twenty years earlier.

All at once, in the 1890s, the scientists began to reshape the fighting ship again. Adolescence had been characteristically awkward. Maturity produced a trimness and balance in line that had been lost for forty years. The metallurgists were chiefly responsible. They even changed the name: 'ironclad' went out of the vocabulary, and 'battleship' (a term which had never quite disappeared) took its place. The French remained loyal longest to the hideous mid-century tradition. Elsewhere, an artist (if still only a primitive) walked hand in hand with the scientist. The Americans laid down their *Indiana* class in 1891, with the elegant symmetry provided by two tall funnels, two masts and two 13-inch gun turrets, one fore and one aft. The British followed with the nine fine battleships of the *Majestic* class with a similar silhouette but funnels tight together side by side; the Germans with their strong and splendid *Kaisers*, the noblest if not the most powerful battleships of their day; the Italians at the end of the decade with a 13,000-tonner carrying the name of the great *Benedetto Brin*, himself the creator of the ugliest fighting ships of all time.

# 5. THE TORPEDO-CARRIER

By the 1880s the accepted omnipotence of the ironclad battleship was over. At the very height of the theoretical contest between guns and armour, the scientists stepped in with a new weapon which in the course of time was to alter entirely the nature of warfare at sea – all calculations, all strategical and tactical tenets, all accepted moral standards. The most destructive weapon of sea warfare in the great maritime struggles of the present century was the unmanned fighting ship, the crewless explosive ram – the self-propelled torpedo.

Naval history since the earliest days has been full of anecdotes about primitive efforts to destroy an enemy fighting ship below the water-line. The ram was the only really effective weapon for accomplishing this, although it sometimes happened in the heat of close Mediterranean galley actions that divers might go over the side to drill holes below the water line of an enemy. With the arrival of gunpowder methods were devised of placing charges against an enemy's hull but there is no record of much success in this direction until the 1700s, and then only on the most modest scale. In the American War of Independence a Captain David Bushnell introduced an underwater boat for 'the purpose of conveying magazines to the bottom of hostile ships and there exploding them'. Drifting buoyant mines, their charge actuated by a clockwork motor, were also used on occasion and to the outrage of their intended victims – for the underwater weapon, in whatever guise, had always been considered as underhand.

Two better known inventors also took a small part in developing further the idea of blowing up fighting ships from underneath with the

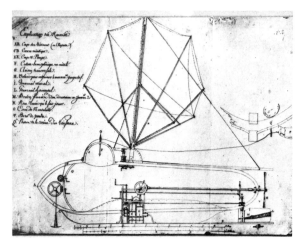
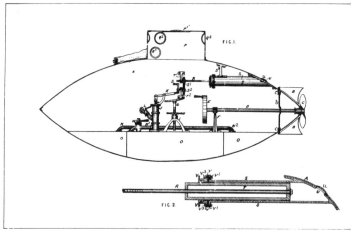

minimum risk and from a safe distance. Robert Fulton offered his scientific services to both Britain and France during the Napoleonic wars. For France he devised a machine 'to impart two carcasses of gunpowder a progressive motion underwater, to a certain point, and there to explode them'. It was tried against the British fleet in the Channel, but without success, so Fulton went over to the enemy and demonstrated the effectiveness of his weapon by blowing up an old brig. Even this was not good enough for the Royal Navy, and Fulton returned in a disgruntled frame of mind to the United States.

Over the next half century a number of experiments were made – most successfully by Samuel Colt the great American gun exponent – with various forms of drifting or towed mines actuated by clockwork or the striking of an exposed bolt against a ship's hull. In the American Civil War the spar torpedo was much favoured for a time, proved effective on a number of occasions, and was taken up by European navies. This weapon was an explosive charge attached to the end of a spar projecting from the bows of a small vessel, and demanded of its operator an exceptional degree of courage. In a naval manual's instruction on the operation of the spar torpedo, the writer noted that its 'guiding principle is that its construction and design render it necessary that wherever the torpedo goes the operator must go too'.[7]

Self-propulsion for the explosive charge was the obvious answer. The locomotive torpedo began its life a little over a hundred years ago. At first it was not intended to be submerged but to operate on the surface, driven by steam or clockwork, and steered by ropes and guide lines after the manner of the Brennan torpedo. A Captain Lupuis of the Austrian Navy was the inventor, but he did not make much progress before he called in a British engineer, Robert Whitehead. Whitehead worked at an engine plant in Fiume, where the machinery that powered the victorious flagship at Lissa was manufactured. When he

Fulton's submarine *Nautilus*, 1800 and (right) the Rev. Garrett's specification for a submarine, submitted to the Patent Office in 1878. Opposite are section plans and elevations. Early submarines kept near the surface at all times

ELEVATION

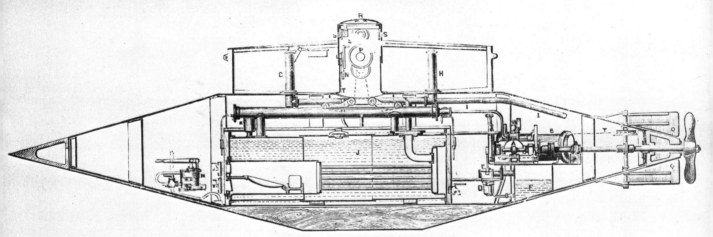

LONGITUDINAL SECTION

SCALE OF FEET

0 1 2 3 4 5 10

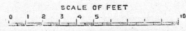

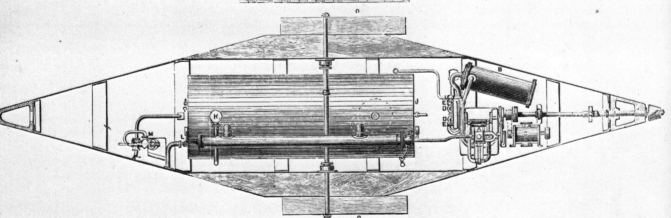

SECTIONAL PLAN

CROSS SECTION IN FRONT OF BOILER

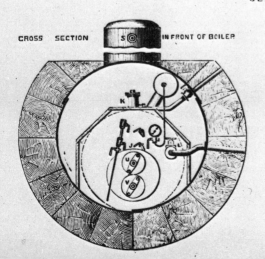

CROSS SECTION THROUGH ENGINE ROOM

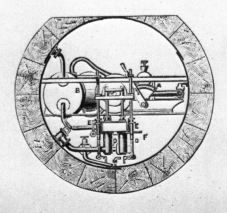

saw Lupuis's weapon he shook his head, said it would not work, and returned to his drawing board to devise a torpedo of his own. His prototype was tested in 1867. It was powered by compressed air, ran at 6 knots *under* the water at a (more or less) uniform depth for 300 yards, and carried an 18-pound charge in the nose. It was an erratic, unreliable weapon, but inevitably as its fearful potential was comprehended, rapid improvements followed. The British Navy, in an uncharacteristic moment of enthusiasm for the novel, bought the manufacturing rights for £15,000, and work on further improvement began at Woolwich. Speed rose to 20 knots and more, the range to 400 yards, and the destructive power of the charge multiplied many times over. Other countries began to buy manufacturing rights, and soon everybody was making torpedoes.

For the first ten years or so of its life, the torpedo was regarded as no more than a modest hazard to warships lying at anchor. Besides the protective steel net, quick-firing light guns were installed on armoured ships for destroying the torpedo's carrier on its approach. The first small influence of the new weapon was being felt by the battle fleet, but the threat remained a modest one until the torpedo acquired a suitable carrier. At first torpedoes were launched from ships' boats or launches, but by 1877 when the British Admiralty bought its first torpedo boat, the *Lightning*, a method had been devised of launching the torpedo from a tube on the deck. Eleven more boats of a type similar to the *Lightning* were ordered the following year. There was a tube right up in the bows and dropping gear abaft the tiny funnel. Speed was 20 knots, displacement a mere 32 tons.

Other naval powers followed the British lead, and among the most enthusiastic were the French, who began building a swarm of little torpedo boats with a speed of 23 knots, carrying a tube in the bows, a second on a turntable aft, and a pair of small guns. France possessed over 200 torpedo boats by 1892, and Russia, Germany and Italy each had over a hundred. All the smaller navies enthusiastically built or bought torpedo boats too, for in the torpedo they recognized the means of balancing up the numerical superiority of an enemy: for, above all, the torpedo offered, for the first time in the history of sea warfare, the intoxicating prospect of destroying an enemy fleet at negligible *matériel* and human cost. The effect of this on the minds of naval commanders, and their chiefs who increasingly controlled their actions from on shore, was profound and enduring. Such was the appalling and ever-growing weight of responsibility bearing down on fleet commanders that the anxiety they felt for the *preservation* of their valuable armoured fleet infected ships' commanders and all ranks. The boldness and aggression so splendidly evidenced in the Napoleonic wars, the War of 1812, the Dutch wars, and back in history to the galley actions of the Mediterranean, greatly diminished. The introduction of the torpedo was one of the chief causes of the cult of preservation rather than destruction in naval warfare from 1880 and right through the First World War.

By the 1890s the frightening potential of this new underwater threat was fully understood, and countermeasures were energetically undertaken. These were of an offensive and defensive nature. First, the new big armoured ships were built with more substantial underwater protection, with double bottoms, armoured bulkheads and more elaborate compartmentation. Then, as it became clear that the fleet might now be attacked at sea and not only at anchor, much larger torpedo boats were designed which could sail with the fleet, attack the enemy with torpedoes, and defend the fleet from similar attack with their own guns. These were at first called torpedo catchers, then torpedo boat destroyers. The first were built in Britain in 1893, displaced around 280 tons, carried three torpedo tubes, and a 12-pounder and three 6-pounder guns. Speed was up to 28 knots, and it was calculated that they could catch any torpedo boat afloat within three hours of sighting.

High speed and the ability to inflict greater damage with a single blow than the largest gun were the unique qualities of the torpedo boat and 'destroyer'. Both increased rapidly during the last years of the century. In 1895 the French boat *Forban* was reported to have maintained 31 knots for an hour, and higher claims were made for a German destroyer. These speeds were accomplished by reciprocating engines. With the coming of the turbine, speeds rose still higher, and the vibration and noise aboard the little boats (which remained wet and cramped) became less intolerable. The turbine-powered *Viper* managed over 37 knots in 1899, and, even more impressive, held over 34 knots for three hours.

By the first years of the new century the rôles of the torpedo boat and the destroyer were clearly defined. They were both weapons of attrition, the smaller for inshore and harbour work (they were sometimes carried on board battleships), the bigger destroyer for sailing with the fleet at sea, defending it and seeking by swift attack in numbers to divert attention and damage the enemy line by launching torpedoes at close range, escaping as quickly as they had come. The size and number of guns mounted by armoured ships for warding off attacks by these new torpedo carriers increased year by year. The *King Edward VII* class of British battleship, laid down in the first years of the new century, carried fourteen 12-pounders, the same number of

3-pounders, and a pair of Maxim guns to fight off the torpedo menace, besides ten 6-inch guns of the secondary armament, which would certainly be used against massed torpedo boat or destroyer attack.

The Whitehead torpedo was first used in large-scale combat during the Russo-Japanese war of 1904–5. Hostilities were opened – as at Pearl Harbor thirty-seven years later – by a surprise Japanese attack on the Russian fleet in Port Arthur. A handful of torpedo boats, in a few minutes of frenzied action in darkness, crippled two of Russia's best battleships and a cruiser, and entirely altered the balance of naval power in the Far East. Later in the war the loss by Japan of two of her six modern battleships in one afternoon by Russian mines suggested to some thinkers that the underwater weapon was to be the future arbiter of war at sea. But these lessons were soon forgotten in the crash of heavy artillery at the Battle of Tsushima – a classic gun duel in which the torpedo took no significant part – which provided a comforting, reassuring sound for those nursing doubts about the future of the big gun and its noble platform. General confidence in the battleship's massive weapons and her menacing profile was undimmed. She might no longer be the splendid sovereign of the seas she had been half a century earlier. Yet in 1905 her greatest days still lay ahead.

The *Hotspur*, 1887, with her anti-torpedo nets

By the outbreak of the First World War, the torpedo boat had been replaced entirely by the destroyer for fleet use. Size, armament and speed had all greatly increased. Above all, the torpedoes themselves possessed a vastly increased power, speed and range. With its ability to destroy a 25,000-ton battleship at a range of 7,000 yards, it was little wonder that the German and British commanders revised their fleet tactics in the event of a torpedo attack: the battle fleet was to turn away, to evade, and in the uncertain visibility of the North Sea, or in the artificially created smokescreen, probably to lose sight of the enemy – as happened at the Battle of Jutland.

These are some representative types of destroyers of this period:

Britain
*Matchless* 1,154 tons. 271 feet overall. Four 21-inch torpedo tubes. 3 × 4-inch guns, 2 × 1-pounder anti-aircraft guns. Speed: 33 knots.

United States
*Aylwin* 1,036 tons. 305 feet overall. Eight 18-inch torpedo tubes. 4 × 4-inch guns. Speed: 30 knots.

France
*Téméraire* 950 tons. 285 feet overall. Four 18-inch torpedo tubes. 4 × 4-inch guns. Speed: 32 knots.

The *Hornet*, 1893, Admiral Fisher's first 'destroyer', was the fastest vessel in the world at her trials, with 28 knots

Above: an Italian 'human torpedo' craft, 1941, and (below) a British version, 1942, with the warhead removed

Model of the *Hoche*, 1880, with anti-torpedo nets

Germany

*S.18* 570 tons. 235 feet overall. Four 19.7-inch torpedo tubes. 2 × 4.1-inch, 1 × 3.4-inch gun. Speed: 33 knots.

The torpedo-carrying destroyer proved its worth during the First World War, but less in the function for which it had been designed than as a makeshift protector of the merchantman against the depredations of the most feared and most effective torpedo carrier of them all, the submarine. The great battle fleets of Germany and Britain, and later of America, could not venture to sea unaccompanied by their flotillas for defence against the destroyers and submarines of the enemy and for attack against his big ships. As the years went by, with only one major and inconclusive fleet engagement, and as the menace of the submarine against the commerce of the Allies grew more dangerous, the British Grand Fleet's destroyers were increasingly drawn from their inactive rôle of protecting a fleet that rarely went to sea, to convoying merchantmen and hunting their hidden attackers. The Germans switched the crews, and the guns too, from their destroyers to their growing fleet of submarines.

The underwater torpedo-carrier, which was to plague the surface fighting ships and destroy merchantmen in millions of tons through two World Wars, had an early history closely similar to that of the torpedo boat. Bushnell, Colt and Fulton all experimented with submersibles in the late 1700s and early 1800s. A number of more or less effective submersibles and semi-submersibles were built later in the century, the best known being the 'Davids' of the American Civil War, which were really small launches carrying a spar torpedo and capable of being trimmed so that only funnel and hatches were above water. A Spaniard called Monturiol built a very advanced submarine boat in 1862, with double hull containing ballast tanks which could be pumped out with compressed air, and steam propulsion, the air being purified by an oxygen-making plant. Then there was the French *Plongeur* of the same period. An Irish-born American, John P. Holland, the French designer, Max Laubeuf, and a brilliant Swede, Torsten Nordenfelt, working independently in their own countries, were jointly instrumental in bringing the submarine from its primitive and highly dangerous experimental form to maturity in the last two decades of the century. Laubeuf placed the ballast tanks outside the pressure hull, and others followed this lead.

Just as the aircraft – also to become such an effective torpedo-carrier – failed to rise safely from the ground until a suitable source of power had been found, so the submarine could sink safely beneath

The USS *Picuda*, submarine

Polaris submarine surfacing

the waves only when a suitable means of propulsion had been devised. For the submarine on the surface the diesel engine with its oil fuel instead of petroleum and explosion by compression instead of ignition was a much safer proposition than the internal combustion engine, which powered the early practical submarines when not submerged. Both these engines were complemented by electric power for submerged use.

In the years before the First World War the range, size and destructive power of the submarine grew with that of the destroyer and the torpedo itself. At first American and French craft were the most advanced. The British and Germans, who were expending such wealth and effort on their surface fleets, were reluctant to accept this new and potentially dangerous threat to their treasured battleships. The mind recoiled from such a sinister and barbarous weapon carrier, as it once had from the explosive shell, while ever-greater and more fearful shell-firing guns were warmly welcomed in the fleet. The eminent British admiral, Sir A. K. Wilson, described the submarine as 'underhand, unfair, and damned un-English', and his contemporary, Lord Charles Beresford, dismissed the submarine as a useless

245

weapon because 'it is always in a fog'. Submariners were regarded with disdain as members of an oil-stained force of outlaws – raffish and socially unacceptable. The demonstrations of the submarine's effectiveness at 'sinking' battleships on manoeuvres were treated unjustly. 'You be damned!' retorted one British admiral to a submarine commander who had three times 'torpedoed' his flagship.

It took the driving force of the radical and powerful Admiral Sir John Fisher to introduce the submarine, built under licence from the Holland company in America, into the British Navy. The German Navy, which in a few years was to come so near to annihilating with its submarines Britain's merchant fleet, was even slower off the mark. On the outbreak of war neither of these two great combatant naval nations possessed much faith in the power of the submarine except as a weapon for coastal defence and offence. It was left to the despised submariners themselves to prove the potential of their craft. By 1915 the submarine had shown itself to be a seaworthy and fearfully destructive new fighting ship far from its home base. Within two years it was the most feared weapon at sea. While the British Grand Fleet remained in Scapa Flow as the pivot of British sea power, controlling by its distant presence the surface of the northern seas, and exercising an almost complete blockade of Germany, German submarines in increasing numbers severely handicapped the Allies' war effort and brought Britain close to starvation and defeat.

Between the wars the pace of submarine development decelerated, although by 1939 it was a more potent weapon than ever, and defences against its hidden power had still not caught up. At one end of the scale were giants, bigger and more powerful than anything their most ardent champions could have envisaged in 1914. During the First World War the British had built a sort of battleship-submarine, armed with a 12-inch gun and an anti-aircraft gun. A few years later a cruiser-submarine armed with four 5.2-inch guns was launched. The French built the famous *Surcouf* with two 8-inch guns and capable of carrying an aircraft. At the other end of the scale, all the leading powers experimented with miniature submarines, manned by a crew of one or two. These consisted in some cases of little more than one torpedo with the pilot filling the place normally occupied by the explosive charge, and a second or third real torpedo secured below. These were called 'chariots'. The Italians built brilliant and very effective submarines carrying limpet mines; the Japanese, characteristically, built suicide submarines, which were simply large torpedoes on which the pilot rode to his target and death. The Japanese were also very clever with their torpedoes, the 'Long Lance' oxygen-

The *Rorqual*, conventional submarine, and (bottom) the USS *Thomas Jefferson* SSBN 618 under way at sea

powered model proving its unique speed, accuracy and destructive power during the early period of the Pacific War.

German submarine development was similarly swift and efficient before and during the Second World War. The 'snorkel' allowed the much more efficient diesel engine to be used under water, and brought the submarine half way towards being a true submarine craft rather than a submersible – this conversion being completed with the introduction of nuclear power. Present-day American, British and Russian nuclear-powered submarines can remain submerged almost indefinitely and release their fearful new weapons without surfacing.

New classes of vessels, some of them bearing old names, appeared just before and during the Second World War. Their chief function was to escort merchantmen convoys and protect them against submarine and air attack. Frigates, sloops, corvettes and destroyer escorts were built in great numbers. They were of modest displacement – from around 1,000 to 2,500 tons – and were equipped with submarine-hunting and destroying devices which have progressively become more elaborate and effective. Today new classes of small fighting ships – such as Aircraft Detection Frigates and Guided Missile Armed Destroyers – carry sophisticated radar apparatus which can locate aircraft and missiles at great range, and numerous anti-aircraft rocket and missile devices and guns. Endurance and good sea-going qualities are considered of greater importance than speed. The primary enemies of all these men-of-war are still the new aerial and submerged weapons, today more elaborate and fearful than ever, which brought about the demise of the armoured gun platform – the battleship and battle cruiser – in the 1940s.

A mine laid by a German merchantman converted for the purpose caused the first British Dreadnought loss in the First World War. Minelaying, and the counter-activity of minesweeping, has called for specialized skills and special ships ever since the Russo-Japanese war of 1904–5 proved the destructive power of the buoyant mine. The great numbers of minelayers and minesweepers which operated in the First World War were mainly converted warships or merchantmen. Fishing trawlers made excellent sweepers, and were in constant operation, often manned by their civilian crews, right through the war. Between the wars special minelaying cruisers modestly armed but possessing high speed, and capable of carrying several hundred mines, were built by many of the great naval powers. The French *Pluton* of 4,800 tons, built in 1929 and typical of its type, was armed with four 5.5-inch and numerous anti-aircraft guns, and could steam at 30 knots.

U-boat surrenders to a Hudson craft', 1941, by Cundall

# 6. THE CRUISER

With the demise of the mixed steam-and-sail screw frigates of the 1860s and 1870s, there emerged a new class of fighting ship intended to fill the many rôles of the old frigate of the Napoleonic wars. Good speed, good endurance, a moderate armament and armour protection to resist the shells of its own kind were all required. As its duties widened, as new weapons and new tactics added greater complexity to sea warfare, the *genus* multiplied in types and numbers. In the last two decades of the 1800s, the cruiser family proliferated into armoured, semi-armoured, belted, protected (first and second class), light cruisers, and scouts. These distinctions were sometimes narrow ones, and even overlapped and were duplicated from navy to navy.

The process of cruiser development in the late 1800s was logical and inevitable. The introduction of armour plate began it all. When the last of the steam-sail frigates received their inevitable plating protection against the new shell gun, they became armoured cruisers. Some were heavily armoured and, like the earlier Fourth Rates of fifty or sixty guns, were fit to stand in the line. The smaller cruiser relied on speed for its protection. When this was matched by more powerful and equally fast armoured cruisers, light armour was applied to these smaller cruisers too. There then emerged the compromise small fighting ship, the protected cruiser, without armour plate on the sides, but with armoured decks and gun positions. These cruisers, too, possessed high speed as their first protection.

These complex, theoretical 'I'll-go-one-better' design battles continued for a number of decades, and right up to the First World War,

The forward guns and bridge of the French cruiser, *Georges Leygues*, 1937

between architect and architect, nation and nation. The French and Italians built with speed as a first requirement; the American Navy, still a mainly coast defence force, demanded greater protection; the British with world-wide imperial commitments had, as always, to compromise most carefully.

Typical cruisers of the 1890s were the French armoured cruiser *Dupuy de Lôme*, the British first class protected cruiser, *Ariadne*, and the German armoured cruiser *Furst Bismarck*.

> *Dupuy de Lôme*, completed 1893, 6,400 tons, 22 knots
> Armament: 2 × 7.6-inch, 6 × 6.4-inch, 4 × 9-pounders, 4 × 18-inch torpedo tubes
> Armour: 4¾-inch belt amidships and on conning tower, 4-inch on gun turrets and bases

> *Ariadne*, completed 1900, 11,000 tons, 20 knots
> Armament: 16 × 6-inch, 12 × 12-pounders, 2 × 18-inch torpedo tubes
> Armour: 12-inch on conning tower, 6-inch on gun casemates, 4-inch armoured deck

> *Furst Bismarck*, completed 1900, 10,700 tons, 19 knots
> Armament: 4 × 9.4-inch, 12 × 6-inch, 10 × 15-pounders, 5 × 17.7-inch torpedo tubes
> Armour: 8-inch belt amidships, tapering to 4-inch at ends, 8-inches on barbettes and turrets and conning tower, and 4-inches for smaller guns.

By the early years of the new century, new cruiser construction among the great powers had settled into a simpler and more distinct pattern of two types: small, light and very fast unarmoured cruisers, and armoured cruisers. For a decade Britain had abstained from building big, heavy armoured cruisers, but French rivalry – still as fierce as ever – had led to several heavily armed French armoured cruisers like the *Dupuy de Lôme* (see above) joining the fleet. These represented a real threat as commerce raiders in the event of war, and Britain was forced to reply with six armoured cruisers (the *Cressy* class), laid down in 1898-9, which carried a pair of 9.2-inch guns (against the contemporary French armoured cruisers' two 7.6-inch) and twelve 6-inch.

As the pace of rearmament increased in the first decade of the 1900s, the size, power and protection of the armoured cruiser rapidly increased. The German *Prinz Adalbert*, *Friedrich Karl*, *Roon* and *Yorck*, completed between 1903 and 1906, were of 9,000 tons and carried fourteen 8.2- and 6-inch guns. These fine ships were followed by the *Scharnhorst* and *Gneisnau* (11,600 tons, 8 × 8.2-inch, 6 × 6-inch, massively protected by 6-inch Krupp armour) which were to fulfil their

A sketch for a cruiser III class Kaiser Wilhelm in 1894, on an Imperial telegraph form

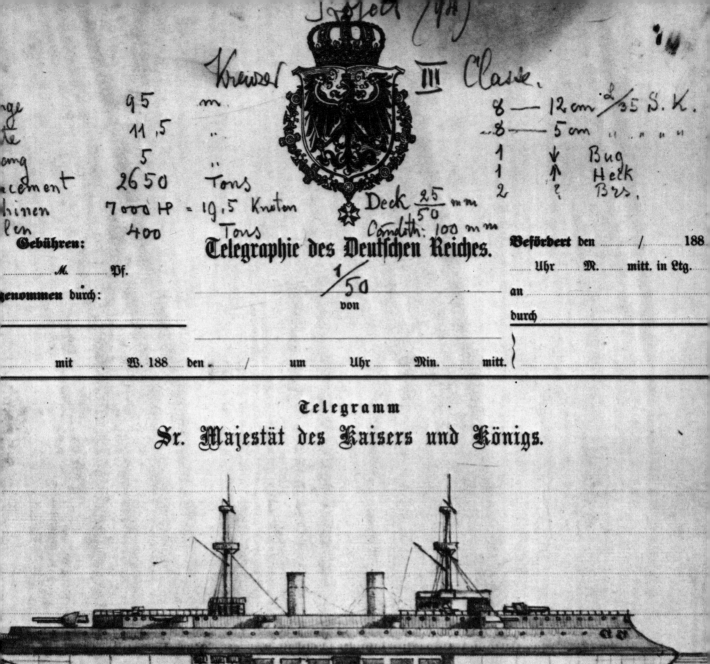

Kreuzer III Classe.

| | | | |
|---|---|---|---|
| änge | 95 | m. | |
| | 11,5 | " | |
| ang | 5 | " | |
| acement | 2650 | Tons | |
| hinen | 7000 HP | = 19,5 Knoten | |
| len | 400 | Tons | |

8 — 12 cm /35 S. K.
8 — 5 cm " " "
1 ↓ Bug
1 ↑ Heck
2 ? Brs.

Deck 25/50 mm
Cmdlth: 100 mm

Telegraphie des Deutschen Reiches.

**Gebühren:**

M. Pf.

genommen durch:

1/50
von

Befördert den ___ / ___ 188

Uhr ___ M. ___ mitt. in Ltg.

an

durch

mit W. 188 den ___ / ___ um ___ Uhr ___ Min. ___ mitt.

### Telegramm
## Sr. Majestät des Kaisers und Königs.

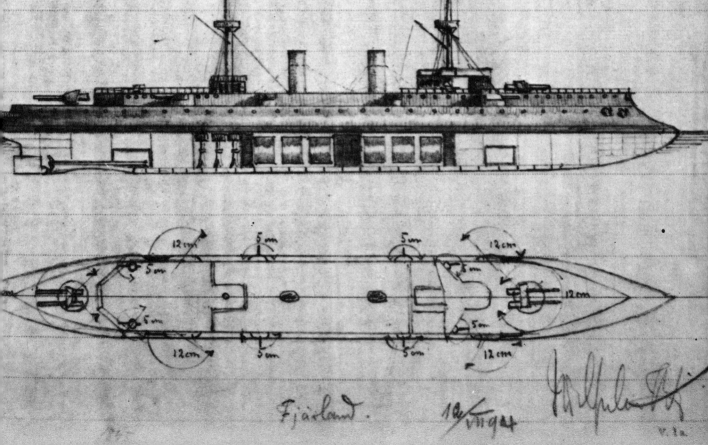

Fjärland. 1⁰ VII 94

rôle as commerce raiders so effectively and prove hard to destroy at the Battle of the Falkland Islands. The German armoured cruiser programme culminated in the greatest of them all, the 15,000-ton *Blücher*, armed with twelve 8.2-inch and eight 6-inch guns, which could steam at 25 knots, and five years after her completion survived an appalling hammering by British 12-inch and 13.5-inch shells at the Dogger Bank before she was sent to the bottom by torpedoes.

The ultimate American armoured cruisers (the *Washington* class) were scarcely smaller than the *Blücher*, boasted four 10-inch guns as their heaviest armament, and were inferior to the German ship only in speed. But the most remarkable of all armoured cruisers originated in Italy, and in the brilliant mind of the greatest naval architect of his day, Colonel Vittorio Cuniberti. His *Vittorio Emanuele* class of four ships, laid down between 1901 and 1903, and described by Fred T. Jane in his annual *Fighting Ships* as 'the ideal armoured cruisers', were almost small, fast battleships, with a displacement of 12,000 tons, a speed of 21 knots (slower than most armoured cruisers but much faster than any battleship), an armament of twelve 8-inch and two 12-inch guns, and a main armoured belt on the waterline no less than 10 inches thick. Part of their secret of high speed, heavy armament and armour lay in Cuniberti's method of girder-like construction and the use of asbestos in place of wood in the interior fittings as another means of saving weight.

The life of the armoured cruiser in this century was a brief and mainly tragic one. She always was a hybrid, and with the *Dreadnought* revolution in 1906, the coming of the Dreadnought-type of all-big-gun cruiser – the battle cruiser – instantly made every armoured cruiser obsolete: dangerously obsolete, for this class of vessel suffered grievously when struck by heavy shell, as at Dogger Bank and Jutland.

The functions of the armoured cruiser were two-fold. Firstly, to act individually as commerce-raiders and commerce-raider destroyers, secondly to operate together with the fleet as a scouting wing. In this second capacity they were intended to be fast enough to escape from the big guns of the battleships and also to deal with light cruisers. The ideal light cruiser, however, could escape from the armoured cruiser, and with its superior speed scout ahead and also help to destroy the destroyer flotillas. The light cruiser of the period before the First World War possessed a modest armament of guns of from 3-inch to 6-inch calibre, was protected only by an armoured deck, and could make from 24 to 26 knots. These were perhaps the most elegant and satisfactory fighting ships built at this time. Representatives of their breed were the 3,750-ton *Birmingham* of the United States Navy, turbine-powered and coal-fuelled to give a speed of 25 knots, and armed with light unprotected guns of 5-inch and 3-inch calibre; the German *Emden* (that devastating raider of 1914) of about the same displacement armed with ten 4.1-inch guns – a most effective and quick-firing weapon – and possessing a speed of 25 knots; and the British *Bristol* class of 1908, which were slightly faster and bigger and carried two 6-inch and ten 4.7-inch guns behind shields.

The light cruisers, most notably the *Southampton* and *Galatea*, performed their scouting functions admirably at the Battle of Jutland in 1916.

The armoured cruiser reappeared in revised and re-named form after the First World War as the Heavy Cruiser. The Washington Treaty of 1922 limited the cruiser to 10,000 tons; over this displacement they became classified as capital ships, which were restricted among the signatories by number, and by size to 35,000 tons. It therefore appeared sensible to build every cruiser to this limit, armed with 8-inch guns (the maximum Treaty calibre), armour them modestly, and give them sufficient speed to escape from the contemporary battleships. The result was a generation of mainly uniform heavy cruisers which by the time war came again were quite as anomalous as their predecessors because the battleship had now caught them up in speed, and the development of airpower had made them even more vulnerable. Nonetheless, by ingenuity, cheating, and designing for local commitments only, some remarkable heavy cruisers were built between the wars. The British and Americans built conservatively. Their defence requirements called for vessels capable of meeting all weather conditions from the North Sea and the Mediterranean, the Indian

The *Ajax*, 1934, in the River Plate

Ocean and the Pacific, to the Atlantic in winter. Provision had to be made for a large fuel capacity, for outstanding seaworthiness, and for comfortable habitation for long periods. Representative of this new breed of heavy cruiser in America were the *Pensacola* of 1929 and the *Augusta* of 1931. They were armed with nine or ten 8-inch guns in centre-line turrets, a still-modest quota of anti-aircraft guns, with a thin skin of armour on the decks and along the waterline, with a speed of 32 knots, a radius of action of 13,000 miles, and several seaplanes for reconnaissance. Their intended rôle was to run down enemy cruisers and destroyers and act as 'eyes of the fleet' as their predecessors had done in the First World War. Their British contemporaries were the 'County' class, completed between 1927 and 1930. These much-criticized flush-decked vessels, with their three funnels and high freeboard, possessed a stately grace about them that was in keeping with the Imperial responsibilities they were designed to uphold. They were the last of the British 'flag-showers', comfortably habitable in all climates, and with an operating range of over 10,000 miles. Like the armoured cruisers they succeeded, they proved highly vulnerable in combat circumstances not envisaged at the time the distinguished architect Sir Eustace Hugh Tennyson d'Eyncourt drew up their design.

Italian strategic requirements were entirely different from those of any other major naval nation. As in the days of Roman and Venetian power, speed and flexibility of operation in the more kindly climatic conditions of the Mediterranean were the first needs. No other fighting ships of other nations, including their fastest destroyers, could match the Italian *incrociatori* of the 1920s and 1930s. The *Trieste* and *Trento* set the pattern. Like the British 'County' class, they carried eight 8-inch guns in paired turrets on the centre line. Their low profile with two squat funnels hinted at once at their remarkable maximum speed of some 38 knots, and they were also better protected with armour than the British ships. But like the galleys of old, they were essentially Mediterranean ships. They could not have withstood the rigours of winter North Atlantic convoy work that the British ships endured in the 1940s, nor could they have remained at sea for so long.

The Japanese and the Germans, while signatories to limiting treaties, and claiming to meet the restrictions they imposed, were quick to discover means of evading them. Some of their 8-inch-gunned heavy cruisers exceeded the treaty displacement of 10,000 tons by almost 50 per cent. The architects' problems of compromise were therefore greatly eased, and both these naval powers produced heavy cruisers as large and formidable as the *Blücher* of 1909, and far better

'Calf Island Lighthouse and HMS *Lion*, battle cruiser', by Neil, and (bottom) the *Lion*, battle cruiser, 1912

Overleaf: 'The convoy to North Africa', 1942, by Eurich. The picture is supposed to show every type of ship in the British Navy at that time. (Bottom) 'A British convoy on its way to Russia', 1942, by Pears

Chas. PEARS.

equipped to match up to the new weapons of destruction devised after their completion. The Japanese *Nati* class completed in the late 1920s carried ten 8-inch and numerous light anti-aircraft guns, four seaplanes on catapults, could achieve over 33 knots and were substantially armoured. Like all their Japanese contemporaries, their low profile, complex superstructure, and heavily raked and often trunked funnels combined to give an appearance of fearsome and intimidating aggressiveness. While the Japanese cruisers were pagoda-like oriental sea fortresses, the German cruisers' silhouette tended towards the unembellished Prussian military citadel, purposeful and business-like. Their heavy cruisers like the new *Blücher*, built in the 1930s, while meeting the treaty limits with their gun-calibre of eight inches – and carrying no more than eight of them – were as heavily protected as the old *Blücher*, 7 or 8 knots faster, and as minutely compartmented and as unsinkable by gunfire as the earlier ship. With a displacement of more than 14,000 tons, they were naturally a vastly more formidable proposition than the English 8-inch-gunned cruisers of the previous decade.

The French never regained in the 1900s their earlier gift for superior ingenuity and technical excellence in naval architecture. Their cruisers between the wars were, however, characterized by good sense, taste and grace. Gone were the hideous 'fierce-face' aspects of the late 1800s, and a number of their fighting ships looked from a distant casual glance like small passenger liners off on a gay cruise. At first the French Ministry of Marine succumbed to the temptation of building up to the 10,000-ton 8-inch-gun limits of the Washington Treaty. The *Duquesne* had a main armament of eight heavy guns, very light protection and a speed intended to match – though it failed – that of the contemporary Italian cruisers. But at the same time France built lighter cruisers carrying 6.1-inch main armament, and vessels like the *Duguay-Trouin*, completed in 1926, set the pattern of cruiser development in the 1930s.

As war in the Atlantic, Pacific and Mediterranean became more imminent in the 1930s, all the great powers likely to be involved authorized massive programmes of cruiser construction. The shadow of the bomber and torpedo 'plane fell heavily over the designers' drawing boards at this time, and cruiser characteristics tended more than ever to high speed, a complement of reconnaissance or bombing catapulted aircraft, an ever-larger number of light anti-aircraft guns and a main armament of 5-inch to 6-inch guns with a high rate of fire capable of being used against air or surface targets. Such a vessel was the United States light cruiser, *Brooklyn*, completed in 1938, which

The *Devonshire* firing a guided missile, and (bottom) the *Devonshire*

261

combined substantial protection against bombs and torpedoes with a speed of 33 knots, fifteen 6-inch guns in five triple centre-line turrets, and numerous batteries of medium and light anti-aircraft guns. Six aircraft were stowed neatly in a hangar and ready for catapulting from her stern. The French were busily building similar vessels at the time of the German invasion in 1940, when the British had already completed numerous 6-inch-gunned light cruisers which were to do invaluable service in numerous capacities during the next five years of war. The most spectacular cruisers of all time were built by the Italians in the late 1930s. Of very light construction, with negligible protection yet formidable dual-purpose gunfire ranging from 5.3-inch to 20 mm., they were capable of well over 40 knots and – it has been said – in a strong headwind could readily outpace their adversary, that antiquated British torpedo bomber, the Swordfish.

Like all its contemporary classes of fighting ship, the iron- and steel-

The USS *Springfield*, CLG 7, 1944

hulled cruiser has suffered from the rapid pace of scientific development. In the First World War the superior guns and speed of the battle cruiser (see below p. 281) made the armoured cruiser a floating coffin in action. In the Second World War the cruiser was forced to sustain the onslaughts of the submarine and the aircraft, especially in the Mediterranean and the Pacific. The cruiser fought back with new radar devices, armoured decks, and more and more anti-aircraft guns. Her class suffered grievously, especially in the Japanese and the British navies.

Some were modified into pure anti-aircraft cruisers and a handful were built exclusively for this rôle. She survives to this day in a number of navies with a mixed armament of guns, rockets and guided missiles, and in her ultimate form as the 14,200-ton nuclear powered guided missile cruiser *Long Beach* with its fearful ram-jet propelled missiles which can carry atomic warheads and engage subsonic or supersonic targets.

The guided missile cruiser USS *Canberra* launching a surface-to-air Terrier missile. The modern ship differs radically from the World War II ship in her large number of radar aerials and her missiles replacing guns

# 7. THE DREADNOUGHT

On 27 May 1905 there took place the first and only decisive fleet action between surface vessels in the life of the steam battleship. Nearly half a century had passed since the French Navy had commissioned the *Gloire*, a century since Trafalgar. Except for the *mêlée* at Lissa, and minor actions and bombardments, the naval architects had been working blindly and speculatively. Perhaps not only the *matériel* but also the principles of all contemporary tactics and strategy in naval warfare were false? Who was to know? There was no sure way of telling until an altogether improbable conflict broke out in the Far East between the new Oriental power of Japan and the old European power of Russia. The naval eyes of the world eagerly followed every move at sea, and the British (sympathetic to the Japanese cause) sent observers to watch the Imperial Japanese Navy at work. The war both on land and sea was decided by an engagement between Admiral Heihachiro Togo and Admiral Zinovi Petrovitch Rozhestvensky which took place in the Straits of Tsushima. The Russian Baltic Fleet, weary in spirit and body after its long and eventful voyage from Europe, was met by Admiral Togo's highly trained and enthusiastic force and almost annihilated. Fire was opened with accuracy at the astonishing range of 9,000 yards. The 12-inch shell proved its fearful destructiveness. It would have been more effective still if the spotting of the fall of shot had not been confused by the explosions of shells from smaller guns. With the capsizing of the first Russian battleship, the *Oslyabya*, after 12-inch shells had peeled off the armour plating and let the water come pouring into her hull, the big gun had proved herself at sea. All

'Warships Week' in Trafalgar Square, 1942, by Rushbury

the predictions of the big gun enthusiasts had been fulfilled. At Tsushima dreadful carnage and damage was committed by the smaller gun at close range. But 12-inch ordnance was the ship-destroyer. No gun of lesser calibre, it was at once and widely claimed, counted for anything in a fleet action. 'The cult of the big bang' was justified, and was to retain its loyal (and influential) adherents for another thirty-five years and more.

From the holocaust of that May afternoon in distant waters, European and American naval thinkers drew the conclusions that were to shape the nature of the fighting ship for the rest of its life. If Tsushima had proved the futility of mixing gun calibres and beyond doubt that only the biggest gun was the ship-destroyer, what was the purpose in mounting anything smaller – except of course some quick-firers to deal with the torpedo craft? Those thinkers who had been advocating for some time privately and occasionally publicly for an all-big-gun battleship saw their beliefs magnificently confirmed.

Like every great step forward in the development over the centuries of the fighting ship, there was nothing wholly 'new' about the single armament or all-big-gun Dreadnought type battleship. People had been thinking about them for years, and as we have noted all-big-gun ships of a grotesque nature were built some thirty years earlier. After years of experiment with every possible heavy gun permutation, a body of opinion in every navy was beginning to recognize that the mixed-armament battleship was nearing the end of its development. In the opening years of the new century battleships with a uniform armament of the largest guns were advocated by the American Bureau of Construction, in Italy by the advanced thinker Colonel Cuniberti, in Britain by Admiral Sir John Fisher. The Germans and even the Russians were known to be thinking along similar lines. Britain, with her overwhelmingly powerful Navy and vast maritime responsibilities, began to recognize the dangers.

It was left to Fisher to take action. This was no time, Fisher concluded, to conform to the traditional British policy of allowing others to move first and answering herself with more numerous ships. Fisher believed that the pace of competition with Germany yearly intensifying would make it national suicide to allow anyone to steal a march on his beloved Royal Navy. On the ninety-ninth anniversary of the Battle of Trafalgar, 21 October 1904, Fisher was appointed First Sea Lord. He immediately set up a Committee on Designs, which drew up plans for the rapid construction of a battleship that would make all others afloat or building obsolete. Less than a year after Fisher took office, this battleship was laid down at Portsmouth.

Fisher had prepared his plans with infinite care as well as unprecedented speed. Many of the vital materials of construction were made
ready beforehand, the ship's guns (the construction of which was such
a long and elaborate process that it often governed the building period
of a heavy ship) were ruthlessly plundered from a pair of mixed-
armament battleships already under construction. Nothing was
allowed to delay the building of the new vessel. She was launched in
a little over four months and was on her trials a year and a day after
her keel had been laid. From stem to stern she was an inspired fighting
ship. Not only did she boast ten heavy guns when no other battleship
carried more than four of the largest calibre; she was also the biggest
battleship in the world, the fastest, and the first large warship anywhere to be turbine-powered – Fisher's final master-stroke. At the
same time she was adequately armoured with a belt eleven inches
thick at the waterline, and was specially protected against torpedo
attack. When she steamed off on her trials – she did 21.6 knots – she
was the cynosure of every navy in the world.

It is true that HMS *Dreadnought* of 1906 created a revolution in naval

The *Dreadnought*, 1906, an all-big-
gun, high-speed battleship; she was
built in a year and a day

architecture. And the drama of the revolution was greatly increased by the magnificently conducted staff work surrounding her construction and the triumphantly strident tone in which her imposing size, speed and gunpower were announced to the world. There were many critics of the *Dreadnought*, which made obsolete not only the existing battleships of Britain's potential enemies but her own as well. And because Britain had so many more than anyone else, the *Dreadnought* represented greater wasted tonnage to the country which had built her than to any of her rivals. The *Dreadnought* controversy raged for years in Britain. But the final, incontrovertible argument in support of Fisher's decision was that *other nations were already building all-big-gun ships too*, although this was not known publicly in Britain at the time. Both the Japanese and the Americans had laid down all-12-inch-gunned battleships early in 1905. Due to supply difficulties, the Japanese ships were not completed for five years, and then had to make-do with mixed 10-inch and 12-inch guns, and the Americans took more than four years to build the *South Carolina* and *Michigan*. But the revolution had already begun, even before the *Dreadnought* herself took to the water, and with her the generic name for a class of battleship which was to endure for as long as her kind.

Like the *Monitor*, the *Gloire* and the *Warrior*, the Dreadnought-type battleship was forged in the fire of international anxiety and competition. In the 1890s and early 1900s, the old rival imperial powers of France and Britain were forced to seek an *entente cordiale* to preserve what they possessed, to retain the balance of European power in their favour, and to stunt the ambitions of the new colonialists. In Europe Germany had made clear her intention to become a great maritime as well as a great colonial and military power, and Admiral Alfred von Tirpitz – Germany's Fisher – was busily implementing the notorious Navy Act of 1900, which provided for no less than thirty-eight battleships.

In America, President Theodore Roosevelt had read and absorbed the lessons in Alfred Thayer Mahan's books and begun to apply his new comprehension of maritime power to the defence policies of the New World, both in the Atlantic and the Pacific. Urgency was added to the American situation by Admiral Togo's victory at Tsushima, and the emergence of Japan as a threat to the United States in the Pacific as potentially alarming as Germany's threat to Britain in Europe. International maritime rivalry on an unprecedented scale – in the North Sea, the Mediterranean, the Atlantic and the Pacific – brought about the Dreadnought revolution and the Dreadnought race that followed it. It was to last in Europe for a decade, in the Far

USS *Michigan*, 1909, was the U.S. Navy's first dreadnought

East for a few years longer, until the Washington Conference brought the insanely expensive competition to a temporary halt. During this time the most technically interesting battleships of all time were constructed in great numbers, each one as it joined the fleet adding to the self-confidence and self-esteem of its creators.

The race itself was inevitable; only the pace was set by Britain. One of Admiral Fisher's many pungent catch phrases, which he repeated in his staccato manner on every possible occasion, was: 'Build few and build fast, each one better than the last.' Britain's shipbuilding resources were unmatched anywhere in the world, and Fisher saw to it that Britain did build fast so that her lead in the drive to Armageddon could be maintained. Some thirty more British Dreadnoughts were completed before the outbreak of war eight years after the *Dreadnought* herself was commissioned. On every lap of the race with Germany, Britain remained ahead numerically and, ship by ship, statistically as well. Britain built Dreadnoughts with not only a more striking silhouette than Germany, but with guns of a larger calibre. The fact that they were not so comprehensively protected as their German contemporaries was not immediately apparent. The finest and most formidable battleships laid down in Britain during this period were of the *Queen Elizabeth* class, mounting eight 15-inch guns (Germany's largest until 1917 were 12-inch), protected by 13-inch armour, and possessing a speed of 25 knots, derived for the first time in a battleship from oil fuel.

It was ships like the five Queen Elizabeths that appeared to justify the continuing maritime arrogance of Britain in the face of the giant Dreadnought competition going on all over the world. Fine-looking ships in great numbers and armed with the greatest guns, and with names like *Valiant*, *Thunderer*, *Hercules* and *Audacious*, could not fail to seem splendid and fearsome and provocative. It was partly for this reason, and also because she was quite lacking in any naval history and tradition, that the spirit of the German Navy in 1914 was tempered by a sense of inferiority. There was little *matériel* reason for this, except on paper. Between 1909 and 1916 von Tirpitz created a magnificent force of fighting ships mainly superior in quality and only slightly inferior in numbers to the British Navy. The rapid construction of the *Dreadnought* upset the German plans as completely as Fisher had intended. Not only had the keels been laid for more mixed-armament battleships, but new ships to compete with the *Dreadnought* would require the widening of the Kiel Canal between the Baltic and the North Sea – a formidably expensive and long undertaking.

The German architects responded with an all-big-gun design that appeared to be inferior to the British contemporaries. While the *Nassau*, completed in 1909, carried twelve 11-inch guns against the *Dreadnought*'s ten 12-inch, only two of the turrets were on the centre line against the *Dreadnought*'s three, and the weight of main armament broadside of the British ship was therefore greater. She was also slower and smaller than her British rival. But the *Nassau* and all her successors scored heavily in their ability to resist both shell and torpedo. The German Dreadnoughts were designed primarily for service in home waters, and like the longships which had fought in the North Sea a thousand years earlier, they were not intended to accommodate their crews for long periods. Human comforts could be largely disregarded, and Tirpitz saw to it that full advantage was taken of this circumstance. The German ships were minutely sub-divided by unpierced watertight bulkheads, and careful attention was paid to the problem of retaining buoyance after a hit below the waistline. 'The whole part of the ship below the waterline,' wrote von Tirpitz, 'was designed to provide for failure to localize the effects of the explosion or for several hits being made . . . endless labour was expended upon details such as the pumping system or the possibility of speedily counteracting a list by flooding corresponding compartments.'[8]

When in port, the German crews may have had to live in barracks; but the careful experimenting to achieve ultimate protection of German armoured ships paid off time and again in two World Wars. The ability to withstand intensive and sustained shellfire came to be recognized in the British Navy as a formidable characteristic of every German Dreadnought. From the *Lützow* at Jutland in 1916 to the *Scharnhorst* in 1943, the story was the same. German heavy ships could be reduced to a shambles by shellfire without succumbing, and it required a number of torpedo hits as well to send them to the bottom. By contrast, British battleships proved themselves fatally vulnerable to mines, a few shell hits sufficed to destroy British battle cruisers in both world wars because they were inadequately protected horizontally against 'plunging fire' (projectiles fired from a great range falling almost vertically).

German Dreadnought development during von Tirpitz's period of office culminated in the battleships *Baden* and *Bayern*, which with their uncompleted sister ships were laid down in answer to the British Queen Elizabeths. Displacement was up to 28,000 tons, speed to over 22 knots, and there were eight 15-inch guns, all on the centre line, four of them in superimposed turrets. Armour plate was almost 13 inches thick on turrets and side belt.

The Atlantic fleet, 1925, led by the *Rodney*

France, Italy, Austria, Hungary, Russia and minor powers like Spain, Turkey, Greece and even the South American States all ordered Dreadnoughts during the height of the fever from 1907 to 1914. Shipbuilders and ordnance works the world over profited, and the output of steel in the industrial nations multiplied many times. But long before the fleets of Germany and Britain clashed in the North Sea, a new and fearsome rivalry for dominance of the Pacific had gathered speed. The Japanese were bursting with self-confidence and eagerness to develop the new technological skills they had recently acquired. And as a result the Americans were becoming increasingly worried about their interests in Asia. The Japanese Navy which had won at Tsushima had been largely built in British yards. Japanese apprentice technicians had watched the riveting of every plate, the construction of every gun. They learned well, and hastened home. While the war with Russia was still raging, the first heavy armoured ships were laid down in Japanese yards – a pair of powerful armoured cruisers with 12-inch and 6-inch guns. The construction of battleships rapidly followed. There was a pause while the country straightened out its finances after her expensive war. Her first two 'pure' Dreadnoughts were laid down in 1909. Six more followed between 1911 and 1913. Nor were these fighting ships pale imitations of foreign practice. They were of ingenious design, were fast and exceptional in their gun-power and protection. The *Fuso* and *Yamashiro* of the 1911–12 Emergency Expansion Programme displaced over 30,000 tons, were 700 feet long, carried an all-centre-line armament of twelve 14-inch guns – supported by sixteen 6-inch – and steamed at 24.7 knots on their trials. By 1920 Japan had completed battleships carrying 16-inch guns – the first in the world – and giant battleships and battle cruisers with 16-inch and even 18-inch guns were being contemplated before the Washington Conference called a halt.

Neither in 1916 nor in 1940 could Japan hope to equal the fighting ship building potential of the United States. Japanese strategy in the Pacific was similar in many respects to that of Germany in the North Sea. Both powers hoped to whittle down the superior strength of the enemy by striking at units or detachments with greater forces and by underwater (mines and submarines) and later air (bombs and torpedoes) attack, avoiding a direct fleet confrontation until the odds were loaded strongly in their favour. Under the inspired leadership of Admiral William Sims, American Dreadnought construction went ahead rapidly from 1906.

The originality of thought in American battleship design, especially from 1905 to 1920, was a marked feature of this period. America's first Dreadnoughts, the *South Carolina* and *Michigan*, were markedly smaller than the British prototype of the breed, and attained a speed no higher than many pre-Dreadnoughts. But they were neat, carefully planned and economical, especially in the layout of their main armament of 12-inch guns. As the eminent authority, William Hovgaard, wrote in *Jane's Fighting Ships* for 1910, 'The ideal arrangement of the *heavy gun turrets* seems to be the American, first adopted in the *Michigan*, where two turrets are placed at each end of the ship in the centre-line, the guns nearest amidships firing over those nearest the ends.' By this means these two American ships could offer a broadside as powerful as that of the *Dreadnought* while saving the weight, space and expense of a fifth heavy turret. Superimposition had been tried with indifferent results in the American Navy before; it was to the greater credit of the Bureau of Construction that they should persevere with an arrangement which possessed so many advantages. Within a few years every naval power was following the American example.

Six Dreadnoughts followed this first American pair, armed with ten or twelve 12-inch guns. Then when Britain introduced the 13.5-inch gun, America went one better with the 14-inch, which first appeared in the *New York* and *Texas* laid down in 1911. Having pioneered superimposition and a multitude of features like the lattice mast (for strength, and rangefinder stability), American architects introduced a new defence feature in their 14-inch-gunned battleships laid down in 1912. Once before, at the height of the guns *versus* armour contest of the 1860s and '70s, designers had been forced to resort to concentrating all their armour weight over the ship's vitals. With the increasing penetrating and explosive power of the new 13.5 and 14-inch guns, it was evidently necessary to revert to a similar disposition of armour plate, unless the battleship were to sink under the weight of its own protective steel. With the *Oklahoma* and *Nevada* the American Navy took the plunge. When they were completed there was armour up to 18 inches thick on the turrets and their trunks, 16 inches on the conning tower, and over 13 inches in a narrow waterline belt and round the funnel base – and almost nothing anywhere else. Seven more 14-inch-gunned Dreadnoughts of up to 32,000 tons, all oil-fuelled and turbine-powered, all virtually invulnerable to shell damage where it mattered, and all with the characteristic businesslike and well-balanced American profile, were built between 1914 and 1921. This massive battleship programme, directed against the threat of war with Japan rather than the actuality of war with Germany (well taken care of by Britain) was completed with a trio of 16-inch-

gunned fighting ships, laid down in answer to the Japanese *Mutsu* and *Nagato*. Further, and still more hyperbolic super-battleships and battle cruisers, of over 40,000 tons and armed with twelve 16-inch guns, were authorized to meet the new Oriental super-battleships being built in Japan. Construction of these was halted in 1922; two of them, the *Saratoga* and *Lexington*, were completed as outsize aircraft carriers.

All the threat of bombs, all the proof by bombing trials of the vulnerability of the battleship to air attack, all the claims made by far-sighted theorists and prophets, could not deter the great powers from building battleships again as soon as they were allowed to by Treaty and felt themselves forced to by the imminence of a new war. The cult of the big bang could not so easily be suppressed; the grandeur and imposing presence of the Dreadnought battleship provided more arguments in its favour than any mere theorizing could refute. The Dreadnought battleship had not done much fighting, it was true (a few minutes, without decision, at Jutland, that was about all), but its strategic influence had scarcely diminished in the minds of the world's defence councils when consideration had again to be given to battleship construction in the 1930s. All the great powers conformed. Between 1930 and 1940 Britain, America, Germany, Japan, France, Italy and Russia all laid down the keels of massive new battleships, varying in displacement from 25,000 to nearly 70,000 tons. The design of all these ships was mainly conservative, and the progress in naval architecture and scientific devices in the years preceding the Second World War did not come near to matching the astonishing achievements of 1906 to 1914. The increasing need to defend the vessel against bombing attack was seen in the large number of anti-aircraft guns, which could if necessary be used also against surface torpedo vessels, the number of aircraft carried on board (for reconnaissance, spotting and counter-attack), and the emphasis on the protection of the decks. The disposition of armour against shellfire generally followed the earlier American trend towards the all-or-nothing principle.

The French followed British practice for the first time, by concentrating all their heavy guns forward. They also reduced weight and expense by mounting four guns to a turret. Their *Dunkerque* and *Strasbourg*, *Richelieu* and *Jean Bart* could manage around 30 knots and were satisfactory enough fighting ships, but they lacked the old spark and originality. The other major powers conformed more closely to their own past tradition. Germany began before Hitler's time by flouting all the rules and laying down 'pocket battleships' which purported to be within the heavy cruiser Washington limit of 10,000 tons

The super-dreadnought USS *Oklahoma*, 1917. The birdcage mast is typical

275

yet carried 11-inch guns, could do 26 knots with diesel engines, and had a radius of action of 10,000 miles. This combination of qualities seemed too good to be true, and so it was, for the *Deutschland* and her sisters actually displaced around 12,000 tons. Germany continued to concentrate on big fast capital ships for commerce raiding rather than ships to stand in the line as she had for the earlier war, and these reached their culmination in the enormously tough and formidable *Bismarck* and *Tirpitz* of some 42,000 tons armed with eight 15-inch guns. Italy built light and fast with her 35,000-ton *Roma*, *Littorio*, *Vittorio Veneto* and *Impero* (the last never completed), which were reputed to be capable of 35 knots but proved to be vulnerable to air attack. The airborne torpedo also demonstrated its deadly power against the *Prince of Wales*, one of the five new 35,000-tonners built by Britain between 1937 and 1942. Although equipped with enormous batteries of anti-aircraft guns of all calibres, they were not enough to fight off the swarming Japanese torpedo and high-level bombers on 10 December 1941: two torpedoes sufficed to cripple the battleship, and three more sent her to the bottom.

After their savage losses by air attack at Pearl Harbor three days before the *Prince of Wales* went down, the Americans were quick to recognize the need to augment drastically their heavy ships' anti-aircraft defences. No nation built battleships of this last generation with such enthusiasm as the Americans. Between 1941 and 1944 ten 16-inch-gunned fighting ships – all immensely strong, very fast and up to 45,000 tons displacement – joined the fleet. Although conceived some thirty years later, they conformed to the design principles laid down by the Bureau of Construction for the old *Michigan* and *South Carolina*. The *Washington*, the *Alabama* and the *Missouri* were still Dreadnoughts. They were still basically gun-platforms, their single calibre heavy armament carried in three instead of four turrets. The main function of their armour plate was to resist enemy shell, their secondary batteries were to ward off other forms of high explosive carrier. But what batteries these were! By this time the aircraft carrier was the new capital ship of naval warfare. But when her aircraft came in to attack a Dreadnought in the Pacific or the Mediterranean, they were met at once by the fire from 150 or more anti-aircraft guns of all calibres before which her 'planes fell like locusts in the line of a poison spray.

In the Second World War the American and British Dreadnoughts accepted with dignity their secondary rôle to the carrier. In the Mediterranean, Atlantic and Pacific they escorted convoys, bombarded shore positions, and acted as protective nursemaids to the

'A destroyer rescuing survivors 1942, by Eurich, and (bottom) the *Ark Royal*, aircraft carrier, 1942, by Ravilious

Overleaf: the *Hermes*, aircraft carrier

carriers, filling the air with shot and shell when the enemy appeared in the sky. Not a single American battleship was lost between 1942 and 1945 to her old enemy, the gun, or to her new enemies, the aircraft bomb and torpedo. In her last great war, the battleship vindicated herself when she was properly protected against her new enemies by her own guns and by the command of the air provided by her new consort, the carrier. Without these advantages she was, by 1941, a hopelessly vulnerable fighting ship. The mighty *Tirpitz* succumbed to the bomb, her sister ship was first crippled and then finished off by the torpedo. In the Mediterranean, British and Italian battleships fell to bombs and torpedoes when command of the air was lost. In the Pacific, the Japanese fleet of battleships – some converted in desperation into semi-aircraft carriers – was whittled away by the dive bomber, the torpedo bomber, and on several occasions and for the last time, by enemy shellfire.

The last phase in the long life of the battleship was concluded on 4 July 1945 when the Japanese *Yamato* blew up and sank beneath a huge cloud of smoke at Leyte Gulf after being struck by some five bombs and ten torpedoes. The *Yamato* class of Japanese battleship were by a wide margin the largest and most heavily-gunned Dreadnoughts ever built – the *ne plus ultra* of their kind: over 70,000 tons at full load, nine 18-inch guns in three triple turrets, and an 18-inch belt of armour and 22 inches on her turrets, speed 27 knots. Four ships in the class were laid down between 1938 and 1940, and they were intended to outrange and out-gun contemporary American battleships, which they could never hope to compete with numerically. The *Yamato* and *Musashi* were completed in 1941 and 1942, the third ship, *Shinano* was completed as the world's largest carrier and was sunk ten days later, and the fourth was scrapped on the stocks. Besides being the biggest Dreadnoughts, these were also the most ill-fated of them all. From the outset they were an embarrassment to their owners. Only the *Yamato* enjoyed a brief period when Japan controlled the air, and for most of the rest of their short lives the two giants were hidden away. When at last they made a desperate appearance within the range of American carrier aircraft, neither their massive batteries nor their tremendous strength could prevail against multiple attack by dive- and torpedo-bomber.

### THE BATTLE CRUISER

The intense battleship competition of the early 1900s which resulted in the all-big-gun *Dreadnought* of 1906 led to a parallel reappraisal of the future function and nature of the big cruiser. The second basic

Detail of 'Bombardment of a coast by HM ships *King George V* and *Duke of York*', 1941, by Eurich

lesson of Tsushima was the importance of superior speed in the successful handling of a battle fleet, which had permitted Togo to 'cross the T' of the Russian column – or to bring his own line across the bows of the enemy in order to bring his full broadsides to bear against the inferior forward Russian fire. The whole Fisher-Cuniberti Dreadnought design principle was based jointly on the all-big-gun matched with superior speed. Cuniberti's own first Dreadnought, the *Dante Alighieri*, possessed a maximum speed of 23 knots, equal to that of most of the armoured cruisers of her day, and the speed of the *Dreadnought* herself was at least two knots above that of any pre-Dreadnought battleship. As one of the chief functions of the armoured cruiser was to act as a fast scout ahead of the main force, a marked increase in speed was clearly demanded of post-Dreadnought ships of this class. When the British Committee on Designs assembled to discuss the nature of Britain's first all-big-gun battleship, it therefore also wisely considered the next stage of development of the armoured cruiser. The result of their deliberations was as epochal as the *Dreadnought* herself – an all-big-gun armoured cruiser of over 17,000 tons, armed with eight 12-inch guns, with very light protection, and an unprecedented speed of 27 knots, derived from turbines of nearly twice the horsepower of the *Dreadnought*'s. Three armoured cruisers of this type, *Invincible*, *Inflexible* and *Indomitable*, were built in Britain under conditions of great secrecy, and joined the fleet in 1908, before any foreign rival had a chance to do anything about them.

These new big armoured cruisers (later called battle cruisers) were to act as super-scouts to the fleet, destroying enemy armoured cruisers with impunity, to hunt down enemy commerce raiders, and to operate with the fleet as a very fast supporting wing, at the van or the rear as the situation demanded. An additional wartime function was assigned to them when German battle cruisers made hit-and-run bombardment raids against the British east coast. Under the command of Admiral Doveton Sturdee at the Battle of the Falkland Islands, and under Admiral Sir David Beatty at the Dogger Bank and Jutland, the British battle cruisers (at great cost) magnificently justified themselves in all these rôles, in spite of their vulnerability and poor shells and gunnery. The absence of adequate protection, especially against long-range plunging fire, was a cruel handicap to every British battle cruiser, from the *Invincible*, blown up at Jutland and the *Queen Mary* (26,350 tons, 8 × 13.5-inch guns) which suffered a similar fate, down to the last of her kind, the 41,000-ton *Hood* (8 × 15-inch guns, 31 knots, completed in 1920) which fell to the guns of the *Bismarck* in the Second World War.

The tough, highly efficient and fast (28 knots) German cruiser *Moltke* of World War I

USS *Alaska*, with 9 12-inch guns and a speed of 33 knots. The U.S. built her only 2 battle-cruisers in World War II

The Japanese battleship, *Yamato* 1941

The Germans considered the requirements of the Dreadnought battle cruiser with greater care, and applied to them many of the qualities of their battleships: structural strength, buoyancy, substantial and shrewdly-applied armour plate, combined with high speed and, by British standards, a modest main armament both in numbers and calibre. German's first battle cruiser, the *von der Tann* (19,100 tons, 8 × 11-inch guns, 26 knots), was a very doughty adversary, and subsequent German ships of this class proved their toughness on many occasions. The *Seydlitz*, *Derfflinger* and *Lützow* all took a terrible hammering at Jutland, yet the first two limped home half full of water and with most of their guns out of action, and only the *Lützow* was so shattered that she had to be sunk by her own side. The *Goeben* survived shells, bombs and mines in the First World War, and was still afloat (as the Turkish *Yavuz*) in excellent condition in 1967, nearly sixty years after she was laid down.

Only the British and Germans showed much enthusiasm for the battle cruiser type, although the Japanese built four early on and later converted them into battleships, and both the Japanese and Americans began to build them before the Washington Treaty was signed. When rearmament got into its stride again in the 1930s, the fast battleship which enjoyed its speed without any marked sacrifice in protection, appeared to have made the type redundant. The Germans built the *Scharnhorst* and *Gneisnau* of 31,000 tons, which were classified as battle cruisers only because of their very high speed of 32 knots, but Britain, which had initiated the class, did not feel tempted to add to the three old units she still possessed. Certainly by 1941 the battle cruiser, that noble, swift and awe-inspiring class of fighting ship, appeared to be extinct. Then to everyone's surprise, America decided to introduce a class of very fast, very light, very powerful cruiser that matched up to all the requirements demanded by the dynamic and percipient Fisher almost forty years earlier. The *Alaska* and *Guam* each carried one more 12-inch gun than the old *Invincible*, were almost 10 knots faster, and were much more fully protected internally. But in the Fisher tradition, they were thinly-skinned, heavily-armed scouts capable of crushing any fighting ship possessing their own speed, and escaping from anything that outgunned them. Both vessels had a busy and dangerous career in the Pacific before returning safely home to be placed in the reserve.

The German battlecruiser
*Derfflinger*, 1911

# 8. THE AIRCRAFT CARRIER

The greatest handicaps suffered by the new torpedo carriers – the torpedo boat, destroyer, submarine and aircraft – were their short range and endurance. The limited fuel capacity of the torpedo boat in the Russo-Japanese war severely restricted its operations. In the First World War the period that the British Grand Fleet and German High Seas fleet could remain at sea was dependent on the endurance of their screening flotillas, and speed too had to be carefully controlled because higher speed resulted in disproportionately higher fuel consumption. All early submarines were severely restricted in their range of operation and were regarded as mainly coastal craft until German U-boats began to appear not only about the British base at Scapa Flow, but even out in the Atlantic. The range of early aircraft was even shorter, and only later in the war were operations across the North Sea by bombing and torpedo-carrying machines carried out.

Of all the new weapon-carriers the aircraft has remained, even to this day, the most restricted in its endurance. In the early days of the torpedo, 'mother ships' had been fitted out expressly to carry very small torpedo boats for launching within close range of the enemy – preferably at night. When, after a number of experiments by German, British and Italian pioneers, the first practical torpedo-carrying aircraft rose from the water (it was a seaplane) in 1914, and Winston Churchill as First Lord of the Admiralty authorized the construction of a flight of them, means were already being considered for extending their range. The seaplane carrier, like the torpedo boat carrier of forty years earlier, provided the solution.

The USS *Ranger* CVA 61 and the USS *England* DLG 22 (out of sight) refuelling from the USS *Sacramento* AOE 1. Ships can again stay at sea indefinitely, as they did in Nelson's day

The British were the leading pioneers in the development of a naval air arm. Men of the calibre of Fisher and Churchill had relentlessly destroyed the reactionary elements in the British Navy; an enthusiasm for technical innovation was further encouraged by the needs of war. On 1 July 1914 a naval air service was formed. In the same year a 7,500-ton collier was bought and converted to carry seaplanes, which were hoisted out by crane, dropped in the sea, and even more hazardously recovered after they had landed again. Later, much faster ships which could keep up with the fleet at sea were similarly converted, and one of these was employed with the British Grand Fleet at Jutland. The Germans at first backed the airship against the heavier-than-air machine, but were soon to recognize the benefits of the smaller, cheaper and nimbler aircraft.

The seaplane carrier was always a makeshift vessel, limited in its capacity for carrying aircraft and in the conditions under which it could operate. It was obviously a much better idea to *launch* aircraft straight into the air while the carrier was moving. The first take-offs from ships were made in Britain and in America before the First World

The *Furious* receiving naval airship S.S.Z. (submarine scout). The *Furious* was capable of carrying a squadron of aircraft in addition to an airship

War. At first short runways were built on the forecastle of battleships. The British Navy built them on top of gun turrets, which could be conveniently turned into wind to shorten the take-off run. Spotting as well as fighter aircraft were employed in this way, and by the end of the war the Grand Fleet could launch as many as 120 aircraft into the air from its carriers, battleships and cruisers and from rafts towed behind fast destroyers; observer balloons towed aloft extended the range of vision of the fleet while at sea.

The next stage of development was to provide a flight deck long enough for pilots to land their aircraft back on board so that the parent vessel did not have to stop to pick them up. Several British ships were converted for this purpose while still under construction. The Italian liner *Conte Rosso* and the Chilean battleship *Almirante Cochrane*, building in Britain, the battle cruiser *Furious* and the cruiser *Cavendish*, were all given long flight decks. Early in 1918, the world's first ship to be designed 'from scratch' as an aircraft carrier, the 11,000-ton *Hermes*, was laid down on the Tyne. She was the archetype of all the numerous carriers built by the great naval powers over the next fifty years – tall, ungainly, lop-sided, with a flush deck extending from stem to stern; hangars below decks, lifts to raise the aircraft to their flying deck; mast, superstructure, bridge and funnel reduced to a minimum and placed on the extreme starboard to allow her 'planes a clear run; guns for defence against aircraft and light surface attack; high speed to reduce to a minimum the length of take-off run. The duties of her aircraft included submarine spotting and destroying, reconnoitring, bombing and torpedoing the enemy, and fighting off similar attack.

In the period between the wars the aircraft carrier acquired growing status. The capital ship of the fleet remained the battleship. But the rapid improvement in speed, range, and destructive potential of the aircraft between 1916 and 1919 proved in numerous bomb and torpedo trials after the war, and the 'battleship holiday' enforced by the Washington Treaty, caused many of the great naval powers to give greater attention to their air arm. The vast spaces of the Pacific Ocean especially seemed to offer a wonderful opportunity for the carrier and her aircraft to prove themselves. Japan, deprived by Treaty of parity in battleships with America, converted some of her forbidden half-completed giant battleships and battle cruisers into vast and fast floating airfields with horizontal funnels. The United States replied by carrying out a similar conversion to the uncompleted hulls of her aborted 35,000-ton battle cruisers, *Lexington* and *Saratoga*, which could carry at 34 knots a hive of around a hundred aircraft, were modestly armoured, and were capable of defending themselves with the gun-

power of a heavy cruiser. The French Ministry of Marine also took the uncompleted hull of a battleship and turned it into the ugly, box-like and rather slow carrier *Béarn*. By the outbreak of war again, Britain had seven carriers in commission, and another half dozen large fleet carriers building. Shortly before his death in 1920, the prophetic Fisher had written, 'By land and sea the approaching prodigious aircraft development knocks out the present fleet, makes invasion practicable, cancels our country being an island, and transforms the atmosphere into the battleground of the future. . . .' By the end of the 1920s it was beginning to appear that the old admiral's last prophecy – like so many of his earlier ones – was coming to pass. In the British, American and Japanese navies, aircraft bombing and torpedoing at sea was becoming an advanced and sophisticated business. The Japanese especially spent heavily on the building of carriers, carrier aircraft and weapons, and the training of flying crews. By 1941 Japan possessed the most powerful and advanced fleet air arm in the world, manned by skilful and dedicated air crews: by airpower alone, it crippled the American Pacific Fleet on 7 December 1941; and from that date until the conclusion of hostilities in 1945, through the desperate combats at Coral Sea, Midway, Guadalcanal, and Leyte Gulf, the torpedo- and dive-bomber (with the submarine) ruled the Pacific, while the carrier was tenderly guarded by her own aircraft, by destroyers and cruisers, and by the Dreadnoughts she had replaced as queen of the fleet. In the first half of 1942 Japanese naval power – through its superbly efficient air arm – dominated the waters of the Pacific and Indian Oceans. When American aircraft in their turn destroyed four Japanese fleet carriers at the Battle of Midway, America within a few hours had regained maritime control because she had achieved control of the air above the sea's surface.

The Americans, Japanese and British all converted ships for carrier use and built new carriers in great numbers. All sorts of makeshifts were resorted to in order to get more aircraft into the air. Turrets were stripped from battleships to make room for runways. More and more aircraft for catapult launching were carried on warships, and even merchantmen. British merchantmen were equipped with a single fighter which could be launched against bombers, the pilot later parachuting into the sea close to his mother ship. Prolonged and bloody campaigns remained to be fought, and many American ships and aircraft were to be destroyed in the years ahead; but from that day in June 1942 at Midway there could be no other outcome than victory for the Americans and their allies.

The introduction from 1945 of jet-powered aircraft with very high

One of the surprise-novelties of the first World War: the seaplane carrier and depot ship *Ark Royal*

The USS *America* CVA 66

wing loadings, and therefore high landing speeds, complicated the problem of 'landing on', always the most difficult and dangerous aspect of carrier flying. Nets and hooks to reduce the landing run had been used since the early days of the carrier, even for slow piston-engined biplanes. The simple remedy now was to 'angle' the flight deck. Take-off was assisted by steam catapults.

It has been argued, especially in Britain where the economy is so precariously poised and defence costs are so high, that the carrier will be as obsolete in the 1970s as the battleships in the 1940s; that the carrier aircraft's duties can be more economically and effectively taken over by shore-based aircraft. The Americans on the other hand continue to pin much faith in the monster carrier – vast, nuclear-powered vessels with an unlimited endurance. They carry a complement of over 4,000 officers and men and supersonic bombers and fighters, and are protected by every conceivable form of anti-aircraft, anti-missile and anti-submarine devices. They are even secure against nuclear fall-out. Although we all pray that sea warfare will never again occur, the construction of such super-carriers make it certain that the long history of the fighting ship will continue at least until the end of this century.

The modern method of sea warfare an amphibious group, includin aircraft carriers, landing cra vehicle and personnel, and tw kinds of helicopters. This pictur shows the *Fearless* and the *Bulwa* with their landing craft, Wessex helicopters of 845 Naval Air Com mando squadron, Whirlwinds the RAF, and Sioux Light heli copters of the Royal Marines an Army. Over 2,000 troops with gun and vehicles are embarked

# Bibliography

*Numbers refer to direct quotations*

## Main References in Part One

1. Oared Fighting Ships by R. C. Anderson (London, 1962)
   The Vikings of Britain by D. F. Capper (London, 1937)
   The Ancient Mariners by Lionel Casson (London, 1959)
7. Sailing Ships by E. Keble Chatterton (London, 1909)
4. A History of Marine Architecture by John Charnock (London, 3 vols, 1800–2)
   Sailing Ships by G. S. Laird Clowes (London, 1932)
   The Warship in History by Philip Cowburn (New York, 1965)
   Le Trireme by L. Fincati (Rome, 2nd ed., 1881)
   Ancient Mariners by C. Daryll Forde (London, 1927)
   The Story of the Ship by Charles E. Gibson (London and New York, 1958)
   The Ship by Björn Landström (London, 1961)
2. Greek and Roman Naval Warfare by W. L. Rodgers (Annapolis, 1937)
6. Naval Warfare under Oars by W. L. Rodgers (Annapolis, 1939)
   Sea Power in Ancient History by A. M. Shepard (London, 1925)
3. Ancient Ships by Cecil Torr (Cambridge, England, 1894)
5. Greece, from the coming of the Hellenes to AD 14 by E. S. Shuckburgh (London, 1905)

## Main References in Part Two

   Ship Models by B. W. Bathe (London, 1964)
12. From Carrack to Clipper by Frank C. Bowen (London, 1948)
3. An History of Marine Architecture by John Charnock (London, 3 vols, 1800–2)
1. Sailing Ships and their Story by E. Keble Chatterton (London, 1909)
5. Sailing Ships: Their History and Development by G. S. Laird Clowes (London, 1932)
15. The Royal Navy: a History by William Laird Clowes and others (London, 7 vols, 1897–1903)
   The Warship in History by Philip Cowburn (New York, 1965)
10. The Story of Sea Warfare by David Divine (London, 1957)
   The Story of the Ship by C. E. Gibson (London, 1958)
2. Famous Sea Fights from Salamis to Jutland by J. R. Hale (London, 8th edn, 1939)
7. The Principall Navigatione, Voiages, and Discoveries of the English Nation by Hakluyt (London, 1589)
14. Rodney by David Hannay (London, 1891)
19. The Ship by Björn Landström (London, 1961)
8. Old Ship Figure-Heads and Sterns by L. G. Carr Laughton (London and New York, 1925)

6. The Navy of Britain: a Historical Portrait by Michael Lewis (London, 1948)
11. Ships and how they Sailed the Seven Seas by Hendrik van Loon (London, 1935)
22. The Trafalgar Roll by R. H. Mackenzie (London, 1913)
16. The Influence of Sea Power upon the French Revolution 1793-1812 by A. T. Mahan (London, 2 vols, 1892)
17. A Naval History of England by G. J. Marcus (London, 1961)
9. The Defeat of the Spanish Armada by Garrett Mattingly (London, 1959)
   Sailing Ships of War 1800-1860 by Alan Moore (London and New York, 1926)
18. The Maritime History of Massachusetts by S. E. Morison (Boston, 1921)
4. A History of the Royal Navy by N. H. Nicolas (London, 2 vols, 1847)
21. The Navy: a History by Fletcher Pratt (New York, 1938)
13. Histoire de la Marine Française by Ch. de la Roncière and G. Clerc-Rampal (Paris, 1934)
   The Strategy of Sea Power by S. W. Roskill (London, 1962)
20. History of the United States Navy, 1775-1897 by J. R. Spears (London, 4 vols, 1898)
   United States Frigate Constitution (Washington, 1932)

## Main References in Part Three

3. The Introduction of the Ironclad Warship by J. P. Baxter (Cambridge, Mass., 1933)
   The Naval Annual, edited by Lord Brassey and others (London, annually)
2. The Navies of the World by Hans Busk (London, 1859)
5. The Royal Navy: a History by William Laird Clowes and others (7 vols, London 1897-1903)
1. Conversations-Lexicon (Leipzig, 1858)
   The Warship in History by Philip Cowburn (New York, 1965)
   Famous Sea Fights from Salamis to Jutland by J. R. Hale (London, 8th edn, 1939)
   The Hunting of Force Z by Richard Hough (London, 1963)
   Dreadnought: a History of the Modern Battleship by Richard Hough (New York, 1964)
   Perchance: a short history of British Aviation by B. J. Hurren (London, 1949)
   Fighting Ships, edited by Fred T. Jane and others (London, annually)
   Land, Sea and Air by Mark Kerr (London, 1927)
   The Ship by Björn Landström (London, 1961)
   The Navy of Britain: a Historical Portrait, by Michael Lewis (London, 1948)
   British Destroyers by E. J. March (London, 1966)
   Admiral Sims and the Modern American Navy by E. E. Morison (New York, 1942)
   British Battleships by Oscar Parkes (London, 1958)
4. The Navy: a History, by Fletcher Pratt (New York, 1938)
6. Modern Ships of War by E. J. Reed and E. Simpson (New York, 1888)
   Histoire de la Marine Française by Ch. de la Roncière and G. Clerc-Rampal (Paris, 1934)
7. Torpedoes and Torpedo Warfare by C. W. Sleeman (London, 1880)
   Submarines by Frederick A. Talbot (London, 1915)
8. My Memoirs by Alfred von Tirpitz (London, 1919)
   History of United States Naval Aviation by A. D. Turnbull and C. L. Lord (New York, 1949)
   The Kaiten Weapon by Yutaka Yokota (New York, 1962)

# List of Illustrations

## Colour

The jacket picture and another of 'The Field of the Cloth of Gold' make a pair by an unknown sixteenth-century artist, which are owned by Her Majesty the Queen and hung at Hampton Court Palace. *Photo: Cooper*

**Page 25:** detail of a naval battle, *from the Naval Battle Room at the Escorial. Photo: Scala*

**Pages 26 and 27 top:** the port of Naples, by Strozzi, *from San Martino, Naples. Photo: Scala*

**Pages 26 and 27 bottom:** the Battle of Lepanto, by Micheli, *from the Palazzo Ducale, Venice. Photo: Scala*

**Page 28:** Portuguese carracks, by Anthoniszoon, *from the National Maritime Museum, Greenwich. Photo: Derrick Witty*

**Page 37:** two details of an oil painting by Breughel of a battle in the Gulf of Naples, *from the Galleria Doria, Rome. Photo: Scala*

**Page 38:** Greek fire from Juan Skylitzes 'Sinopsis Historiarum', *from the Biblioteca Nacional, Madrid. Photo: Mas*

**Page 38:** Venetian shipyard, 1517, eighteenth-century Venetian school, *from the Museo Storia Veneziana, Venice. Photo: Scala*

**Page 55:** the Oseberg ship, *from Universitetets Oldsaksamling, Oslo*

**Page 56:** Norman soldiers, *from the Bibliotheque Nationale, Paris. Photo: Freeman*

**Page 65:** Portuguese carracks, by Anthoniszoon, *from the National Maritime Museum, Greenwich. Photo: Derrick Witty*

**Page 66:** 'Equipping the Argo', *from MS Douce 353, f 31, roll 165E no. 10, from the Bodleian Library, Oxford*

**Page 67 top:** 'Argonauts land at Colchos', *from MS Douce 353, f 31, roll 165E no. 11, from the Bodleian Library, Oxford*

**Page 67 bottom left:** early sixteenth-century ship, *from MS Ashmole 1504, f 20v, roll 156B no. 37 164C/11, from the Bodleian Library, Oxford*

**Page 67 bottom right:** 'Henry I's nightmare', *from MS C.C.C. 157, f 383, roll 132 no. 14, by courtesy of the President and Fellows of Corpus Christi College, Oxford*

**Page 68:** the *Great Harry*, 1546, from the Anthony Anthony Rolls, *by courtesy of the Master and Fellows of Magdalene College, Cambridge. Photo: Edward Leigh*

**Page 101:** two illustrations from 'Fragments of Ancient Shipwrightry', *by courtesy of the Master and Fellows of Magdalene College, Cambridge. Photo: Edward Leigh*

**Pages 102 and 103:** detail of the first of a pair of Armada paintings by Vroom. *Photo by courtesy of 'The Connoisseur'*

**Page 104 top:** the second of a pair of Armada paintings by Vroom. *Photo by courtesy of 'The Connoisseur'*

**Page 104 bottom:** detail of a portrait of Queen Elizabeth I, *from the Woburn Abbey Collection with kind permission of His Grace the Duke of Bedford*

**Page 121:** the *Resolution*, by Van de Velde II, *from the National Maritime Museum, Greenwich*

**Pages 122 and 123:** Dutch men of war and yacht, by Van de Velde II, *from the National Maritime Museum, Greenwich*

**Page 124:** the *Sovereign of the Seas* and Peter Pett, anon, *from the National Maritime Museum, Greenwich. Photo: Derrick Witty*

**Page 141 top:** the *Santa Brigida*, by Whitcombe, *by courtesy of Oscar and Peter Johnson Limited, Lowndes Lodge Gallery, London*

**Page 141 bottom:** the Battle of La Hogue by Van Diest, *from the National Maritime Museum, Greenwich*

**Pages 142 and 143:** the *Royal George*, by Clevely, *from the National Maritime Museum, Greenwich. Photo: Derrick Witty*

**Page 144:** the Battle of 1 June by de Loutherbourg, *from the National Maritime Museum, Greenwich Hospital Collection*

**Page 153 top:** frigate action, *from the Musée de la Marine, Paris. Photo: Jacqueline Hyde*

**Page 153 bottom:** brigs fighting, *from the Musée de la Marine, Paris. Photo: Jacqueline Hyde*

**Page 154:** the *Chesapeake* and the *Shannon*, by Elmes, *from the National Maritime Museum, Greenwich*

**Page 171:** the *Albemarle*, *official U.S. Navy photo*

**Page 172 top:** the *Erie*, by Camilierre, *official U.S. Navy photo*

**Page 172 bottom:** the *Constellation*, by de Simone, *official U.S. Navy photo*

**Page 181 top:** the *Java* and the *Constitution*, by Pocock, *from the National Maritime Museum, Greenwich*

**Page 181 bottom:** the *United States* and *Macedonian*, by Coates, *official U.S. Navy photo*

**Pages 182 and 183:** the *Serapis* and *Bonhomme Richard*, by Paton, *official U.S. Navy photo*

**Page 184:** the *Constitution* and the *Guerrière*, by Birch, *official U.S. Navy photo*

**Page 201:** the *Victory*, by Swaine, *from the National Maritime Museum, Greenwich*

**Pages 202 and 203:** Trafalgar by Wilson, *by courtesy of Oscar and Peter Johnson Limited, Lowndes Lodge Gallery, London*

## Monochrome

**Page 221 left:** the Battle of Hampton Roads, by Currier and Ives, *from the Bettman Archive Inc., New York;* right, the *Novgorod, from the Mansell Collection, London*

**Page 222:** the *Warrior, from the Imperial War Museum, London*

**Page 224:** transverse section of the *Warrior. Photo: Science Museum, London*

**Page 225:** the *Minotaur. Photo: Science Museum, London*

**Page 227:** the *Warrior,* by Dutton, *from the National Maritime Museum, Greenwich*

the *Gloire,* by Le Breton, *from the National Maritime Museum, Greenwich*

the *Conqueror,* 1883

the *Glatton, from the 'Illustrated Penny Almanack' for 1879*

**Page 233:** the *Devastation, from the Imperial War Museum, London*

the *Inflexible, from the Imperial War Museum, London*

the *Royal Sovereign, from the Imperial War Museum, London*

the *Majestic, from the Imperial War Museum, London*

**Page 236 left:** Fulton's submarine *Nautilus. Photo: Science Museum, London;* right, the Rev. Garrett's submarine

**Page 237:** elevations and plans of the Rev. Garrett's submarine. *Lent to the Science Museum, London, by C. Cochrane & Co., Birkenhead*

**Page 240:** the *Hotspur, from the Imperial War Museum, London*

**Page 241:** the *Hornet, from the Imperial War Museum, London*

**Page 242:** the *Hoche, from the Musée de la Marine, Paris*

**Page 243:** the Italian and English 'human torpedo' craft. *Photos: Science Museum, London*

**Page 244:** the USS *Picuda, official U.S. Navy photo*

**Page 245:** Polaris submarine. *Photo: Camera Press, London*

**Page 250:** the *Georges Leygues. Photo: Laurence Dunn*

**Page 253:** Kaiser Wilhelm's sketch for a cruiser, *from the Bundesarchiv, Germany*

**Page 255:** the *Ajax. Photo: Science Museum, London*

**Page 262:** the USS *Springfield* CLG 7, *official U.S. Navy photo*

**Page 263:** the USS *Canberra* DLG, *official U.S. Navy photo*

**Page 264:** 'Warships Week', by Rushbury, *from the Imperial War Museum, London. Photo: Derrick Witty*

**Page 267:** the *Dreadnought. Photo: Science Museum, London*

**Page 269:** the USS *Michigan, official U.S. Navy photo*

**Page 271:** the Atlantic fleet. *Photo: Science Museum, London*

**Page 274:** the USS *Oklahoma. Photo: Radio Times Hulton Picture Library*

**Page 283:** the *Moltke, from the Imperial War Museum, London*

the USS *Alaska, official U.S. Navy photo*

the *Yamato. Photo: Science Museum, London*

**Page 284:** the *Derfflinger, from the Imperial War Museum, London*

**Page 286:** the USS *Ranger* CVA 61 refuelling, *official U.S. Navy photo*

**Page 288:** the *Furious, from the Imperial War Museum, London*

**Page 290 top:** the *Ark Royal. Photo: Radio Times Hulton Picture Library, London*

**Page 290 bottom:** the USS *America* CVA 66, *official U.S. Navy photo*

**Page 292:** amphibious group, *Crown copyright*

**End papers:** 'Group of Vessels' by Van de Velde. *Photo: Scala, Milan*

## ACKNOWLEDGMENTS

I would like to thank Lieutenant-Commander P. K. Kemp and his Staff at the Historical Department of the Navy Department in London; and Rear-Admiral E. M. Eller and members of his staff at the Department of Naval History in Washington D.C. for all their assistance. I am also grateful to those who have read and made suggestions on the manuscript, and especially Commander W. B. Rowbotham, whose fund of knowledge on all things naval seems limitless.

For the inclusion of extracts from copyright material I am grateful to Mrs John D. Clark for permission to use extracts from *The Navy: A History* by Fletcher Pratt; to Messrs George Allen and Unwin (*The Navy of Britain: A Historical Portrait* by Michael Lewis); to Messrs Longmans, Green (*A Naval History of England* by G. J. Marcus); to the Controller of Her Majesty's Stationery Office (*Sailing Ships: Their History and Development* by G. S. Laird Clowes); to Messrs Methuen *Famous Sea Fights from Salamis to Jutland* by J. R. Hale); to the Director of Publications at the U.S. Naval Institute, Annapolis, Maryland (*Greek and Roman Naval Warfare* © 1937 by the U.S. Naval Institute, and *Naval Warfare under Oars* © 1940 by the U.S. Naval Institute, both by Admiral William Ledyard Rogers); and R. C. Anderson, Esq. (*Oared Fighting Ships* by R. C. Anderson).

The producers would like to thank Commander George Naish, deputy director of the National Maritime Museum, Greenwich, for his invaluable help and advice in selecting pictures and writing captions.

# Index

Headings in italics are names of ships or foreign words. Important references are given first. '. . . (2)' after page-references mean two occurrences on the same page. 'mgn' = marginal note